A Concise Bibliography
for Students of English

A Concise Bibliography for Students of English

FIFTH EDITION

By Arthur G. Kennedy and Donald B. Sands

Revised by William E. Colburn

Stanford University Press

STANFORD, CALIFORNIA   1972

A Concise Bibliography for Students of English was originally compiled by Professor Arthur G. Kennedy of Stanford University and published in 1940. Revised editions followed in 1945 and 1954. A Fourth Edition was prepared after Professor Kennedy's death by Donald B. Sands and published in 1960. The present edition, published in 1972, is the work of William E. Colburn.

Stanford University Press
Stanford, California
© 1972 by the Board of Trustees of the
Leland Stanford Junior University
Printed in the United States of America
Cloth ISBN 0-8047-0804-5
Paper ISBN 0-8047-0813-4
LC 77-183889

For
my family, who made it possible
my colleagues, who made it necessary
my students, who made it worthwhile

W.E.C.

January 1972

Preface

When any work appears in five editions throughout three decades, it is likely to incorporate many changes. In a work intended as a guide and companion to advanced undergraduates and graduate students in English, those changes should reflect what has been happening in that field of study, and perhaps beyond. Decisions on what to include and exclude are not easily made in works of this sort, and earlier editors of this one understandably tended to be inclusive at the borderline, with the result that each edition was larger than its predecessor and more complex in organization. The fourth edition had over 5,000 entries, grouped into 228 categories, covering a wide range of associated disciplines and related areas as well as the fields of English and American literature.

The present edition represents a deliberate effort to return to the idea of conciseness, to recognize that there are practical limits within which students must operate. I have not tried to compile a record of everything that has been written that might be of some value, but rather to offer a list of older works of demonstrated usefulness to the student and new works that show great promise. I have kept material in languages other than English to a minimum, along with material in ancillary fields and works of narrow specialization. I have further reduced the number of categories by treating works on the drama and on the theater together, and by drawing national distinctions only when necessary. In the Modern Period, for example, nothing is gained by distinguishing between American and British plays and novels.

As in previous editions, works devoted to single authors do not appear, and as a practical necessity no work that deals with fewer than three authors has been included. An exception to this admittedly arbitrary rule is the listing of periodicals devoted to a single author (Section 111). Periodical essays have not been included, but whenever possible reprinted collections of specialized articles have been listed.

The most significant change from the previous edition occurs in connection with material in Linguistics and Folklore. In the last decade these fields have grown immeasurably, the movement being away from the literary toward the scientific. In many schools, new departments have developed out of what had been part of the English department. The recent decision of the Modern Language Association to divide the annual bibliography into four sections, one devoted to Linguistics, is evidence of what has happened. Linguistics and Folklore have become full-fledged disciplines; they now have their own problems of terminology, organization, categorization, schools, areas, approaches. To do justice to either of these fields now would require a work three times the size of this edition and call for a committee of compilers rather than an individual. Consequently, only basic works in these areas, and only those of most interest to students of literature, are included.

In the fourth edition there was a marked movement away from older to more recent works. In this edition that movement has been accelerated. Works that have been superseded no longer appear; on the other hand, some works that have not yet "proved" themselves are included just because they are provocative, controversial, even perverse. If some sections seem disproportionately longer than others, it is the result of greater activity in those areas. The length of the section on modern fiction, for example, suggests that even if the novel is dead, there are many who insist upon paying it their final respects.

This new edition also recognizes the increasing importance of literature written in English throughout the world. Some of this is most difficult to categorize. Whenever the work relates to the British or Commonwealth traditions, it is so labeled; otherwise, it is placed, rather uncomfortably, in Section 121 as World Literature. The literature of Canada (in English) presents special problems. Not too long ago Canadians resented the arrogating to themselves of the label "American" by the people of the United States. Now they prefer that some distinction be drawn. And, of course, the term "Commonwealth Literature," as it is now used, is not really appropriate. Therefore, wherever possible works are designated as Canadian. Inevitably, however, in a few instances "American" must be understood to include Canadian literature as well as that of the United States.

Only in recent years has the importance of black literature been generally recognized, and studies in this area are now mushrooming. In this edition such works have been completely integrated. If there appears to be a concentration of black literature studies at the end of some sections, it is the result of the chronological arrangement, but might well serve as a reminder of that belated recognition.

The organization of the present edition is as simple as the material will allow, from the general to the more specific within each of the three parts. In Part 1, "The Literature," the arrangement follows the course that the student is likely to pursue in the investigation of a literary problem—from general bibliographies to specific bibliographies and guides, next to general surveys, and finally to general studies in a specific literary period. Part 2, "The Book," deals with the physical means by which literature is preserved and transmitted. First to be considered is the book as object—its early forms, production, distribution, preservation, and collection. Then follows consideration of the book in specialized forms, most importantly the periodical. Part 3, "The Profession," is concerned with the technology of the study of literature—theory, practice, methods of research, scholarly writing, and tools of the trade for the student and teacher.

For invaluable help in the preparation of this new edition thanks are due to many of the staff of the libraries of Georgia State University and Emory University, to the Georgia State University Foundation, Inc., to the Cartography Laboratory of Georgia State University, and especially to my friend, colleague, and sailing companion Arthur E. Waterman.

WILLIAM E. COLBURN

Contents

A Note to the Reader

Generally, the items in each section are arranged in order of publication of the latest edition, except that bibliographies, guides, and periodicals appear at the beginning. In a few sections a more appropriate alphabetical arrangement or one based upon the chronology of the material covered is used. Also, separately published works, indexes for example, that are directly associated with major works appear with them.

Works are listed in one place only. A work that deals with two periods, for example the Medieval and the Renaissance, will appear only under the first. Works that deal with more than two periods or with more than one genre or form appear in those sections designated as General Studies.

Periodicals that concentrate on, or carry a serial bibliography for, a particular period or genre appear in the appropriate section. They may be located by reference to the Index of Periodicals.

In addition to the usual bibliographical information, the entries include Dewey Decimal class numbers and LC call numbers, if the work has received Library of Congress cataloguing. Many works are not, or have not yet been, catalogued by the Library of Congress; also some works, particularly periodicals, often are not assigned Dewey numbers. In a few cases, the decimal number has been taken from the *British National Bibliography*. For libraries using the Dewey System, the individual book number, determined by the library, must be added by the reader to what is here given.

There are two circumstances in which these numbers, of either system, may not correspond to the numbers used by an individual library. First, if the library itself catalogued the work before Library of Congress cataloguing became available, its classification may be somewhat different. Second, because of changes in the system, quite frequently a reprint of an older work will be catalogued by the Library of Congress differently than the original. If the library has no reason to acquire the reprint, it is not likely to discover the change. It is always the latest cataloguing that appears here.

Libraries treat periodicals in various ways. Often they are not catalogued under either the Dewey or the LC system, but are arranged alphabetically or by some unique plan. Also practice differs as to whether annuals are treated as "books" or as periodicals.

Part One. The Literature

1. General Works–Literature in English

§1. Comprehensive Bibliographies

1.1 Besterman, Theodore. *A World Bibliography of Bibliographies and of Bibliographical Catalogues, Calendars, Abstracts, Digests, Indexes, and the Like.* 4th ed. 5 vols. Geneva, 1965-66. (Orig. ed. 1939.)
016.01   Z1002 B5684

1.2 Courtney, William P. *A Register of National Bibliography. With a Selection of the Chief Bibliographical Books and Articles Printed in Other Countries.* 3 vols. London, 1905-12. Rpt. N.Y., 1967.
015   Z1002 C86

1.3 Northup, Clark S. *A Register of Bibliographies of the English Language and Literature. With Contributions by Joseph Quincy Adams and Andrew Keogh.* New Haven, 1925. Rpt. N.Y., 1962. Cornell Studies in English.
016.01642   Z2011 N87

1.4 Van Patten, Nathan. *An Index to Bibliographies and Bibliographical Contributions Relating to the Work of American and British Authors, 1923-1932.* Stanford, 1934. Rpt. N.Y., 1967, 1970, 1971.
016.82   Z1225 A1 V2

1.5 *Bibliographic Index. A Cumulative Bibliography of Bibliographies.* 1938- . 2/yr and annual cumulation. 1937-68 cumulated in 8 vols.
016.016   Z1002 B593

1.6 Eager, Alan R. *A Guide to Irish Bibliographical Material. Being a Bibliography of Irish Bibliographies and Some Sources of Information.* London, 1964.
016.91415   Z2031 E16

1.7 Borchardt, Dietrich H. *Australian Bibliography. A Guide to Printed Sources of Information.* 2nd ed. Melbourne, 1966. (Orig. ed. 1963.)
016.9194   Z4011 B65

1.8 New Zealand Library Assoc. *A Bibliography of New Zealand Bibliographies.* Preliminary ed. Wellington, 1967.
016.01691931   Z4101 A1 N4

§2. Selective Bibliographies

2.1 Spargo, John W. *A Bibliographical Manual for Students of the Language and Literature of England and the United States. A Short-Title List.* 3rd ed. N.Y., 1956. (Orig. ed. 1939.)
016.82   Z2011 S73

2.2 Pinto, Vivian De S., ed. *A Reference Library. English Language and Literature.* 3rd ed. London, 1962. (Orig. ed. 1920.) English Assoc. Pamphlet 66.
016.82   Z2011 E58

2.3 Bateson, Frederick W. *A Guide to English Literature.* 2nd ed. London, 1967; N.Y., 1968. (Orig. ed. 1965.)
016.82   Z2011 B32

2.4 *A Student's Guide to British and American Literature.* Ed. David McPherson and Robert L. Montgomery. Austin, Tex., 1967.

2.5 Wright, Andrew H. *A Reader's Guide to English and American Literature.* Glenview, Ill., 1970.
016.82   Z2011 W73

2.6 Altick, Richard D., and Andrew Wright. *Selective Bibliography for the Study of English and American Literature.* 4th ed. N.Y., 1971. (Orig. ed. 1960.)
016.8207   Z2011 A4

2.7 Bond, Donald F. *A Reference Guide to English Studies.* 2nd ed. Chicago, 1971. (Orig. ed. 1962.)
016.01682   Z1002 B72

§3. Comprehensive Serial Bibliographies

3.1 Gray, Richard A., ed. *Serial Bibliographies in the Humanities and Social Sciences.* Ann Arbor, 1969. A bibliography of bibliographies.
016.01605   Z1002 G814

3.2 *American Year Book. A Record of Events and Progress.* 1910-20, 1925-50. 36 vols.
E171 A585

3.3 American Year Book. *Literature and Language Bibliographies from the American Year Book, 1910-1919.* Ed. Arnold N. Rzepecki. Ann Arbor, 1970.

3.4 *Year's Work in English Studies.* 1921 (for 1919/20)- . Annual.
405.842   PE58 E6

3.5 *Annual Bibliography of English Language and Literature.* Modern Humanities Research Association. 1921- .
016.42   Z2011 M69

3.6 *MLA International Bibliography of Books and Articles on the Modern Languages and Literatures.* 1922-1968 as June issue of *PMLA.* Formerly *American Bibliography.* 1969- . Annual in 4 vols.
Z7006 M64

3.7 *Quarterly Check-List of Literary History: English, American, French, German. An International Index of Current Books, Monographs, Brochures and Separates.* 1958- .
Z6513 Q35

3.8 *Abstracts of English Studies.* 1958- . 10/yr. Coverage of more than 1,100 periodicals.   PR 8164 0314

§4. Subject Indexes

4.1 Ireland, Norma O. *An Index to Indexes. A Subject Bibliography of Published Indexes.* Boston, 1942.
016.01   Z6293 I7

4.2 Peddie, Robert A. *Subject Index of Books Published Before 1880.* London, 1933. Three supplements . . . *Up to and Including 1880.* 3 vols. London, 1935-48. Rpt. 1962.
016   Z1035 P38

4.3 *The A.L.A. Index. An Index to General Literature, Biographical, Historical, and Literary Essays and Sketches, Reports, etc.* 2nd ed. Boston, 1901. (Orig. ed 1893.) *Supplement, 1900-1910.* Chicago, 1914. Rpt. Ann Arbor, 1970-71, in 2 vols. plus orig. author index.
040   AI3 A32

4.4 British Museum. *Subject Index of the Modern Works Added to the Library of the British Museum in the Years 1881-1900.* 3 vols. Ed. George K. Fortescue. London 1902-3. Ten *Supplements, 1901-1960.* London, 1906-65. Rpt. of orig. and supplements through 1940, 14 vols., 1965-66.
Z1035 B8613

4.5 London Library. *Subject Index of the London Library, St. James Square, London.* Ed. Charles T. H. Wright. London, 1909. *Additions, 1909-1953.* 3 vols., 1923-55. Rpt. in 4 vols. Nendeln, Liechtenstein, 1968.
Z921 L613

4.6 *Library of Congress Catalog. Books: Subjects.* 3/yr with annual cumulation and the following:
1950-1954. 20 vols. Ann Arbor, 1955.

1955-1959. 22 vols. N.Y., 1960.
1960-1964. 25 vols. Ann Arbor, 1965.
1965-1969. 42 vols. Ann Arbor, 1970.
Z881 U49 A22

4.7 *Essay and General Literature Index. An Author and Subject Index to Essays and Composite Works.* 1934- . 2/yr with annual cumulation. Cumulations, 1900-1969, in 7 vols.
016   AI3 E752

§5. Guides, Glossaries, Etc.

5.1 Shipley, Joseph T. *Encyclopedia of Literature.* N.Y., 1946.
809   PN41 S52

5.2 Pei, Mario A., and Frank Gaynor, eds. *Liberal Arts Dictionary in English, French, German, Spanish.* N.Y., 1952.
703   PB333 P4

5.3 Beckson, Karl E., and Arthur Ganz. *A Reader's Guide to Literary Terms. A Dictionary.* N.Y., 1960.
803   PN41 B33

5.4 Thrall, William F., and Addison Hibbard. *A Handbook to Literature.* Rev. ed. by C. Hugh Holman. N.Y., 1960. (Orig. ed. 1936.)
803   PN41 T5

5.5 Magill, Frank N., ed. *Cyclopedia of Literary Characters.* N.Y., 1963.
803   PN44 M3

5 6 Benet, William Rose. *The Reader's Encyclopedia.* 2nd ed. N.Y., 1965. (Orig. ed. 1948.)
803   PN41 B4

5.7 Scott, Arthur F. *Current Literary Terms. A Concise Dictionary of Their Origin and Use.* N.Y., 1965.
803   PN44.5 S3

5.8 Barry, Raymond W., and A. J. Wright. *Literary Terms. Definitions, Explanations, Examples.* San Francisco, 1966.
801.4   PN44.5 B33

5.9 Lanham, Richard A. *A Handlist of Rhetorical Terms. A Guide for Students of English Literature.* Berkeley, 1968.
423.1   PE1445 A2 L3

5.10 Liberman, Myron M., and Edward E. Foster. *A Modern Lexicon of Literary Terms.* Glenview, Ill., 1968.
801.4   PN44.5 L46

● *Penguin Companion to Literature.* 4 vols. Harmondsworth, Eng., 1969; N.Y., 1971.
803   PN41 P44

   5.11 I. *English.* ed. David Daiches.
820.9   PN849 C5 P4

   5.12 II. *European.* Ed. Anthony K. Thorlby.
809.894   PN41 P43

   5.13 III. *American.* Ed. Malcolm Bradbury et al.
809   PN843 P4

   5.14 IV. *Classical and Byzantine.* Ed. Donald R. Dudley. *Oriental and African.* Ed. David M. Lang.
809   PA31 P4

5.15 Ruttkowski, Wolfgang V., and R. E. Blake. *Glossary of Literary Terms in English, German, and French, with Greek and Latin Derivations of Terms for the Student of General and Comparative Literature.* Bern, 1969.
803   PN44.5 R8

5.16 Myers, Robin, ed. *A Dictionary of Literature in the English Language from Chaucer to 1940.* 2 vols. London, 1970-71.
016.82   Z2010 M9

5.17 Shipley, Joseph T., ed. *Dictionary of World Literary Terms, Forms, Technique, Criticism.* Rev. ed. Boston, 1970. (Orig. ed. as *Dictionary of World Literature,* N.Y., 1943.)
803   PN41 S5

5.18 Abrams, Meyer H. *A Glossary of Literary Terms.* 3rd ed. N.Y., 1971. (Orig. ed. by Dan S. Norton and Peters Rushton, N.Y., 1941.)
803   PN44.5 A2

5.19 Barnet, Sylvan, Morton Berman, and William Burto. *A Dictionary of Literary, Dramatic, and Cinematic Terms.* 2nd ed. Boston, 1971. (Orig. ed. *The Study of Literature,* 1960.)
801.4   PN44.5 B3

5.20 Lemon, Lee T. *A Glossary for the Study of English.* N.Y., 1971.
803   PN44.5 L4

§6. Biographical Reference (Writers)
   See also §120

6.1 Adams, Oscar F. *A Dictionary of American Authors.* 5th ed. Boston, 1905. (Orig. ed. 1897.) Rpt. Detroit, 1969; Kennebunkport, Me., 1970.
015.73   Z1224 A22

6.2 Kunitz, Stanley J., and Howard Haycraft. *British Authors of the Nineteenth Century.* N.Y., 1936. Rpt. 1955.
928.2   PR451 K8

6.3 Russell, Josiah C. *Dictionary of Writers of Thirteenth Century England.* London, 1936. Rpt. N.Y., 1971. Spec. Supp. 3, Bull. of the Inst. of Hist. Research.
928.2   D1 L65

6.4 Kunitz, Stanley J., and Howard Haycraft, eds. *American Authors, 1600-1900. A Biographical Dictionary of American Literature.* N.Y., 1938. Rpt. 1949.
928.1   PS21 K8

6.5 Millett, Fred B. *Contemporary American Authors. A Critical Survey and 219 Bio-Bibliographies.* N.Y., 1940. Rpt. 1944, 1970.
810.9005   PS221 M5

6.6 Kunitz, Stanley J., and Howard Haycraft. *Twentieth Century Authors. A Biographical Dictionary of Modern Literature.* N.Y., 1942. Rpt. 1950. *First Supplement* by S. J. Kunitz and Vineta Colby. N.Y., 1955.
928   PN771 K86

6.7 Wallace, William S. *A Dictionary of North American Authors Deceased Before 1950.* Toronto, 1951. Rpt. Detroit, 1968.
810.9   PS128 W3

6.8 Kunitz, Stanley J., and Howard Haycraft. *British Authors Before 1800. A Biographical Dictionary.* N.Y., 1952. Rpt. 1956.
928.2   PR105 K9

6.9 Browning, David C. *Everyman's Dictionary of Literary Biography English and American.* London & N.Y., 1958.
928.2   PR19 B7

6.10 *Contemporary Authors. A Bio-Bibliographical Guide to Current Authors and Their Works.* 1962- . 2/yr.
928.1   Z1224 C6

6.11 *The Author's and Writer's Who's Who.* 5th ed. N.Y., 1963. (Orig. ed. 1934.)
928.2   Z2001 A91

6.12 Hetherington, John A. *Forty-Two Faces.* London, 1963. Rpt. Freeport, N.Y., 1969. Australian prose writers.
928.2899994   PR9453 H4

6.13 Sylvestre, Guy, et al., eds. *Canadian Writers. A Biographical Dictionary.* Rev. ed. Toronto, 1966. (Orig. ed. 1964.)
PR9127 S9

6.14 Cleeve, Brian T., ed. *Dictionary of Irish Writers.* Cork, 1967.
820.99415   PR8727 C5

6.15 French, Warren G., and Walter E. Kidd, eds. *American Winners of the Nobel Literary Prize*. Norman, Okla., 1968.
810.9005   PS121 F65

6.16 Harte, Barbara, and Carolyn Riley. *Two Hundred Contemporary Authors. Bio-Bibliographies of Selected Leading Writers of Today with Critical and Personal Sidelights*. Detroit, 1969.
809.04   PN771 H28

6.17 Nobel Lectures. *Literature, 1901-1967, Including Presentation Speeches and Laureates' Biographies*. Ed. Horst Frenz. Amsterdam, 1969.
808.9   PN771 F74

6.18 *International Who's Who in Poetry*. 2nd ed. by Ernest Kay. London, 1970. (Orig. ed. by Geoffrey Handley-Taylor, 1958.)
928   PS324 I5

Anonymous Authorship

6.19 Cushing, William. *Anonyms. A Dictionary of Revealed Authorship*. Cambridge, Mass., 1889. Rpt. Waltham, Mass., 1963.
Z1045 C98

6.20 Halkett, Samuel, and John Laing. *Dictionary of Anonymous and Pseudonymous English Literature*. 9 vols. New ed. by James Kennedy et al., Edinburgh, 1926-62. (Orig. ed. in 4 vols., 1882-88.) Rpt. N.Y., 1971.
014.2   Z1065 H18

6.21 Stonehill, Charles A., et al. *Anonyma and Pseudonyma*. 4 vols. London, 1926-27. Rpt. in 2 vols., Pound Ridge, N.Y., 1969.
014.1   Z1065 S882

6.22 Taylor, Archer, and Fredric J. Mosher. *The Bibliographical History of Anonyma and Pseudonyma*. Chicago, 1951.
014   Z1041 T3

§7. General Literary Studies

7.1 Dudley, Fred A., ed. *The Relations of Literature and Science. A Selected Bibliography, 1930-1967*. Ann Arbor, 1968.
016.809   Z6511 D8

7.2 Modern Language Association. *Literature and Society, 1950-1955. A Selective Bibliography*. Ed. Thomas F. Marshall et al. Coral Gables, Fla., 1956.
——*... 1956-1960.* 1962.
——*... 1961-1965.* Ed. Paul J. Carter and George K. Smart. 1967.
016.809933   Z6511 M62

•

7.3 *Essays and Studies in Honor of Carleton Brown.* London & N.Y., 1940. Rpt. Freeport, N.Y., 1969.
809   PN501 B7

7.4 Highet, Gilbert. *The Classical Tradition. Greek and Roman Influences on Western Literature.* N.Y., 1949.
809   PN883 H5

● *English Studies Today.* Lectures and Papers . . . International Association of University Professors.

> **7.5** *1st Conference,* Magdalen College, 1950. London & Bern, 1951.

> **7.6** *Second Series.* 3rd Conference, Lausanne & Bern, August 1959. Ed. G. A. Bonnard. Bern, 1961.

> **7.7** *Third Series.* 5th Conference, Edinburgh & Glasgow, August 1962. Ed. G. I. Duthie. Edinburgh, 1964.

> **7.8** *Fourth Series.* 6th Conference, Venice, August 1965. Ed. Ilva Cellini and Giorgio Melchiori. Rome, 1966.
> 420.82   PE25 E5

7.9 Auerbach, Erich. *Mimesis. The Representation of Reality in Western Literature.* Trans. Willard R. Trask. Princeton, 1953. (Orig. German ed. Bern, 1946.)
809   PN56 R3 A83

7.10 Brett-James, Antony. *The Triple Stream. Four Centuries of English, French, and German Literature, 1531-1930.* Cambridge, 1953.
802   PN524 B8

7.11 Pritchett, Victor S. *Books in General.* N.Y., 1953. Rpt. Westport, Conn., 1970.
809.03   PN710 P68

7.12 Jarrett-Kerr, Martin. *Studies in Literature and Belief.* N.Y., 1954. Rpt. Freeport, N.Y., 1970.
808.84931   PN49 J37

7.13 Meyerhoff, Hans. *Time in Literature.* Berkeley, 1955. Rpt. 1960, 1967.
809   PN49 M43

7.14 Simpson, Alan. *Puritanism in Old and New England.* Chicago, 1955. Rpt. 1961.
285.9   BX9321 S55

7.15 Abrams, Meyer H., ed. *Literature and Belief.* English Institute Essays, 1957. N.Y., 1958.
808.1   PE1010 E5

7.16 West, Rebecca [Cicily I. Fairfield]. *The Court and the Castle. Some Treatments of a Recurrent Theme.* New Haven, 1957. Rpt. N.Y., 1971.
809.03   PN45 W45

7.17 Bayley, John O. *The Characters of Love. A Study in the Literature of Personality.* London, 1960. Rpt. N.Y., 1963.
809.93   PN56 L6 B3

7.18 Steiner, George. *The Death of Tragedy.* N.Y., 1961. Rpt. 1963.
809.2   PN1892 S7

7.19 Spitzer, Leo. *Essays on English and American Literature.* Ed. Anna Hatcher. Princeton, 1962.
820.9   PR99 S6

7.20 Rogers, Katharine M. *The Troublesome Helpmate. A History of Misogyny in Literature.* Seattle, 1966.
809.933   PN56 W6 R6

7.21 Brophy, Brigid, et al. *Fifty Works of English (and American) Literature We Could Do Without.* London, 1967.
820.9   PR86 B7

7.22 Ellmann, Mary. *Thinking About Women.* N.Y., 1968.
809.933   PN56 S5 E4

7.23 *The Rarer Action. Essays in Honor of Francis Fergusson.* Ed. Alan Cheuse and Richard Koffler. New Brunswick, N.J., 1970.
809   PN36 F4

7.24 Reisner, Robert G. *Graffiti. Two Thousand Years of Wall Writing.* N.Y., 1971.
001.55   GT95 R4

§8. Studies in Style
See also Poetry, §27, and Prose, §33

8.1 Milic, Louis T. *Style and Linguistics. An Annotated Bibliography.* N.Y., 1967.
016.808   Z6514 S8 M49

8.2 Bailey, Richard W., and Lubomír Dolezel, eds. *An Annotated Bibliography of Statistical Stylistics.* Ann Arbor, 1968.
016.80802   Z6514 S8 B34

8.3 Bailey, Richard W., and Dolores M. Burton. *English Stylistics. A Bibliography.* Cambridge, Mass., 1968.
016.808   Z2015 S7 B2

●

8.4 *Language and Style. An International Journal.* 1968-   . 4/yr.
808.005   PN203 L35

●

8.5 Conference on Style. Indiana Univ. 1958. *Style in Language.* Ed. Thomas A. Sebeok. Cambridge, Mass., 1960.
808   PN203 C6

8.6 Frye, Northrop. *The Well-Tempered Critic.* Bloomington, Ind., 1963.
801.9   PN203 F7

8.7 Ullmann, Stephen. *Language and Style. Collected Papers.* Oxford & N.Y., 1964.
412   PN203 U4

8.8 Bridgman, Richard. *The Colloquial Style in America.* N.Y., 1966. Rpt. 1968.
818.0809   PS371 B7

8.9 Fowler, Roger, ed. *Essays on Style and Language. Linguistics and Critical Approaches to Literary Style.* London & N.Y., 1966.
801.9   PN203 F6

8.10 Leed, Jacob, ed. *The Computer and Literary Style. Introductory Essays and Studies.* Kent, O., 1966.
801.950184   PN98 E4 L4

8.11 Erdman, David V., and Ephim G. Fogel, eds. *Evidence for Authorship. Essays on Problems of Attribution with an Annotated Bibliography of Selected Readings.* Ithaca, N.Y., 1966.
809   PR61 E7

8.12 Miles, Josephine. *Style and Proportion. The Language of Prose and Poetry.* Boston, 1967.
808.042   PE1421 M5

8.13 Milic, Louis T. *Stylists on Style. A Handbook with Selections for Analysis.* N.Y., 1969.
820.9   PE1421 M53

8.14 Hough, Graham G. *Style and Stylistics.* London & N.Y., 1969.
808.20   PN203 H65

8.15 Freeman, Donald C., ed. *Linguistics and Literary Style.* N.Y., 1970.
808   PN203 F67

8.16 Watson, George G., ed. *Literary English Since Shakespeare.* N.Y., 1970.
820.9   PR83 W38

§9. Scholarly Journals

These are general journals. Specialized journals are listed in the appropriate sections.

9.1 *Anglia. Zeitschrift für englische Philologie.* 1877-   . 4/yr.
PE3 A6

9.2 *Englische Studien. Zeitschrift für englische Philologie.* 1877-1944. 76 vols. 4/yr.
PE3 E6

9.3 Royal Society of Canada. *Transactions.* Section II: *Literature, History . . .* 1882- . Irreg.
AS42 R6

9.4 *PMLA. Publications of the Modern Language Association of America.* 1884- . 6/yr including Directory issue. See 3.6.
PB6 M6

9.5 *JEGP. Journal of English and Germanic Philology. Devoted to the English, German, and Scandinavian Languages and Literatures.* 1897- . 4/yr.
PD1 J7

9.6 *Modern Language Review. Official Journal of the Modern Humanities Research Association.* 1905- . 4/yr.
PB1 M65

9.7 *Essays and Studies by Members of the English Association.* 1910- . Annual.
820.4   PR13 E4

9.8 *Texas Studies in English.* 1911-58. 37 vols. Annual.
820.9   PR13 T4

9.9 *Neophilologus.* Groningen. 1916- . 4/yr.
PB9 N4

9.10 *English Studies. A Journal of English Letters and Philology.* Amsterdam. 1919- . 6/yr.
PE1 E55

9.11 *Essays by Divers Hands. Being the Transactions of the Royal Society of Literature of the United Kingdom.* 1921- . Annual.
808.008   PN22 R6

9.12 *Review of English Studies. A Quarterly Journal of English Literature and the English Language.* 1925- .
820.5   PR1 R4

9.13 *Studia Neophilologica. A Journal of Germanic and Romanic Philology.* Uppsala. 1928- . 2/yr.
405   PB5 S7

9.14 *Revue des langues vivantes.* Brussels. 1932- . 6/yr.

9.15 *Etudes anglaises. Grande-Bretagne, Etats-Unis.* 1937- . 4/yr.
820.9   PR1 E8

9.16 *Journal of the Warburg and Courtauld Institutes.* 1937- . Annual.
062   AS122 L8515

9.17 *English Institute Essays.* 1939- . Annual. Until 1942 *English Institute Annual.* Beginning in 1963 catalogued separately under editor and title.
420.6373   PE1010 E5

9.18 *Tulane Studies in English.* 1949- . Annual.
820.9   PR13 T8

9.19 *Anglo-Welsh Review.* 1950- . 2/yr.
891.6605

9.20 *Humanities Association [of Canada] Bulletin.* 1951- . 4/yr.

9.21 *Literary Criterion.* India. 1952- . 2/yr.
PR1 L5

9.22 *AUMLA. Journal of the Australasian Universities Language and Literature Association.* 1953- . 2/yr.
PB1 A2

9.23 *Zeitschrift für Anglistik und Amerikanistik.* 1953- . 4/yr.
PR1 Z4

9.24 *Literature East and West.* 1954- . 4/yr.
PN2 L67

9.25 *Ball State University Forum.* 1960- . 4/yr.
LH1 B18 F6

9.26 *Studies in English.* Mississippi. 1960- . Annual.
PR5 M5 A55

9.27 *Studies in English Literature, 1500-1900.* 1961- . 4/yr.
PR1 S82

9.28 *Papers on Language and Literature. A Journal for Scholars and Critics of Language and Literature.* 1965- . 4/yr.
PR1 P3

9.29 *Literary Monographs.* 1967- . Annual or biennial.
820   PR13 L55

9.30 *Massachusetts Studies in English.* 1967- . 2/yr.

9.31 *Southern Literary Journal.* 1968- . 2/yr.

9.32 *Studies in the Literary Imagination.* 1968- . 2/yr.

9.33 *Hartford Studies in Literature.* 1969- . 3/yr.
805   PN2 H3

9.34 *New Literary History. A Journal of Theory and Interpretation.* 1969- . 3/yr.
820.1   PR1 N44

9.35 *Western Canadian Studies in Modern Languages and Literature.* 1969- . Annual.

9.36 *British Studies Monitor.* 1970- . 3/yr.

9.37 *Review of National Literatures.* 1970- . 2/yr.

9.38 *English Literary Renaissance.* 1971- . 3/yr.

9.39 *Journal of Narrative Technique.* 1971- . 3/yr.
820.9   PE1425 J68

§10. Humanistic and Interdisciplinary Journals

In various degrees, these journals provide articles and reviews of interest to the student of literature.

10.1 *Quarterly Review.* 1809-1967. 305 vols.
AP4 Q2

10.2 *Dublin Review.* 1836-1969. 242 vols. Incorporated with *The Month.*
AP4 D8

10.3 *Daedalus. Journal of the American Academy of Arts and Sciences.* 1846- . 4/yr.
Q11 B7

10.4 *Notes and Queries. For Readers and Writers, Collectors and Librarians.* 1849- . 12/yr.
AG305 N7

10.5 *The Month. A Review of Christian Thought and World Affairs.* 1864- . 12/yr.
AP4 M65

10.6 *Harvard Advocate.* 1866- . 6/yr.
LH1 H3 A2

10.7 *Hermathena. A Dublin University Review.* 1873- . 2/yr.
AS121 H5

10.8 *Durham University Journal.* 1876- . 3/yr.
AS121 D8

10.9 *Twentieth Century.* 1877- . 4/yr.
AP4 N7

10.10 *Cambridge Review. A Journal of University Life and Thought.* 1879- . 6/yr.
378.42   LH5 C2 C3

10.11 *Yale Review.* 1892- . 4/yr.
AP2 Y2

10.12 *South Atlantic Quarterly.* 1902- .
AP2 S75

10.13 *Aberdeen University Review.* 1913- . 2/yr.
LH5 A3

10.14 *Canadian Forum. An Independent Journal of Opinion and the Arts.* 1920- . 12/yr.
AP5 C125

10.15 *Dublin Magazine. A Quarterly Review of Literature, Science and Art.* 1923-58. 33 vols.
052   AP4 D77

10.16 *Modern Schoolman. A Quarterly Journal of Philosophy.* 1925- .

10.17 *Thought. A Review of Culture and Idea.* 1926-   . 4/yr.
AP2 T333

10.18 *Furman Studies.* 1928-   . 2/yr. irreg.
051   AS36 F86

10.19 *Aryan Path.* Bombay. 1930-   . 12/yr.
BP500 A8

10.20 *American Scholar. A Quarterly for the Independent Thinker.* Phi Beta Kappa. 1932-   .
371.852   AP2 A4572

10.21 *Science and Society. An Independent Journal of Marxism.* 1936-   . 4/yr.
305   H1 S25

10.22 *Huntington Library Quarterly. A Journal for the History and Interpretation of English and American Civilization.* 1937-   .
027.479493   Z733 S24 Q

10.23 *Journal of the History of Ideas. A Quarterly Devoted to Cultural and Intellectual History.* 1940-   .
105   B1 J75

10.24 *Main Currents in Modern Thought. A Cooperative Journal to Promote the Free Association of Those Working Toward the Integration of All Knowledge Through the Study of the Whole of Things.* 1940-   . 5/yr.
051   AP2 M252

10.25 *Meanjin Quarterly. A Review of Arts and Letters in Australia.* 1940-   .
AP7 M4

10.26 *Bucknell Review. A Scholarly Journal of Letters, Arts and Science.* 1941-   . 3/yr.
AP2 B887

10.27 *Humanist.* 1941-   . 6/yr.
144   B821 A1 H8

10.28 *Canadian Modern Language Review.* 1944-   . 4/yr.

10.29 *Emory University Quarterly.* 1945-67.
378.758   AS36 E6

10.30 *Science and Public Affairs. Bulletin of the Atomic Scientists.* 1945-   . 10/yr.
341   TK9145 A84

10.31 *New South. A Quarterly Review of Southern Affairs.* 1946-   .
309.175   HN79 A2 N4

10.32 *Mississippi Quarterly. The Journal of Southern Culture.* 1947-   .
051   AS30 M58 A2

10.33 *Pacific Spectator. A Journal of Interpretation.* 1947-56.
10 vols. 4/yr.
051   AP2 P176

10.34 *Renascence. Essays on Values in Literature.* 1948-   . 2/yr.
PN2 R4

10.35 *Literature and Psychology. The Quarterly Newsletter of General
Topics Ten of the Modern Language Association.* 1951-   .
PN49 L5

10.36 *Boston University Journal. A Review of Current Graduate and
Research Activities.* 1952-   . 3/yr. Until 1969 *Boston Univ. Graduate
Journal.*
AS36 B6 A25

10.37 *Encounter. Literature, Arts, Current Affairs.* 1953-   . 12/yr.
052   AP4 E44

10.38 *Dissent.* 1954-   . 6/yr.
335.05   HX1 D58

10.39 *History of Ideas News Letter.* 1954-60. 5 vols. 4/yr.
AS30 H5

10.40 *Overland. Temper Democratic, Bias Australian.* 1954-   . 4/yr.
AP7 O9

10.41 *Aylesford Review. A Carmelite Quarterly.* 1955-68. 9 vols.

10.42 *Forum.* Houston. 1956-   . 3/yr.

10.43 *Centennial Review.* 1957-   . 4/yr.
051   AS30 C45

10.44 *Renaissance and Modern Studies.* 1957-   . Annual.
042   AS121 R4

10.45 *Arts in Society. The Arts and the Human Environment.* 1958-   .
3/yr.
N81 A893

10.46 *Discourse. A Review of the Liberal Arts.* 1958-70. 13 vols. 4/yr.
AS30 C6 A2

10.47 *Texas Quarterly.* 1958-   .
051   AP2 T269

10.48 *Massachusetts Review. A Quarterly of Literature, the Arts, and
Public Affairs.* 1959-   .
051   AS30 M3 A22

10.49 *Ohio University Review. Contributions in the Humanities.* 1959-
70. Annual. Succeeded by *Ohio Review.* 1971-   . 3/yr.
082   AS30 O4 A2

10.50 *Texas Studies in Literature and Language. A Journal of the Humanities.* 1959- . 4/yr.
820.5   AS30 T4

10.51 *American Studies.* 1960- . 2/yr. Until 1971 *Midcontinent American Studies Journal.*
E169.1 M6215

10.52 *Midway. A Magazine of Discovery in the Arts and Sciences.* 1960-70. 11 vols. 4/yr.
AP2 M553

10.53 *Dublin Magazine.* 1961- . 4/yr. Until 1964 *The Dubliner.*
PR8844 D8

10.54 *Topic. A Journal of the Liberal Arts.* 1961- . 2/yr.
AS30 T6

10.55 *American Notes and Queries.* 1962- . 10/yr. Previous series 1888-92; 1895-96; 1941-50.
AG305 A5

10.56 *Louisiana Studies.* 1962- . 4/yr.
F366 L935

10.57 *Michigan Quarterly Review. A Magazine of University Perspectives and General Intelligence.* 1962- .
AS30 M48

10.58 *Southern Quarterly. A Scholarly Journal of Studies in the Humanities and Social Sciences.* 1962- .
AS30 S658

10.59 *Alaska Review.* 1963- . 2/yr.

10.60 *South Dakota Review.* 1963- . 4/yr.
AP2 S76

10.61 *Art and Literature. An International Review.* 1964-67. 12 nos. 4/yr.
805   PN6014 A75

10.62 *Tri-Quarterly. A National Journal of Arts, Letters and Opinions.* 1964- . 3/yr.
PS508 C6 T7

10.63 *University of Dayton Review.* 1964- . 3/yr.

10.64 *Approach Magazine.* Oxford. 1965- . 3/yr.

10.65 *Humanitas. Journal of the Institute of Man.* 1965- . 3/yr.
BF1 H84

10.66 *Appalachian Review.* 1966-68. 3 vols. 4/yr.
AP2 A576

10.67 *Barat Review. A Journal of the Liberal Arts.* 1966- . 2/yr.
AS36 B3 A2

10.68 *DeKalb Literary Arts Journal. The Magazine of Literature and the Arts of DeKalb College.* 1966- . 4/yr.

10.69 *Western American Literature.* 1966- . 4/yr.

10.70 *Arlington Quarterly. A Journal of Literature, Comment and Opinion.* 1967- .

10.71 *Center Magazine. A Publication of the Center for the Study of Democratic Institutions.* 1967- . 6/yr.

10.72 *Journal of American Studies.* 1967- . 2/yr. Succeeds British Assoc. for American Studies *Bulletin,* 1956-66.
973.05   E172 B72

10.73 *Journal of Black Culture.* 1967- . 4/yr.

10.74 *Journal of Popular Culture.* 1967- . 4/yr.

10.75 *Malahat Review. An International Quarterly of Life and Letters.* 1967- .

10.76 *Mosaic. A Journal for the Comparative Study of Literature and Ideas.* 1967- . 4/yr.
809   PN2 M68

10.77 *Mundus Artium. A Journal of International Literature and the Arts.* 1967- . 3/yr.

10.78 *Southern Humanities Review.* 1967- . 4/yr.

10.79 *American Studies in Scandinavia.* 1968- . 2/yr.

10.80 *Soundings. An Interdisciplinary Journal.* 1968- . 4/yr. Supersedes *Christian Scholar,* 1917-67.
BV1460 C6

10.81 *Studies in the Humanities.* Indiana, Pa. 1969- . 2/yr.

10.82 *Twentieth Century Studies.* 1969- . 2/yr.
052   AS121 T9

10.83 *Big Rock Candy Mountain.* 1970- . 6/yr.

10.84 *Canadian Review of American Studies.* 1970- . 2/yr.
301.2973071   F1029.5 U6 C35

10.85 *Contempora.* 1970- . 6/yr.

10.86 *Enlightenment Essays.* 1970- . 4/yr.

10.87 *Irish University Review. A Journal of Irish Studies.* 1970- . 2/yr.
052

10.88 *Erasmus Review. A Journal of the Humanities.* 1971- . 5/yr.

2. British Literature

§11. Bibliographies

11.1 Howard-Hill, Trevor H. *Bibliography of British Literary Bibliographies*. London, 1969.
016.01682   Z2011 H6

11.2 Bateson, Frederick W., ed. *The Cambridge Bibliography of English Literature.* Vol. I: 600-1600; Vol. II: 1660-1800; Vol. III: 1800-1900; Vol. IV: Index. N.Y. & Cambridge, 1941. Vol. V: *Supplement, A.D. 600-1900.* Ed. George G. Watson. Cambridge, 1957.
016.82   Z2011 B28

11.3 *New Cambridge Bibliography of English Literature.* Ed. George G. Watson. Vol. II: *1660-1800,* 1971. Vol. III: *1800-1900,* 1969. N.Y. & Cambridge.
016.82   Z2011 N45

●

11.4 Brown, Stephen J. *A Guide to Books on Ireland.* Dublin & N.Y., 1912. Rpt. N.Y., 1970.
016.89162   Z2031 B86

11.5 Miller, Edmund M. *Australian Literature. A Bibliography to 1938. Extended to 1950, Edited, with a Historical Outline and Descriptive Commentaries, by Frederick T. Macartney.* Rev. ed. Sydney. 1956. (Orig. ed. 1940.)
016.8289994   Z4021 M5

11.6 Canton, E. Berthe. *Bibliography of West Indian Literature, 1900-1957.* Port of Spain, 1957.

11.7 *National Bibliography of Indian Literature, 1901-1953* [in the Humanities]. Ed. B. S. Kesavan and V. Y. Kulkarni. 2 vols. New Delhi, 1962.
Z3201 N3

11.8 *New Zealand Writing. A Selective List of Poetry, Prose Fiction, and Criticism in Print, 1967.* Wellington [?].
016.82099931   Z4111 N48

11.9 Blake, Leslie J. *Australian Writers.* Adelaide, 1968.
820   Z4021 B55

11.10 Harmon, Maurice. *Modern Irish Literature, 1800-1967. A Reader's Guide.* Chester Springs, Pa., 1968.
016.82   Z2037 H3

§12. Guides

12.1 Goode, Clement T., and Edgar F. Shannon. *An Atlas of English Literature.* N.Y., 1925.
PR109 G6

12.2 *Annals of English Literature, 1475-1950. The Principal Publications of Each Year Together with an Alphabetical Index of Authors with Their Works.* 2nd ed. rev. and updated by Robert W. Chapman. Oxford, 1961. (Orig. ed. by Jyotish C. Ghosh and Elizabeth G. Withycombe, 1935.)
016.82   Z2011 A5

12.3 Barnhart, Clarence L. *The New Century Handbook of English Literature.* Rev. ed. N.Y., 1967. (Orig. ed. 1956.)
820.3   PR19 N4

12.4 Harvey, Paul. *Oxford Companion to English Literature.* 4th ed. Rev. by Dorothy Eagle. Oxford, 1967. (Orig ed. 1932.)
820.3   PR19 H3

12.5 *Concise Oxford Dictionary of English Literature.* Ed. Dorothy Eagle. 2nd ed. London, 1970. (Orig. ed. 1939.)
820.3   PR19 C65

12.6 Johnston, Kevin W. Grahame. *Annals of Australian Literature.* London, 1970.
016.82   Z4021 J6

12.7 Jones, Joseph J. *Authors and Areas of the West Indies.* Austin, Tex., 1970.
810.99729   PR9320 J6

§13. Historical Surveys: British Isles

13.1 *The Cambridge History of English Literature.* Ed. Adolphus W. Ward and Alfred R. Waller. 14 vols. + Index. Cambridge & N.Y., 1907-17; Index, 1927. Rpt. without bibliographies 1932.
PR83 C22

13.2 Gwynn, Stephen L. *Irish Literature and Drama in the English Language. A Short History.* London, 1936. Rpt. Folcroft, Pa., 1969.
820.9   PR8711 G8

● *Introductions to English Literature.* Gen. ed. Bonamy Dobrée. London. Orig. ed. 1938-40.

    13.3 I. *The Beginnings of English Literature to Skelton, 1590,* by William L. Renwick and Harold Orton. 3rd ed. 1966.
820.902   PR83 R37

    13.4 II. *The English Renaissance, 1510-1688. With a Chapter on Literature and Music by Bruce Pattison,* by Vivian de S. Pinto. 3rd ed. 1966.
820.903   PR83 I6

    13.5 III. *Augustans and Romantics, 1689-1830,* by Henry Dyson and John Butt. 3rd ed. 1961.
820.908   PR83 I6

    13.6 IV. *The Victorians and After, 1830-1914,* by Edith C. Batho and Bonamy Dobrée. 3rd ed. 1962.
820.903   PR83 I6

    13.7 V. *The Present Age. After 1920,* by David Daiches. 1958. Rpt. 1969. (Replaced Edwin Muir, *The Present Age, from 1914,* 1939.) American title *The Present Age in British Literature,* Bloomington, Ind., 1958.
820.90091   PR471 D3

● *Oxford History of English Literature.* Oxford, 1945-　.

    13.8 I. Pt. 1. *English Literature Before the Norman Conquest.* In prep.

    13.9 Pt. 2. *Middle English Literature.* In prep.

    13.10 II. Pt. 1. *Chaucer and the Fifteenth Century,* by Henry S. Bennett. Corr. ed. 1948. (Orig. ed. 1947.) Rpt. 1954.
821.17   PR225 B43

    13.11 Pt. 2. *English Literature at the Close of the Middle Ages,* by Edmund K. Chambers. 1945. Rpt. 1957.
820.902   PR291 C5

    13.12 III. *English Literature in the Sixteenth Century Excluding Drama,* by Clive S. Lewis. 1954.
820.903   PR411 L4

    13.13 IV. Pt. 1. *The English Drama, 1485-1585,* by Frank P. Wilson and George K. Hunter. 1968.
822.209   PR641 W58

    13.14 Pt. 2. *The English Drama, 1585-1642.* In prep.

    13.15 V. *English Literature in the Earlier Seventeenth Century, 1600-1660,* by Douglas Bush. 2nd ed., 1962. (Orig. ed. 1945.)
820.903   PR431 B8

13.16 VI. *English Literature of the Late Seventeenth Century,* by James R. Sutherland. 1969.
820.9004   PR437 S9

13.17 VII. *English Literature in the Early Eighteenth Century, 1700-1740,* by Bonamy Dobrée. 1959.
820.903   PR445 D6

13.18 VIII. *The Mid-Eighteenth Century.* In prep.

13.19 IX. *English Literature, 1789-1815,* by William L. Renwick. 1963.
820.903   PR447 R4

13.20 X. *English Literature, 1815-1832,* by Ian R. Jack. 1963.
820.93   PR457 J24

13.21 XI. *The Mid-Nineteenth Century.* In prep.

13.22 XII. *Eight Modern Writers,* by John I. M. Stewart. 1963.
820.904   PR461 S8

• *A History of English Literature.* Gen. ed. Hardin Craig. N.Y.,1950. Rpt. in 2 vols. with New Pref., 1962.

13.23 I. *Old and Middle English Literature, from the Beginnings to 1485,* by George K. Anderson.

13.24 II. *The Literature of the English Renaissance, 1485-1660,* by Hardin Craig.

13.25 III. *The Literature of the Restoration and the Eighteenth Century, 1660-1798,* by Louis Bredvold.

13.26 IV. *The Literature of the Nineteenth and Early Twentieth Centuries, 1798 to the First World War,* by Joseph W. Beach.
820.9   PR85 C682

13.27 Wittig, Kurt. *The Scottish Tradition in Literature.* Edinburgh, 1958.
820.9   PR8511 W5

• *Pelican Guides to English Literature.* Ed. Boris Ford. London.

13.28 I. *The Age of Chaucer.* 1954, rev. 1961.

13.29 II. *The Age of Shakespeare.* 1955, rev. 1961.

13.30 III. *From Donne to Marvell.* 1956, rev. 1962.

13.31 IV. *From Dryden to Johnson.* 1957, rev. 1962.

13.32 V. *From Blake to Byron.* 1957, rev. 1962.

13.33 VI. *From Dickens to Hardy.* 1958, rev. 1963.

13.34 VII. *The Modern Age.* 1961, rev. 1963.
820.9   PR83 F6

• *A Literary History of England.* Ed. Albert C. Baugh et al. 2nd ed. N.Y. & London, 1967. (Orig. ed. 1948.) Both eds. also in 4 vols.

13.35 I. *The Middle Ages. The Old English Period to 1100*, by Kemp Malone, and *The Middle English Period, 1100-1500*, by Albert C. Baugh.

13.36 II. *The Renaissance, 1500-1660*, by Charles F. T. Brooke.

13.37 III. *The Restoration and Eighteenth Century, 1660-1789*, by George Sherburn.

13.38 IV. *The Nineteenth Century and After, 1789-1939*, by Samuel C. Chew.
820.9   PR83 B3

13.39 O'Connor, Frank [Michael O'Donovan]. *A Short History of Irish Literature. A Backward Look.* N.Y., 1967.
820.9   PB1306 O3

13.40 Armour, Richard W. *English Lit Relit. A Short History of English Literature from the Precursors (Before Swearing) to the Pre-Raphaelites and a Little After* . . . N.Y., 1969.
820.207   PR86 A7

13.41 Power, Patrick C. *A Literary History of Ireland.* Cork, 1969. Rpt. 1971.
820.99415   PR8711 P6

13.42 Daiches, David. *A Critical History of English Literature.* 2 vols. 2nd ed. N.Y., 1970. (Orig. ed., London and N.Y., 1960. Rpt. London, 1968, in 4 vols.)
820.9   PR83 D29

13.43 Garlick, Raymond. *An Introduction to Anglo-Welsh Literature.* Cardiff, 1970.
820.9   PR8911 G3

• *The History of Literature in the English Language.* London, 1970-

   13.44 Vol. I: *The Middle Ages.* Ed. Whitney F. Bolton. 1970.
820.9001   PR166 B6

   13.45 Vol. II: *English Poetry and Prose 1540-1674.* Ed. Christopher Ricks. 1970.
820.9   PR533 E5

   13.46 Vol. III: *English Drama to 1710.* Ed. Christopher Ricks. 1971.
822.009

   13.47 Vol. IV: *Dryden to Johnson.* Ed. Roger Lonsdale. 1971.
820.9

   13.48 Vol. V: *The Romantics.* In prep.

   13.49 Vol. VI: *The Victorians.* Ed. Arthur Pollard. 1970.
820.9008   PR463 P6

   13.50 Vol. VII: *The Twentieth Century.* Ed. Bernard Bergonzi. 1970.
820.90091   PR473 B4

13.51 Vol. VIII: *American Literature to 1900.* Ed. Marcus Cunliffe. In prep.

13.52 Vol. IX: *American Literature since 1900.* Ed. Marcus Cunliffe. In prep.

13.53 Vol. X: *Commonwealth Literature.* In prep.

13.54 Vol. XI: *The English Language.* Ed. Whitney F. Bolton. In prep.

13.55 Sampson, George. *The Concise Cambridge History of English Literature. With Additional Chapters on the Literature of the United States of America and the Mid-Twentieth-Century of the English-Speaking World by R[eginald] C. Churchill.* 3rd ed. Cambridge, 1970. (Orig. ed. 1941.)
820.9   PR85 S34

13.56 Tibble, Anne. *The Story of English Literature. A Critical Survey.* London, 1971.
820.9   PR83 T5

§14. Historical Surveys: The Commonwealth

14.1 *English Studies in Africa.* 1958- . 2/yr. Annual Bibliography.
PR1 E6

14.2 *Australian Literary Studies.* 1963- . 2/yr. Annual bibliography.
PR9400 A86

14.3 *Journal of Commonwealth Literature.* 1965- . 2/yr. Annual bibliography.
820.05   PR1 J67

●

14.4 McCormick, Eric H. *New Zealand Literature. A Survey.* London, 1959.
820.9   PR9606 M3

14.5 Hadgraft, Cecil. *Australian Literature. A Critical Account to 1955.* London, 1960.
820.9   PR9411 H3

14.6 Green, Henry M. *A History of Australian Literature Pure and Applied. A Critical Review of All Forms of Literature Produced in Australia from the First Books Published After the Arrival of the First Fleet Until 1950, with Short Accounts of Later Publications Up to 1960.* 2 vols. Sydney, 1961. Rpt. with corrections 1962, 1966, 1968.
820   PR9411 G7

14.7 Dutton, Geoffrey, ed. *The Literature of Australia.* Harmondsworth, Eng., 1964.
820.9   PR9414 D8

14.8 Friederich, Werner P. *Australia in Western Imaginative Prose Writings, 1600-1960. An Anthology and a History of Literature.* Chapel Hill, N.C., 1967. U. of N.C. St. in Comp. Lit. 40.
809.933   PN56.3 A9 F7

14.9 Barnes, Richard J., ed. *The Writer in Australia. A Collection of Literary Documents, 1856 to 1964.* Melbourne & N.Y., 1969.
820.9994   PR9411 B3

14.10 Wilkes, Gerald A., and John C. Reid, eds. *The Literatures of the British Commonwealth: Australia and New Zealand.* University Park, Pa., 1971.
820.9   PR9412 W5

§15. General Studies

15.1 *An English Miscellany Presented to Dr. Furnivall in Honour of His Seventy-Fifth Birthday.* Oxford, 1901. Rpt. N.Y., 1969.
820.9   PR14 E57

15.2 MacDonagh, Thomas. *Literature in Ireland. Studies Irish and Anglo-Irish.* Dublin, 1916. Rpt. London, 1961; Pt. Washington, N.Y., 1970.
821   PR8711 M3

15.3 Allen, Beverley S. *Tides in English Taste, 1619-1800. A Background for the Study of Literature.* 2 vols. Cambridge, Mass., 1937. Rpt. N.Y., 1958.
701.17   N6766 A4

15.4 Wellek, René. *The Rise of English Literary History.* Chapel Hill, N.C., 1941. Rpt. N.Y., 1966.
820.903   PR401 W4

15.5 McManaway, James G., et al., eds. *Joseph Quincy Adams. Memorial Studies.* Washington, D.C., 1948.
820.903   PR423 F6

15.6 Thomson, James A. K. *The Classical Background of English Literature.* London & N.Y., 1948. Rpt. N.Y., 1962.
820.9   PR127 T5

15.7 Thomson, James A. K. *Classical Influences on English Poetry.* London & N.Y., 1951. Rpt. N.Y., 1956, 1962.
821.09   PR127 T53

15.8 Norton, Dan S., and Peters Rushton. *Classical Myths in English Literature.* N.Y., 1952. Rpt. 1970.
292   BL313 N6

15.9 Tillyard, Eustace M. W. *The English Epic and Its Background.* N.Y., 1954. Rpt. 1966.
809.13   PR125 T5

15.10 Williams, Raymond. *Culture and Society, 1780-1950.* London & N.Y., 1958.
914.2   DA533 W6

15.11 Birley, Robert. *Sunk Without Trace. Some Forgotten Masterpieces Reconsidered.* London & N.Y., 1962.
820.9   PR99 B43

15.12 Speirs, John H. *The Scots Literary Tradition. An Essay in Criticism.* 2nd ed. London, 1962. (Orig. ed. 1940.)
821.09   PR8561 S65

15.13 MacLure, Millar, and Frank W. Watt, eds. *Essays in English Literature from the Renaissance to the Victorian Age, Presented to A. S. P. Woodhouse, 1964.* Toronto, 1964.
820.9   PR14 M3

15.14 Gillie, Christopher. *Character in English Literature.* London & n.y., 1965.
820.93   PR149 C37 G5

15.15 Ehrstine, John W., et al. *On Stage and Off. Eight Essays in English Literature.* Pullman, Wash., 1968.
820.9   PR14 O5

15.16 *The Morality of Art. Essays Presented to G. Wilson Knight by His Colleagues and Friends.* Ed. Douglas W. Jefferson. London & N.Y., 1969.
820.9   PR14 M6

15.17 *Librarianship and Literature. Essays in Honour of Jack Pafford.* Ed. Alexander T. Milne. London, 1970.
020.942   Z665 L57

15.18 Sprigg, Christopher S. [pseud. Christopher Caudwell]. *Romance and Realism. A Study in English Bourgeois Literature.* Ed. Samuel Hynes. Princeton, 1970.
820.9   PR401 S7

§16. General Studies: The Commonwealth

16.1 *Southerly. A Review of Australian Literature.* 1939-   . 4/yr.
820.5   AP7 S6

•

16.2 Mulgan, Alan. *Literature and Authorship in New Zealand.* London, 1943. Rpt. Folcroft, Pa., 1971.
820.9   PR9606 M8

16.3 Srinivasa Iyengar, K. R. *Indo-Anglian Literature.* Bombay, 1943.
820.9   PR9706 S7

16.4 Srinivasa Iyengar, K. R. *The Indian Contribution to English Literature*. Bombay, 1945.
820.9   PR9706 S68

16.5 Ingamells, Rex. *Handbook of Australian Letters*. Melbourne, 1949.
820.9   PR9413 I4

16.6 McLeod, Alan L., ed. *The Commonwealth Pen. An Introduction to the Literature of the British Commonwealth*. Ithaca, N.Y., 1961.
820.9   PR9080 M3

16.7 Srinivasa Iyengar, K. R. *Indian Writing in English*. London, 1962.
820.9   PR9706 S69

16.8 Times Literary Supplement. *A Language in Common. Special No., Aug. 10, 1962.* Rpt. for NCTE. London, 1963.
828.995   PR99 T57

16.9 *Commonwealth Literature. Unity and Diversity in a Common Culture. Extracts from the Proceedings of a Conference Held at Bodington Hall, Leeds, 9-12 September 1964, Under the Auspices of the University of Leeds.* Ed. John Press. London & N.Y., 1965.
820.9   PE13 C6

16.10 Jones, Joseph J. *Terranglia. The Case for English as World-Literature*. N.Y., 1965.
820.9   PR471 J65

16.11 Ewers, John K. *Creative Writing in Australia. A Selective Survey.* 5th ed. Melbourne, 1966. (Orig. ed. 1945.)
820.903   PR9412 E9

16.12 Harris, Wilson. *Tradition, the Writer and Society. Critical Essays.* Port of Spain & London, 1967.
801   PR6058 A692 T7

16.13 James, Louis, ed. *The Islands in Between. Essays on West Indian Literature*. London, 1968.
820   PR9320.5 J3

16.14 Roderick, Colin A. *Suckled By a Wolf. Or, The Nature of Australian Literature*. Sydney, 1968.
820.9   PR9416 R6

16.15 McCutchion, David. *Indian Writing in English. Critical Essays.* Calcutta, 1969.
820.9954   PR9708 M3

16.16 Moore, Gerald. *The Chosen Tongue. English Writing in the Tropical World*. London, 1969.
820.9913   PR9320.5 M6

16.17 Wilkes, Gerald A. *Australian Literature. A Conspectus.* Sydney, 1969.

16.18 Goodwin, Kenneth, ed. *National Identity. Papers Delivered at the Commonwealth Literature Conference, University of Queensland, 9th-15th August, 1968.* London & Melbourne, 1970.

16.19 Srinivasa Iyengar, K. R. *Two Cheers for the Commonwealth. Talks on Literature and Education.* N.Y., 1970.
820.9   PR99 S69

16.20 Walsh, William. *A Manifold Voice. Studies in Commonwealth Literature.* N.Y., 1970.
820.9   PR9080 W3

16.21 Moore, Tom Inglis. *Social Patterns in Australian Literature.* Berkeley & Sydney, 1971.

16.22 Verghese, C. Paul. *Problems of the Indian Creative Writer in English.* Bombay, 1971.
820.9954   PR9706 V4

§17. Language: Historical Surveys

17.1 McKnight, George H. *Modern English in the Making.* N.Y., 1928. Rpt. as *The Evolution of the English Language. From Chaucer to the Twentieth Century.* N.Y., 1968.
420.9   PE1075 M3

17.2 Jespersen, Otto. *Growth and Structure of the English Language.* 9th ed. London, 1938. (Orig. ed. 1905.) Rpt. Oxford, 1948; N.Y., 1955, 1968.
420.9   PE1075 J4

17.3 Robertson, Stuart. *The Development of Modern English.* Rev. by Frederic G. Cassidy. 2nd ed. N.Y., 1954. (Orig. ed. 1934.)
420.9   PE1075 R57

17.4 Baugh, Albert C. *A History of the English Language.* 2nd ed. N.Y., 1957. (Orig. ed. 1935.)
420.9   PE1075 B3

17.5 Bryant, Margaret M. *Modern English and Its Heritage.* 2nd ed. N.Y., 1962. (Orig. ed. 1948.)
420.9   PE1072 B75

17.6 Bloomfield, Morton W., and Leonard Newmark. *A Linguistic Introduction to the History of English.* N.Y., 1963.
420.9   PE1075 B5

17.7 Baker, Sidney J. *The Australian Language. An Examination of the English Language and English Speech as Used in Australia, from Convict Days to the Present, with Special Reference to the Growth of Indigenous Idiom and Its Use by Australian Writers.* 2nd ed. Sydney, 1966. (Orig. ed. 1945.)
427.994   PE3601 B3

17.8 Bolton, Whitney F. *A Short History of Literary English.* London, 1967.
820.9   PE1075 B64

17.9 Strang, Barbara M. H. *A History of English.* London, 1970.
420.9   PE1075 S85

17.10 Pyles, Thomas. *The Origins and Development of the English Language.* 2nd ed. N.Y., 1971. (Orig. ed. 1964.)
420.9   PE1075 P9

§18. Language: Special Topics

18.1 Morris, Edward E. *Austral English. A Dictionary of Australasian Words, Phrases, and Usages. With Those Aboriginal-Australian and Maori Words Which Have Become Incorporated in the Language and the Commoner Scientific Words That Have Had Their Origin in Australasia.* London, 1898. Rpt. Detroit, 1968.
427.993   PE3601 M8

18.2 Wright, Joseph. *The English Dialect Dictionary. Being the Complete Vocabulary of All Dialect Words Still in Use, or Known to Have Been in Use During the Last Two Hundred Years.* 6 vols. London, 1898-1905.
          PE1766 W8

18.3 Yule, Henry, and Arthur C. Burnell. *Hobson-Jobson. A Glossary of Colloquial Anglo-Indian Words and Phrases, and of Kindred Terms, Etymological, Historical, Geographical and Discursive.* New ed. by William Crooke. London, 1903. (Orig. ed. 1886.) Rpt. N.Y. & London, 1968.
422.491   PE3501 Y78

✓ **18.4** Murray, James A. H., et al., eds. *The Oxford English Dictionary. Being a Corrected Re-Issue . . . of "A New English Dictionary on Historical Principles Founded Mainly on the Materials Collected by the Philological Society."* 13 vols. London, 1933. (Orig. ed. in 10 vols., 1884-1928.) *The Compact Edition of the OED.* 2 vols. 1971.
423   PE1625 M7

18.5 Little, William, et al., eds. *The Shorter Oxford English Dictionary on Historical Principles.* 3rd ed. 2 vols. London, 1944. Rpt. with Rev. Addenda, 1955, 1962. (Orig. ed. 1933.)
423   PE1625 M72

18.6 Bailey, Dudley, ed. *Introductory Language Essays.* N.Y., 1965.
420.82   PE1072 B3

18.7 Brook, George L. *English Dialects.* 2nd ed. London, 1965. (Orig. ed. 1963.)
427   PE1711 B7

18.8 Fowler, Henry W. *A Dictionary of Modern English Usage.* 2nd ed. Rev. by Ernest Gowers. N.Y. & Oxford, 1965. (Orig. ed. 1926.)
423   PE1628 F65

18.9 Greenwood, Joseph A. *Find It in Fowler. An Alphabetical Index . . .* Princeton, 1969.
423   PE1628 F65

18.10 Klein, Ernest. *A Comprehensive Etymological Dictionary of the English Language. Dealing with the Origin of Words and Their Sense Development Thus Illustrating the History of Civilization and Culture.* 2 vols. N.Y., 1966-67. 1 vol. ed. 1971.
422.03   PE1580 K47

18.11 Onions, Charles T., et al., eds. *The Oxford Dictionary of English Etymology.* London & N.Y., 1966.
422.03   PE1580 O5

18.12 Ramson, William S. *Australian English. An Historical Study of the Vocabulary, 1788-1898.* Canberra, 1966.
427.994   PE3601 R3

18.13 Turner, George W. *The English Language in Australia and New Zealand.* London, 1966.
427.994   PE3601 T8

18.14 Cassidy, Frederic G., and Robert B. Le Page, eds. *Dictionary of Jamaican English.* London & N.Y., 1967.
427.97292   PE3313 Z5 C3

18.15 Partridge, Eric. *A Dictionary of the Underworld British and American. Being the Vocabularies of Crooks, Criminals, Racketeers, Beggars and Tramps, Convicts, the Commercial Underworld, the Drug Traffic, the White Slave Traffic, Spivs.* 3rd ed. London, 1968. (Orig. ed. 1949.)
427.09   PE3726 P3

18.16 Quirk, Randolph. *Essays on the English Language. Medieval and Modern.* Bloomington, Ind., & Harlow, Eng. 1968.
420   PE1072 Q49

18.17 Cook, Albert B. *Introduction to the English Language. Structure and History.* N.Y., 1969.
420.9   PE1075 C6

18.18 Wall, C. Edward, and Edward Przebienda, eds. *Words and Phrases Index. A Guide to Antedatings, New Words, New Compounds, New Meanings, and Other Published Scholarship Supplementing the Oxford English Dictionary, Dictionary of Americanisms, Dictionary of American English and Other Major Dictionaries of the English Language.* 4 vols. Ann Arbor, 1969.
016.423   PE1689 W3

18.19 Partridge, Eric. *A Dictionary of Slang and Unconventional English. Colloquialisms and Catch-Phrases, Solecisms and Catachreses, Nicknames, Vulgarisms, and Such Americanisms as Have Been Naturalized.* 7th ed. 2 vols. London & N.Y., 1970. (Orig. ed. 1937.)

427.09   PE3721 P3

18.20 Partridge, Eric. *Slang To-Day and Yesterday. With a Short Historical Sketch and Vocabularies of English, American, and Australian Slang.* 4th ed. N.Y., 1970. (Orig. ed. 1933.)

427.09   PE3711 P3

18.21 Ramson, William S., ed. *English Transported. Essays on Australasian English.* Canberra, 1970.

427.99   PE3601 R33

3. Literature of the United States and Canada

§19. Bibliographies: General and Literary

19.1 *American Quarterly.* 1949- Annual bibliography of articles on American Studies.
051   AP2 A3985

19.2 *Jahrbuch für Amerikastudien.* 1956- . Heidelberg. Bibliography.
E169.1 J33

19.3 *American Studies. An International Newsletter.* 1965- . American Studies Assoc. 3/yr.
E175.8 A58

•

19.4 American Studies Assoc. *Bibliography of American Culture, 1493-1875.* Ed. David R. Weimer. Ann Arbor, 1957.
016.9173   Z1215 A585

19.5 Basler, Roy P., et al. *A Guide to the Study of the United States of America. Representative Books Reflecting the Development of American Life and Thought.* Washington, D.C.: Library of Congress, 1960.
016.9173   Z1215 U53

19.6 Tanghe, Raymond. *Bibliography of Canadian Bibliographies.* Toronto, 1960. *Supplement 1961,* 1962, and *Supplement 1962,* 1964.
016.01571   Z1365 A1 T3

19.7 Howes, Wright, ed. *U.S.iana (1650-1950). A Selective Bibliography in Which Are Described 11,620 Uncommon and Significant Books Relating to the Continental Portion of the United States.* 2nd ed. N.Y., 1962. (Orig. ed. 1954.)
016.973   Z1215 H75

19.8 McGill University Library. *The Lawrence Lande Collection of Canadiana in the Redpath Library of McGill University. A Bibliography Collected, Arranged, and Annotated by Lawrence Lande.* Montreal, 1965.
Z1365 M14

19.9 Welsch, Erwin K. *The Negro in the United States. A Research Guide.* Bloomington, Ind., 1965.
Z1361 N39 W4

19.10 Harvard University. *Canadian History and Literature.* Widener Library Shelflist No. 20. Cambridge, Mass., 1968.
016.9171   Z1365 H3

19.11 Miller, Elizabeth W., ed. *The Negro in America. A Bibliography.* 2nd ed. by Mary L. Fisher. Cambridge, Mass., 1970. (Orig. ed. 1966.)
016.30145196073   Z1361 N39 M5

19.12 Porter, Dorothy B. *The Negro in the United States. A Selected Bibliography.* Washington, D.C., 1970.
016.9173097496   Z1361 N39 P59

Carnegie System .   •

19.13 *American Literature. A Journal of Literary History, Criticism and Bibliography.* 1929-   . 4/yr with bibliography of periodical literature.
810.5   PS1 A6 - A 5/2 L 7757 (2nd floor)

   19.14 Marshall, Thomas F. *An Analytical Index to "American Literature," Volumes I-XXX, March, 1929-January, 1963.* Durham, N.C., 1963.
Z1225 A4

19.15 *University of Toronto Quarterly. A Canadian Journal of the Humanities.* 1931-   . Annual survey "Letters in Canada."
051   AP5 U55

19.16 *Canadian Literature/Littérature canadienne. A Quarterly of Criticism and Review.* 1959-   . Annual bibliography.
PR9100 C25

   19.17 Bell, Inglis F., and Susan W. Port. *Canadian Literature, 1959-1963. A Checklist of Creative and Critical Writings.* Vancouver, 1966.
016.8098971   Z1375 B4

19.18 *American Literary Scholarship; An Annual.* 1965-   . Ed. James Woodress, 1965-69, J. Albert Robbins, 1970-
814.008   PS3 A47

19.19 *American Literature Abstracts. A Review of Current Scholarship in American Literature.* 1967- . 2/yr.
016.81   PS1 A63

•

19.20 Morgan, Henry J. *Bibliotheca canadensis. Or, A Manual of Canadian Literature.* Ottawa, 1867. Rpt. Detroit, 1968.
810.9   Z1374 M6

19.21 Johnson, Merle D. *American First Editions.* 4th ed. by Jacob Blanck. N.Y., 1942. (Orig. ed. 1929.)
016.0944   Z1231 F5 J6

19.22 Leary, Lewis G. *Articles on American Literature, 1900-1950.* Durham, N.C., 1954. Rpt. 1970.
016.81   Z1225 L49

19.23 Blanck, Jacob N. *Bibliography of American Literature.* New Haven, 1955- .
016.81   Z1225 B55

19.24 Watters, Reginald E. *A Check List of Canadian Literature and Background Materials, 1628-1950. Being a Comprehensive List of the Books Which Constitute Canadian Literature Written in English, Together with a Selective List of Other Books by Canadian Authors Which Reveal the Backgrounds of That Literature.* Toronto, 1959. New ed. in prep.
013.971   Z1375 W3

    19.25 Roy, George R., and Michael Gnarowski, eds. *Canadian Poetry. A Supplementary Bibliography.* Quebec, 1964.

19.26 Maldonado, Anita F. *Index to Articles on American Literature, 1951-1959.* Boston, 1960.
Z1225 P4

19.27 Stovall, Floyd H., ed. *Eight American Authors. A Review of Research and Criticism.* N.Y., 1956. Rpt. with Bibliographical Supplement by J. Chesley Mathews, 1963.
810.903   PS201 S8

19.28 Watters, Reginald E., and Inglis F. Bell, eds. *On Canadian Literature, 1806-1960. A Check List of Articles, Books, and Theses on English-Canadian Literature, Its Authors, and Language.* Toronto, 1966.
016.8109   Z1375 W33

19.29 Davis, Richard B., ed. *American Literature Through Bryant, 1585-1830.* Goldentree Bibliographies. N.Y., 1969.
016.8109   Z1225 D3

19.30 Rubin, Louis D., ed. *A Bibliographical Guide to the Study of Southern Literature. With an Appendix Containing Sixty-Eight Additional Writers of the Colonial South by J. A. Leo Lemay.* Baton Rouge, La., 1969.
016.81   Z1225 R8

19.31 Ryan, Pat M. *Black Writing in the U.S.A. A Bibliographic Guide.* Brockport, N.Y., 1969.
013.973   Z1361 N39 R98

19.32 Gohdes, Clarence L. *Bibliographical Guide to the Study of the Literature of the U.S.A.* 3rd ed. Durham, N.C., 1970. (Orig. ed. 1959.)
016.81   Z1225 G6

19.33 Hirschfelder, Arlene B., ed. *American Indian Authors. A Representative Bibliography.* N.Y., 1970.
016.81   Z7118 H55

19.34 Leary, Lewis G. *Articles on American Literature, 1950-1967.* Durham, N.C., 1970.
016.8109   Z1225 L492

19.35 Nilon, Charles H. *Bibliography of Bibliographies in American Literature.* N.Y., 1970.
016.01681   Z1225 A1 N5

19.36 Turner, Darwin T., ed. *Afro-American Writers.* Goldentree Bibliographies. N.Y., 1970.
016.81080917496   Z1361 N39 T78

19.37 Brown University Library. *Dictionary Catalog of the Harris Collection of American Poetry and Plays.* 13 vols. Boston, 1972.

§20. Guides

20.1 *The Reader's Encyclopedia of American Literature.* Ed. Max J. Herzberg. N.Y., 1962.
810.3   PS21 R4

20.2 Hart, James D. *Oxford Companion to American Literature.* 4th ed. N.Y., 1965. (Orig. ed. 1941.)
810.3   PS21 H3

20.3 Story, Norah. *The Oxford Companion to Canadian History and Literature.* Toronto, 1967.
810.3   PR9106 S7

20.4 Jones, Joseph J., and Johanna Jones. *Authors and Areas of Canada.* Austin, Tex., 1970.
810.9971   PR9127 J6

20.5 Waterman, Arthur E. *A Chronology of American Literary History.* Columbus, O., 1970.
810.202   PS94 W3

§21. Historical Surveys

21.1 *Resources for American Literary Study.* 1971- . 2/yr.

•

21.2 Wendell, Barrett. *A Literary History of America.* N.Y., 1900. Rpt. Detroit, 1968.
810.9   PS88 W4

21.3 Trent, William P., et al. *The Cambridge History of American Literature.* 4 vols. N.Y., 1917-21. Rpt. in 3 vols. 1933; rpt. in 1 vol. 1943, 1946.
810.9   PS88 C3

21.4 Boynton, Percy H. *A History of American Literature.* Boston, 1919. Rpt. N.Y., 1970.
820.9   PS92 B65

21.5 Parrington, Vernon L. *Main Currents in American Thought. An Interpretation of American Literature from the Beginnings to 1920.* Vol. I: 1620-1800 *The Colonial Mind;* Vol. II: 1800-1860 *The Romantic Revolution in America;* Vol. III: 1860-1920 *The Beginnings of Critical Realism in America.* 3 vols. N.Y., 1927. Rpt. in 1 vol. 1930, 1939, 1958. Rpt. of vols. 1 and 2, 1954. Rpt. in 3 vols. 1958.
810.9   PS88 P33

21.6 Quinn, Arthur H., ed. *The Literature of the American People. An Historical and Critical Survey.* N.Y., 1951.
810.9   PS88 Q5

21.7 Wilson, Edmund. *The Shock of Recognition. The Development of Literature in the United States Recorded by the Men Who Made It.* 2nd ed. N.Y., 1955. (Orig. ed. 1943.) Rpt. in 2 vols., 1957.
810.82   PS55 W5

21.8 Brooks, Van Wyck, and Otto L. Bettmann. *Our Literary Heritage. A Pictorial History of the Writer in America.* N.Y., 1956.
810.903   PS92 B73

21.9 Pacey, William C. Desmond. *Creative Writing in Canada. A Short History of English-Canadian Literature.* 2nd ed. Toronto, 1961. (Orig. ed. 1952.) Rpt. 1967.
PR9111 P3

21.10 Spiller, Robert E., et al. *Literary History of the United States.* 2 vols. 3rd ed. N.Y., 1963. (Orig. ed. in 3 vols., 1948.) Includes bibliography of orig. ed. with 1959 Bibliography Supplement by Richard Ludwig. Supplement II, 1972.

810.9   PS88 L522

21.11 Klinck, Carl F., ed. *Literary History of Canada. Canadian Literature in English.* Toronto, 1965.

PR9111 K4

21.12 Littlejohn, David. *Black on White. A Critical Survey of Writing by American Negroes.* N.Y., 1966. Rpt. 1969.

810.9   PS153 N5 L5

21.13 Cunliffe, Marcus F. *The Literature of the United States.* 3rd ed. London & Baltimore. 1967. (Orig. ed. 1954.)

810.9   PS92 C8

§22. General Literary Studies

22.1 Lawrence, D[avid] H. *Studies in Classic American Literature.* N.Y., 1923. Latest rpt. 1964. Also *The Symbolic Meaning. The Uncollected Versions of "Studies in Classic American Literature."* Ed. Armin Arnold. Fontwell, England, 1962; N.Y., 1964.

810.9   PS121 L3

22.2 Dondore, Dorothy A. *The Prairie and the Making of Middle America. Four Centuries of Description.* Cedar Rapids, Ia., 1926. Rpt. N.Y., 1961.

F351 D672

22.3 Nelson, John H. *The Negro Character in American Literature.* Lawrence, Kan., 1926. Rpt. College Park, Md., 1968; N.Y., 1970.

810.93   PS173 N4 N4

22.4 Hazard, Lucy L. *The Frontier in American Literature.* N.Y., 1927. Rpt. 1961.

810.9093   PS169 F7 H3

22.5 Smith, Charles A. *Southern Literary Studies. A Collection of Literary, Biographical, and Other Sketches. With a Biographical Study by F. Stringfellow Barr.* Chapel Hill, N.C., 1927. Rpt. Pt. Washington, N.Y., 1967.

810.9975   PS261 S5

22.6 Foerster, Norman, ed. *The Reinterpretation of American Literature. Some Contributions Toward the Understanding of Its Historical Development.* N.Y., 1928. Rpt. 1959.

810.9   PS88 F6

22.7 Brawley, Benjamin G. *The Negro in Literature and Art in the United States.* N.Y., 1930. Rpt. 1971.
810.9896073   PS153 N5 B65

22.8 Boynton, Percy H. *The Rediscovery of the Frontier.* Chicago, 1931. Rpt. N.Y., 1968, 1970.
813.0093   PS169 F7 B6

22.9 Rourke, Constance M. *American Humor. A Study of the National Character.* N.Y., 1931. Rpt. Garden City, N.Y., 1953. Rpt. N.Y., 1971.
817.09   PS430 R6

22.10 Knight, Grant C. *American Literature and Culture.* N.Y., 1932.
810.9   PS88 K6

22.11 Keiser, Albert. *The Indian in American Literature.* N.Y., 1933. Rpt. 1970.
810.93   PS173 I6 K4

22.12 Brown, Sterling A. *The Negro in American Fiction. Negro Poetry and Drama.* Washington, D.C., 1937. Rpt. Pt. Washington, N.Y., 1968; N.Y., 1969.
813.0093   PS374 N4 B7

22.13 Mersand, Joseph. *Traditions in American Literature. A Study of Jewish Characters and Authors.* N.Y., 1939. Rpt. Pt. Washington, N.Y., 1968.
810.99174924   PS153 J4 M4

22.14 Cargill, Oscar. *Intellectual America. Ideas on the March.* N.Y., 1941. Rpt. 1968.
810.9   PS88 C37

22.15 Smith, Henry N. *Virgin Land. The American West as Symbol and Myth.* Cambridge, Mass., 1950. Rpt. with new Preface, 1970.
978   F591 S65

22.16 Horton, Rod W., and Herbert W. Edwards. *Backgrounds of American Literary Thought.* N.Y., 1952.
810.9   PS88 H6

22.17 Fishman, Solomon. *The Disinherited of Art. Writer and Background.* Berkeley, 1953.
801   PN85 F5

22.18 Fiedler, Leslie A. *An End to Innocence. Essays on Culture and Politics.* Boston, 1955. Rpt. 1957.
973.9204   E169.1 F5

22.19 Spiller, Robert E. *The Cycle of American Literature. An Essay in Historical Criticism.* N.Y., 1955. Rpt. 1957, 1967, 1969.
810.9   PS88 S6

22.20 Butcher, Margaret J. *The Negro in American Culture. Based on Materials Left by Alain Locke.* N.Y., 1956.
325.260973   E185.82 B89

22.21 Brooks, Van Wyck. *The Dream of Arcadia. American Writers and Artists in Italy, 1760-1915.* N.Y., 1958.
914.5   DG457 A6 B7

22.22 Feidelson, Charles, and Paul Brodtkorb, eds. *Interpretations of American Literature.* N.Y., 1959.
810.9   PS121 F4

22.23 Conference of Negro Writers. *The American Negro Writer and His Roots.* N.Y., 1960.
809.8   PS153 N5 C6

22.24 Green, Martin B. *A Mirror for Anglo-Saxons. A Discovery of America, a Rediscovery of England.* N.Y., 1960.
917.3   E169.1 G74

22.25 Howard, Leon. *Literature and the American Tradition.* Garden City, N.Y., 1960.
810.9   PS88 H65

22.26 Kwiat, Joseph J., and Mary C. Turpie, eds. *Studies in American Culture. Dominant Ideas and Images.* Minneapolis, 1960.
917.3   E169.1 K85

22.27 Parry, Albert. *Garrets and Pretenders. A History of Bohemianism in America.* Rev. ed. N.Y., 1960. (Orig. ed. 1933.)
917.3   PS138 P3

22.28 McDermott, John F., ed. *Research Opportunities in American Cultural History.* Lexington, Ky., 1961.
973.072   E175 M3

22.29 Sanford, Charles L. *The Quest for Paradise. Europe and the American Moral Imagination.* Urbana, Ill., 1961.
917.3   E169.1 S245

22.30 Green, Martin B. *Re-Appraisals. Some Commonsense Readings in American Literature.* London, 1963.
813.009   PS121 G7

22.31 Robinson, Cecil. *With the Ears of Strangers. The Mexican in American Literature.* Tucson, Ariz., 1963.
810.93   PS173 M4 R6

22.32 Baritz, Loren, *City on a Hill. A History of Ideas and Myths in America.* N.Y., 1964.
917.3   E169.1 B225

22.33 Curti, Merle E. *The Growth of American Thought.* 3rd ed. N.Y., 1964. (Orig. ed. 1943.)
917.3   E169.1 C87

22.34 Fishwick, Marshall W., ed. *American Studies in Transition.* Philadelphia, 1964.
917.3   E169.1 F543

22.35 Marx, Leo. *The Machine in the Garden. Technology and the Pastoral Ideal in America.* N.Y., 1964. Rpt. 1967.
917.3   E169.1 M35

22.36 Moore, Geoffrey H. *American Literature and the American Imagination.* Hull, Eng., 1964.
810.8   PS124 M6

22.37 Thorp, Willard. *American Humorists.* Minneapolis, 1964. Univ. of Minn. Pamphlets on American Writers, 42.
                    PS430 T4

22.38 Walker, William E., and Robert L. Welker, eds. *Reality and Myth. Essays in American Literature in Memory of Richmond Croom Beatty.* Nashville, Tenn., 1964.
810.9   PS121 W25

22.39 Clough, Wilson O. *The Necessary Earth. Nature and Solitude in American Literature.* Austin, Tex., 1965.
810.93   PS163 C6

22.40 Grant, Douglas. *Purpose and Place. Essays on American Writers.* London & N.Y., 1965.
810.9   PS121 G68

22.41 Hubbell, Jay B. *South and Southwest. Literary Essays and Reminiscences.* Durham, N.C., 1965.
810.9   PS121 H83

22.42 Jones, Howard M. *The Theory of American Literature.* 2nd ed. Ithaca, N.Y., 1965. (Orig. ed. 1948.)
810.9   PS31 J6

22.43 Krause, Sydney J., ed. *Essays on Determinism in American Literature.* Kent, O., 1965.
                    PS121 K7

22.44 Malin, Irving. *Jews and Americans.* Carbondale, Ill., 1965.
820.93   PS508 J4 M32

22.45 Spiller, Robert E. *The Third Dimension. Studies in Literary History.* N.Y., 1965.
810.9   PS121 S6

22.46 Tanner, Tony. *The Reign of Wonder. Naïvety and Reality in American Literature.* Cambridge, Eng., 1965.
810.9   PS88 T25

22.47 Wilson, Edmund. *O Canada. An American's Notes on Canadian Culture.* N.Y., 1965.
809.971   PR9153 W5

22.48 Gross, Seymour L., and John E. Hardy, eds. *Images of the Negro in American Literature.* Chicago, 1966.
810.93   PS173 N4 G7

22.49 Hill, Herbert, ed. *Anger, and Beyond. The Negro Writer in the United States.* N.Y., 1966.
810.9   PS153 N5 H5

22.50 Lee, Robert E. *From West to East. Studies in the Literature of the American West.* Urbana, Ill., 1966.
810.9978   PS374 W4 L4

22.51 Nye, Russel B. *This Almost Chosen People. Essays in the History of American Ideas.* E. Lansing, Mich., 1966.
917.3   E175.3 N9

22.52 Poirier, Richard. *A World Elsewhere. The Place of Style in American Literature.* N.Y., 1966.
810.9   PS88 P6

22.53 Simon, Myron, and Thornton H. Parsons, eds. *Transcendentalism and Its Legacy.* Ann Arbor, 1966.
810.93   PS169 T7 S5

22.54 Smithline, Arnold. *Natural Religion in American Literature.* New Haven, 1966.
810.93   PS166 S4

22.55 Stone, Edward. *Voices of Despair. Four Motifs in American Literature.* Athens, O., 1966.
PS88 S8

22.56 *Essays on American Literature in Honor of Jay B. Hubbell.* Ed. Clarence Gohdes. Durham, N.C., 1967.
810   PS121 E8

22.57 Jones, Howard M. *Belief and Disbelief in American Literature.* Chicago, 1967.
810.93   PS169 B5 J6

22.58 Levin, David. *In Defense of Historical Literature. Essays on American History, Autobiography, Drama, and Fiction.* N.Y., 1967.
810.92   PS169 H5 L4

22.59 Miller, James E. *Quests Surd and Absurd. Essays in American Literature.* Chicago, 1967.
810.9   PR453 M5

22.60 Rubin, Louis D. *The Curious Death of the Novel. Essays in American Literature.* Baton Rouge, La., 1967.
813.03   PS121 R78

22.61 Bier, Jesse. *The Rise and Fall of American Humor.* N.Y., 1968.
817.009   PS430 B47

22.62 Cohen, Hennig, ed. *The American Culture. Approaches to the Study of the United States.* Boston, 1968.
917.303 E169.1 C617

22.63 Cohen, Hennig, ed. *The American Experience. Approaches to the Study of the United States.* Boston, 1968.
917.3 E169.1 C618

22.64 Conference on American Culture, 1967. *Frontiers of American Culture.* Ed. Ray B. Browne et al. W. Lafayette, Ind., 1968.
390 E169.1 C694

22.65 Earnest, Ernest P. *Expatriates and Patriots. American Artists, Scholars, and Writers in Europe.* Durham, N.C., 1968.
810.9 E184.2 E15

22.66 *Essays in American and English Literature Presented to Bruce Robert McElderry, Jr.* Ed. Max F. Schulz et al. Athens, O., 1968.
820.9 PS121 E79

22.67 Fiedler, Leslie A. *The Return of the Vanishing American.* N.Y., 1968.
813.0093 PS374 W4 F5

22.68 Gilbert, James B. *Writers and Partisans. A History of Literary Radicalism in America.* N.Y., 1968.
917.30391 E169.1 G48

22.69 Merideth, Robert, ed. *American Studies. Essays on Theory and Method.* Columbus, O., 1968.
917.303071 E169.1 M56

22.70 Spiller, Robert E. *The Oblique Light. Studies in Literary History and Biography.* N.Y., 1968.
810.9 PS121 S58

22.71 *The American Writer in England. An Exhibition Arranged in Honor of the Sesquicentennial of the University of Virginia.* Fwd. Gordon N. Ray. Intro. C. Waller Barrett. Charlottesville, Va., 1969.
016.810 Z1225 A64

22.72 Bigsby, Christopher W., ed. *The Black American Writer.* 2 vols. Deland, Fla., 1969.
810.9917496 PS153 N5 B5

22.73 Browne, Ray B., and Donald Pizer, eds. *Themes and Directions in American Literature. Essays in Honor of Leon Howard.* W. Lafayette, Ind., 1969.
810.9 PS15 T5

22.74 Cook, Mercer, and Stephen E. Henderson. *The Militant Black Writer in Africa and the United States.* Madison, Wis., 1969.
896 PS153 N5 C65

22.75 Minter, David L. *The Interpreted Design as a Structural Principle in American Prose.* New Haven, 1969. Yale Pubs. in Amer. St. 16.
810.9   PS362 M5

22.76 Mukherjee, Sujit, and D. V. K. Raghavacharyulu, eds. *Indian Essays in American Literature. Papers in Honour of Robert E. Spiller.* Bombay, 1969.
810.9   PS55 M8

22.77 Pearce, Roy H. *Historicism Once More. Problems and Occasions for the American Scholar.* Princeton, 1969.
810.9   PS88 P37

22.78 Bewley, Marius. *Masks and Mirrors. Essays in Criticism.* N.Y., 1970.
820.9   PS121 B54

22.79 *Challenges in American Culture.* Ed. Ray B. Browne et al. Bowling Green, O., 1970. American Studies Association.
917.303   E169.1 C43

22.80 Haslam, Gerald W. *Forgotten Pages of American Literature.* Boston, 1970.
810.809174   PS508 I5 H3

22.81 Jones, Douglas G. *Butterfly on Rock. A Study of Themes and Images in Canadian Literature.* Toronto, 1970.
810.9   PR9111 J6

22.82 Singh, Raman K., and Peter Fellowes, eds. *Black Literature in America. A Casebook.* N.Y., 1970.
810.80917496   PS508 N3 S5

22.83 Williams, Kenny J. *They Also Spoke. An Essay on Negro Literature in America, 1787-1930.* Nashville, Tenn., 1970.
810.9917496   PS153 N5 W5

22.84 Anderson, Quentin. *The Imperial Self. An Essay in American Literary and Cultural History.* N.Y., 1971.
820.9003   PS201 A5

22.85 Gross, Theodore L. *The Heroic Ideal in American Literature.* N.Y., 1971.
8).9352   PS169 H4 G7

22.86 Guttmann, Allen. *The Jewish Writer in America. Assimilation and the Crisis of Identity.* N.Y., 1971.
810.98924   PS153 J4 G8

22.87 Johnson, Lemuel A. *The Devil, the Gargoyle, and the Buffoon. The Negro as Metaphor in Western Literature.* Pt. Washington, N.Y., 1971.
809.93352   PN56.3 N4 J6

22.88 Miller, Ruth, ed. *Backgrounds to Blackamerican Literature.* Scranton, Pa., 1971.
917.30696073   E185 M68

§23. Language Studies
See also §§17-18

23.1 Bartlett, John R. *Dictionary of Americanisms. A Glossary of Words and Phrases Usually Regarded as Peculiar to the United States.* 4th ed. Boston, 1877. (Orig. ed. 1848.) Rpt. of 2nd ed. (1859), N.Y., 1968.
PE2835 B3

23.2 Krapp, George P. *The English Language in America.* 2 vols. N.Y., 1925. Rpt. 1960.
427.97   PE2808 K7

23.3 Craigie, William A., et al. *A Dictionary of American English on Historical Principles.* 4 vols. Chicago, 1936-44. Rpt. 1960.
427.9   PE2835 C72

23.4 Mencken, Henry L. *The American Language. An Inquiry into the Development of English in the United States.* 4th ed. N.Y., 1936. *Supplement I,* 1945. *Supplement II,* 1948. (Orig. ed. 1919.) Rpt. 1941, 1947. Abr. ed. by Raven I. McDavid, N.Y., 1963.
427.973   PE2808 M4

23.5 Wentworth, Harold. *American Dialect Dictionary.* N.Y., 1944.
427.9   PE2835 W4

23.6 Mathews, Mitford M., ed. *A Dictionary of Americanisms on Historical Principles.* 2 vols. Chicago, 1951. Rpt. in 1 vol. 1956. Abr. ed. 1966.
427.9   PE2835 D5

23.7 Marckwardt, Albert H. *American English.* N.Y., 1958.
427.9   PE2808 M3

23.8 Davies, David L., ed. *Glossary and Handbook of Canadian-British Words.* Vancouver, 1967.
427.971   PE3243 D3

23.9 Wentworth, Harold, and Stuart B. Flexner, eds. *Dictionary of American Slang.* Supplemented ed. N.Y., 1967. (Orig. ed. 1960.)
427.09   PE3729 U5 W4

4. Poetry

§24. Bibliographies, Guides, Indexes

24.1 Serle, Percival. *A Bibliography of Australasian Poetry and Verse, Australia and New Zealand.* Melbourne, 1925.
Z4011 S48

•

24.2 Opie, Iona, and Peter Opie. *Oxford Dictionary of Nursery Rhymes.* London, 1951. Rpt. with corrections 1952.
PZ8.3 O6 Ox

24.3 *Granger's Index to Poetry. Fifth Edition, Completely Revised and Enlarged, Indexing Anthologies Published Through June 30, 1960.* Ed. William F. Bernhardt. N.Y., 1962. (Orig. ed. 1904.) *Supplement- . . . from July 1, 1960, to December 31, 1965.* Ed. William F. Bernhardt and Kathryn W. Sewny. N.Y., 1967.
808.81   PN1021 G7

24.4 Cuthbert, Eleanora I. *Index of Australian and New Zealand Poetry.* N.Y., 1963.
016.821   Z4024 P7 C8

24.5 Spender, Stephen, and Donald Hall, eds. *The Concise Encyclopedia of English and American Poets and Poetry.* N.Y., 1963.
821.003   PR19 S6

24.6 Preminger, Alexander S., et al. *Encyclopedia of Poetry and Poetics.* Princeton, 1965.
809.103   PN1021 E5

24.7 Crum, Margaret, ed. *First-Line Index of English Poetry, 1500-1800, in Manuscripts of the Bodleian Library, Oxford.* 2 vols. Oxford, 1969.
821.0016   Z2014 P7 F5

§25. Surveys

25.1 Courthope, William J. *A History of English Poetry.* 6 vols. London, 1895-1910. Rpt. N.Y., 1962.
821.09   PR502 C8

25.2 Grierson, Herbert J., and James C. Smith. *A Critical History of English Poetry.* 2nd ed. London, 1947. (Orig. ed. 1944.) Rpt. 1970.
821.09   PR502 G76

25.3 Kinsley, James, ed. *Scottish Poetry. A Critical Survey.* London, 1955.
821.09   PR8561 K5

25.4 Pearce, Roy H. *The Continuity of American Poetry.* Princeton, 1961.
811.09   PS303 P4

25.5 Reeves, James. *A Short History of English Poetry, 1340-1940.* London & N.Y., 1961.
821.09   PR502 R45

25.6 Waggoner, Hyatt H. *American Poets, from the Puritans to the Present.* Boston, 1968. Rpt. N.Y., 1970.
811.009   PS303 W3

§26. General Studies

26.1 Bradley, Andrew C. *Oxford Lectures on Poetry.* London, 1909. Freq. rpts.
820.9   PN1031 B7

26.2 Elton, Oliver. *The English Muse. A Sketch.* London, 1933. Rpt. 1950.
821.09   PR502 E4

26.3 Housman, Alfred E. *The Name and Nature of Poetry.* N.Y., 1933.
809.1   PN1111 H7

26.4 De Selincourt, Ernest. *Oxford Lectures on Poetry.* Oxford, 1934. Rpt. Freeport, N.Y., 1967.
821.009   PR502 D4

26.5 Empson, William. *Some Versions of Pastoral.* London, 1935. Rpt. Norfolk, Conn., 1950.
820.9   PR149 P3 E6

26.6 Leavis, Frank R. *Revaluation. Tradition and Development in English Poetry.* London, 1936. Rpt. 1949, 1953, 1956, 1959; N.Y., 1963.
821.09   PR503 L4

26.7 Bush, Douglas. *Mythology and the Romantic Tradition in English Poetry.* Cambridge, Mass., 1937. Rpt. N.Y., 1963. Reissued with new Preface, 1969. Harvard Studies in English, Vol. 18.
821   PR508 M9 B85

26.8 Coombes, Archie J. *Some Australian Poets.* Sydney, 1938. Rpt. Freeport, N.Y., 1970.
821.009   PR9414 C6

26.9 Ransom, John C. *The World's Body.* N.Y., 1938. Rpt. Baton Rouge, La., 1968.
808.1   PN1136 R3

26.10 Fairchild, Hoxie N. *Religious Trends in English Poetry.* 6 vols. N.Y., 1939-68.
821.09   PR508 R4 F3

26.11 Knight, George W. *The Burning Oracle. Studies in the Poetry of Action.* London & N.Y., 1939.
821.09   PR502 K55

26.12 Redding, Jay S. *To Make a Poet Black.* Chapel Hill, N.C., 1939. Rpt. College Park, Md., 1968.
810.93   PS153 N5 R4

26.13 Thomson, George D. *Marxism and Poetry.* London, 1945.
808.1   PN1126 T5

26.14 Tillyard, Eustace M. W. *Poetry Direct and Oblique.* Rev. ed. London, 1945. (Orig. ed. 1934.) Rpt. 1948; N.Y., 1959.
8081.   PN1031 T5

26.15 Stauffer, Donald A. *The Nature of Poetry.* N.Y., 1946. Rpt. 1962.
808.1   PN1031 S78

26.16 Brooks, Cleanth. *The Well Wrought Urn. Studies in the Structure of Poetry.* N.Y., 1947. Rpt. 1956.
821.09   PR502 B7

26.17 Tate, Allen. *On the Limits of Poetry. Selected Essays, 1928-1948.* N.Y., 1948. Rpt. Freeport, N.Y., 1970.
809.1   PN710 T33

26.18 Tillyard, Eustace M. W. *Five Poems, 1470-1870. An Elementary Essay on the Background of English Literature.* London, 1948. Rpt. as *Poetry and Its Background. Illustrated by Five Poems, 1470-1870.* London & N.Y., 1961, 1970.
821.009   PR502 T5

26.19 Graves, Robert. *The Common Asphodel. Collected Essays on Poetry—1922-1949.* London, 1949. Rpt. N.Y., 1970.
809.1   PR503 G65

26.20 Bush, Douglas. *Science and English Poetry. An Historical Sketch, 1590-1950.* N.Y., 1950. Rpt. 1967.
821.009   PR508 S3 B8

26.21 Read, Herbert E. *Phases of English Poetry.* Rev. ed. London & Norfolk, Conn., 1950. (Orig. ed. 1928.) Rpt. Westport, Conn., 1972.
821.009   PR502 R4

26.22 Vivante, Leone. *English Poetry and Its Contribution to the Knowledge of a Creative Principle.* Pref. T. S. Eliot. London, 1950. Rpt. Carbondale, Ill., 1963.
821.09   PR503 V5

26.23 Day, Arthur G. *The Sky Clears. Poetry of the American Indians.* N.Y., 1951. Rpt. Lincoln, Neb., 1964.
897   E98 P74 D3

26.24 Bowra, Cecil M. *Heroic Poetry.* London, 1952. Rpt. 1961.
808.13   PN1303 B67

26.25 Empson, William. *Seven Types of Ambiguity.* 3rd ed. London, 1953. (Orig. ed. 1930.) Rpt. N.Y., 1955, 1957.
808.1   PN1031 E5

26.26 Whalley, George. *Poetic Process.* London, 1953. Rpt. Cleveland, 1967.
808.1   PN1042 W45

26.27 Eliot, T[homas] S. *The Three Voices of Poetry.* N.Y., 1954.
808.1   PN1064 E6

26.28 Wimsatt, William K. *The Verbal Icon. Studies in the Meaning of Poetry. And Two Preliminary Essays Written in Collaboration with Monroe C. Beardsley.* Lexington, Ky., 1954.
808.1   PN1031 W517

26.29 Davie, Donald. *Articulate Energy. An Inquiry into the Syntax of English Poetry.* London, 1955. Rpt. 1966; St. Clair Shores, Mich., 1971.
821.009   PR502 D3

26.30 Buckley, Vincent. *Essays in Poetry, Mainly Australian.* Carlton, Australia, 1957. Rpt. Freeport, N.Y., 1969.
821.009   PR9471 B8

26.31 Eliot, T[homas] S. *On Poetry and Poets.* London & N.Y., 1957. Rpt. N.Y., 1961.
808.1   PN511 E435

26.32 Press, John. *The Chequer'd Shade. Reflections on Obscurity in Poetry.* London, 1958. Rpt. 1963.
808.1   PN1031 P72

26.33 Ciardi, John. *How Does a Poem Mean?* Boston, 1959.
821.082   PS586 C53

26.34 Nicolson, Marjorie H. *Mountain Gloom and Mountain Glory. The Development of the Aesthetics of the Infinite.* Ithaca, N.Y., 1959. Rpt. N.Y., 1963.
809.93   PR508 N3 N5

26.35 Brett, Raymond L. *Reason and Imagination. A Study of Form and Meaning in Four Poems.* London & N.Y., 1960.
821.09   PR3558 B7

26.36 Bullough, Geoffrey. *Mirror of Minds. Changing Psychological Beliefs in English Poetry.* Alexander Lectures 1959-60. Toronto & London, 1962.
821.09   PR508 P9 B8

26.37 Ludwig, Richard M., ed. *Aspects of American Poetry. Essays Presented to Howard Mumford Jones.* Columbus, O., 1962.
811.09   PS305 L8

26.38 Bush, Douglas. *Mythology and the Renaissance Tradition in English Poetry.* Rev. ed. N.Y., 1963. (Orig. ed. Minneapolis, 1932.)
821.309   PR508 M9 B8

26.39 Greene, Thomas M. *The Descent from Heaven. A Study in Epic Continuity.* New Haven, 1963.
809.13   PN1303 G7

26.40 Harding, Denys C. *Experience into Words. Essays on Poetry.* London & Toronto, 1963. Rpt. Freeport, N.Y., 1971.
821.009   PR503 H25

26.41 Eliot, T[homas] S. *The Use of Poetry and the Use of Criticism. Studies in the Relation of Criticism to Poetry in England.* 2nd ed. London, 1964. (Orig. ed. 1933.)
821   PN1031 E47

26.42 *American Poetry.* Stratford-upon-Avon Studies, 7. London & N.Y., 1965.
811.509   PS303 A54

26.43 Beaty, Jerome, and William H. Matchett. *Poetry from Statement to Meaning.* N.Y., 1965.
808.1   PN1042 B4

26.44 Foster Poetry Conference. *English Poetry in Quebec. Proceedings . . . October 12-14, 1963.* Ed. John Glassco. Montreal, 1965.
811.5409   PR9291 Q4 F6

26.45 Hope, Alec D. *The Cave and the Spring. Essays on Poetry.* Adelaide, 1965. Rpt. Chicago, 1970.
809.1   PN1042 H57

26.46 Woodhouse, Arthur S. P. *The Poet and His Faith. Religion and Poetry in England from Spenser to Eliot and Auden.* Chicago, 1965.
821.0091   PR508 R4 W6

26.47 Wright, Judith. *Preoccupations in Australian Poetry.* Melbourne & N.Y., 1965.
821.009   PR9461 W7

26.48 Bateson, Frederick W. *English Poetry. A Critical Introduction.* 2nd ed. London & N.Y., 1966. (Orig. ed. 1950.)
821.009   PR504 B36

26.49 Martz, Louis L. *The Poem of the Mind. Essays on Poetry, English and American.* N.Y., 1966. Rpt. 1969.
811.009   PS305 M3

26.50 Barnes, Terence R. *English Verse. Voice and Movement from Wyatt to Yeats.* Cambridge, 1967.
821.009   PR401 B3

26.51 Bush, Douglas. *Pagan Myth and Christian Tradition in English Poetry.* Philadelphia, 1968.
821.0093   PR508 M9 B86

26.52 Calderwood, James L., and Harold E. Toliver, eds. *Perspectives on Poetry.* N.Y., 1968.
809.1   PN1055 C34

26.53 McAuley, James P. *The Personal Element in Australian Poetry.* Sydney, 1970.

26.54 Forster, Leonard W. *The Poet's Tongues. Multilingualism in Literature.* London, 1971.

26.55 Scott, Nathan A. *The Wild Prayer of Longing. Poetry and the Sacred.* New Haven, 1971.
246   BL65 C8 S36

§27. Prosody, Form, Style
See also §8 and §50

27.1 Omond, Thomas S. *English Metrists. Being a Sketch of English Prosodical Criticism During the Last Two Hundred Years.* Oxford, 1921. Rpt. N.Y., 1968.
426   PE1501 O53

27.2 Baum, Paull F. *The Principles of English Versification.* Cambridge, Mass., 1922. Rpt. Hamden, Conn., 1969.
426   PE1505 B25

27.3 Saintsbury, George. *A History of English Prosody. From the Twelfth Century to the Present Day.* 2nd ed. 3 vols. London, 1923. (Orig. ed. 1906-10.)
426.09   PE1505 S163

27.4 Abercrombie, Lascelles. *The Theory of Poetry.* London, 1924. Rpt. N.Y., 1968.
808.1   PN1031 A25

52 / *Poetry*

27.5 Schramm, Wilbur L. *Approaches to a Science of English Verse.*
Iowa City, Ia., 1925.
426   PE1505 S33

27.6 Graves, Robert. *The English Ballad. A Short Critical Survey.*
London, 1927. Rpt. N.Y., 1971.
821.04   PR1181 G7

27.7 Lanz, Henry. *The Physical Basis of Rime. An Essay on the Aesthetics of Sound.* Stanford & London, 1931. Rpt. N.Y., 1968.
416   PN1059 R5 L3

27.8 Gerould, Gordon H. *The Ballad of Tradition.* N.Y. & Oxford, 1932. Rpt. 1959.
PN1376 G4

27.9 Durling, Dwight L. *Georgic Tradition in English Poetry.* N.Y., 1935. Rpt. Pt. Washington, N.Y., 1964. Columbia Univ. Studies in English and Comp. Lit., 121.
821.509   PR509 D5 D8

27.10 Shuster, George N. *The English Ode from Milton to Keats.* N.Y., 1940. Columbia Univ. Studies in English and Comp. Lit., 150.
821.09   PR509 O3 S55

27.11 Miles, Josephine. *Major Adjectives in English Poetry from Wyatt to Auden.* Berkeley, 1946. Rpt. in *The Vocabulary of Poetry. Three Studies.* 1946. Univ. of Calif. Pubs. in English, Vol. 12, No. 3.
PE11 C3

27.12 Pottle, Frederick A. *The Idiom of Poetry.* Rev. ed. Ithaca, N.Y., 1946. (Orig. ed. 1941.) Rpt. Bloomington, Ind., 1963.
808.1   PN1055 P6

27.13 Freeman, Rosemary. *English Emblem Books.* London, 1948. Rpt. N.Y. 1966.
821.00915   PR535 E5 F7

27.14 Shapiro, Karl J. *A Bibliography of Modern Prosody.* Baltimore, 1948.
016.426   Z2014 P7 S5

27.15 Miles, Josephine. *The Continuity of Poetic Language. The Primary Language of Poetry, 1540's-1940's.* Berkeley, 1951. Rpt. N.Y., 1965. Univ. of Calif. Pubs. in English, Vol. 19, Nos. 1-3.
821.009   PE1541 M48

27.16 Barfield, Arthur Owen. *Poetic Diction. A Study in Meaning.* New ed. London, 1952. (Orig. ed. 1928.) Rpt. N.Y., 1964.
808.1   PN1031 B3

27.17 Fussell, Paul. *Theory of Prosody in Eighteenth-Century England.* New London, Conn., 1954. Rpt. Hamden, Conn., 1966. Conn. College Monographs, 5.
426   PE1505 F8

27.18 Groom, Bernard. *The Diction of Poetry from Spenser to Bridges.* Toronto, 1955.
821.09   PR508 D5 G7

27.19 Frye, Northrop, ed. *Sound and Poetry.* English Institute Essays, 1956. N.Y., 1957.
404   PE1010 E5

27.20 Berry, Francis. *Poets' Grammar. Person, Time, and Mood in Poetry.* London & N.Y., 1958.
821.09   PR502 B43

27.21 Duncan, Joseph E. *The Revival of Metaphysical Poetry. The History of a Style, 1800 to the Present.* Minneapolis, 1959. Rpt. N.Y., 1969.
821.009   PR581 D8

27.22 Miles, Josephine L. *Renaissance, Eighteenth Century, and Modern Language in English Poetry. A Tabular View.* Berkeley, 1960.
821.09   PR508 L3 M5

27.23 Pollard, Arthur. *English Hymns.* London, 1960. Writers and Their Work, 123.
245.2   BV312 P6

27.24 Friedman, Albert B. *The Ballad Revival. Studies in the Influence of Popular on Sophisticated Poetry.* Chicago, 1961.
821.04   PR507 F85

27.25 Thompson, John. *The Founding of English Metre.* N.Y., 1961.
426   PE1505 T46

27.26 Foerster, Donald M. *The Fortunes of Epic Poetry. A Study in English and American Criticism, 1750-1950.* Washington, D.C., 1962.
821.03   PN1303 F6

27.27 Hodgart, Matthew J. *The Ballads.* 2nd ed. London & N.Y., 1962. (Orig. ed. 1950.)
821.04   PR507 H7

27.28 Nowottny, Winifred. *The Language Poets Use.* N.Y., 1962.
808.1   PN1031 N6

27.29 Gross, Harvey S. *Sound and Form in Modern Poetry. A Study of Prosody from Thomas Hardy to Robert Lowell.* Ann Arbor, 1964. Rpt. 1968.
426   PE1505 G7

27.30 Hamer, Enid H. *The Metres of English Poetry.* 4th ed. London & N.Y., 1964. (Orig. ed. London, 1930.)
426   PE1505 H3

27.31 Miles, Josephine. *Eras and Modes in English Poetry.* 2nd ed. Berkeley, 1964. (Orig. ed. 1957.)
821.09   PR502 M48

27.32 Fussell, Paul. *Poetic Meter and Poetic Form.* N.Y., 1965.
808.1   PE1505 F78

27.33 Hamilton, George R. *English Verse Epigrams.* London, 1965.
Writers and Their Work, 188.
821.009   PR509 E73 H3

27.34 Shapiro, Karl J., and Robert Beum. *A Prosody Handbook.* N.Y., 1965.
416   PN1042 S57

27.35 Cruttwell, Patrick. *The English Sonnet.* London, 1966. Writers and Their Work, 191.
821.009   PR509 S7 C83

27.36 Gross, Harvey S., ed. *The Structure of Verse. Modern Essays on Prosody.* Greenwich, Conn., 1966.
808.1   PN1042 G7

27.37 Baker, William E. *Syntax in English Poetry, 1870-1930.* Berkeley, 1967.
821.809   PR595 L3 B3

27.38 Davie, Donald. *Purity of Diction in English Verse.* New ed. N.Y. & London, 1967. (Orig. ed. London, 1953.)
821.009   PR555 L3 D3

27.39 Fowler, David C. *A Literary History of the Popular Ballad.* Durham, N.C., 1968.
821.04   PR507 F6

27.40 Deutsch, Babette. *Poetry Handbook. A Dictionary of Terms.* 3rd ed. N.Y., 1969. (Orig. ed. 1957.)
808.1   PN44.5 D4

27.41 Heath-Stubbs, John F. *The Ode.* London, 1969.
821.04   PR509 O3 H4

27.42 Heath-Stubbs, John. *The Pastoral.* London, 1969.
821.008022   PN1421 H4

27.43 Leech, Geoffrey N. *A Linguistic Guide to English Poetry.* Harlow, Eng., 1969.
821.009   PR508 L3 L4

27.44 Piper, William B. *The Heroic Couplet.* Cleveland, 1969.
821.008   PR509 H4 P5

27.45 Solt, Mary E., and Willis Barnstone, eds. *Concrete Poetry. A World View.* Bloomington, Ind., 1969.
808.81   PN6110 C77 S6

27.46 Brower, Reuben A., ed. *Forms of Lyric. Selected Papers from the English Institute* [*1968 & 1969*]. N.Y., 1970.
821.00914   PR509 L8 B8

27.47 Fraser, George S. *Metre, Rhyme and Free Verse.* The Critical Idiom, 8. London, 1970.
426   PE1505 F7

27.48 Malof, Joseph. *A Manual of English Meters.* Bloomington, Ind., 1970.
426   PE1505 M3

27.49 DeFord, Sara, and Clarinda H. Lott. *Forms of Verse.* N.Y., 1971.
808.1   PE1505 D4

27.50 Halle, Morris, and Samuel J. Keyser. *English Stress. Its Form, Its Growth, and Its Role in Verse.* N.Y., 1971.
421.6   PE1139 H27

27.51 Merchant, Paul. *The Epic.* The Critical Idiom, 17. London, 1971.
809.13   PN56 E65 M4

5. Drama and Theater

§28. Bibliographies and Indexes

28.1 Clarence, Reginald, pseud. [H. J. Eldredge]. *The Stage Cyclopaedia. A Bibliography of Plays. An Alphabetical List of Plays . . . of the English Stage . . . Extending over a Period of Upwards of 500 Years.* London, 1909. Rpt. N.Y., 1970.
016.822   Z2014 D7 E4

28.2 *Dramatic Index.* 1909-52. 4/yr with annual cumulation as Part II of *Annual Magazine Subject Index.* Rpt. as *Cumulated Dramatic Index, 1909-1949.* 41 vols. in 2. Boston, 1965.
051   Z5781 C8

28.3 Firkins, Ina T. *Index to Plays, 1800-1926.* N.Y., 1927. *Supplement,* 1935. Rpt. N.Y., 1971.
016.80882   Z5781 F57

28.4 Greg, Walter W. *A Bibliography of the English Printed Drama to the Restoration.* 4 vols. London, 1939-59. Rpt. 1962, 1970. Bibliographical Society Illustrated Monograph, 24.
016.822   Z2014 D7 G78

28.5 Baker, Blanch M. *Theatre and Allied Arts. A Guide to Books Dealing with the History, Criticism, and Technic of the Drama and Theatre and Related Arts and Crafts.* Rev. ed. N.Y., 1952. (Orig. ed. *Dramatic Bibliography,* N.Y., 1933. Rpt. 1968.) Rpt. 1967.
016.792   Z5781 B18

28.6 Stratman, Carl J. *A Bibliography of British Dramatic Periodicals, 1720-1960.* N.Y., 1962.
Z5783 S8

28.7 Bergquist, George W., ed. *Three Centuries of English and American Plays, a Checklist. England: 1500-1800; United States: 1714-1830.* N.Y., 1963.
016.821   Z2014 D7 B45

28.8 Harbage, Alfred. *Annals of English Drama, 975-1700. An Analytical Record of All Plays, Extant or Lost, Chronologically Arranged and Indexed.* Rev. by Samuel Schoenbaum. London, 1964. (Orig. ed. Philadelphia, 1940.)
016.822   Z2014 D7 H25

28.9 Dukore, Bernard F., ed. *A Bibliography of Theatre Arts Publications in English, 1963.* Washington, D.C., 1965.
016.792   Z5781 A48

28.10 Stratman, Carl J. *Bibliography of the American Theatre, Excluding New York City.* Chicago, 1965.
016.7920973   Z1231 D7 S8

28.11 Coleman, Arthur, and Gary R. Tyler. *Drama Criticism. A Checklist of Interpretation Since 1940.* Vol. I. *English and American Plays,* Denver, 1966; Vol. II, *Classical and Continental Plays,* Chicago, 1971.
016.822009   Z1231 D7 C6

28.12 Stratman, Carl J., ed. *Bibliography of English Printed Tragedy, 1565-1900.* Carbondale, Ill., 1966.
016.822051   Z2014 D7 S83

28.13 *Theatre Books in Print.* 2nd ed. by A. E. Santaniello. N.Y., 1966. (Orig. ed. 1963.) New ed. in prep.
016.791   Z5781 S2

28.14 Angotti, Vincent L. *Source Materials in the Field of Theatre. An Annotated Bibliography and Subject Index to the Microfilm Collection.* Ann Arbor, 1967.
016.792   Z5781 A57

28.15 Gohdes, Clarence L. *Literature and Theatre of the States and Regions of the U.S.A. An Historical Bibliography.* Durham, N.C., 1967.
016.8109   Z1225 G63

28.16 New York Public Library. Research Libraries. *Catalog of the Theatre and Drama Collections.* 21 vols. Boston, 1967.
016.700   Z5785 N56

28.17 Palmer, Helen H., and Jane A. Dyson, eds. *American Drama Criticism. Interpretations, 1890-1965 Inclusive, of American Drama Since the First Play Produced in America.* Hamden, Conn., 1967. *Supplement I: to January, 1969,* 1970.
016.7920973   Z1231 D7 P3

28.18 Litto, Fredric M. *American Dissertations on the Drama and the Theatre. A Bibliography.* Kent, O., 1969.
016.8092   Z5781 L56

28.19 Ryan, Pat M. *American Drama Bibliography. A Checklist of Publications in English.* Ft. Wayne, Ind., 1969.
016.812   Z1231 D7 R92

58 / *Drama and Theater*

28.20 Arnott, James F., and John W. Robinson. *English Theatrical Literature, 1559-1900. A Bibliography Incorporating Robert W. Lowe's "A Bibliographical Account of English Theatrical Literature" Published in 1888.* London, 1970.
016.7920942   Z2014 D7 A74

28.21 *Chicorel Theater Index to Plays in Anthologies, Periodicals, Discs and Tapes.* Ed. Marietta Chicorel. N.Y., 1970– .
Z5781 C5

28.22 Hatch, James V. *Black Image on the American Stage. A Bibliography of Plays and Musicals, 1770-1970.* N.Y., 1970.
016.812008   Z5784 N4 H35

28.23 Long, Eugene H. *American Drama from Its Beginning to the Present.* Goldentree Bibliographies. N.Y., 1970.
016.812   Z1231 D7 L64

28.24 Stratman, Carl J. *American Theatrical Periodicals, 1798-1967. A Bibliographical Guide.* Durham, N.C., 1970.
016.7902   Z6935 S75

28.25 Hunter, Frederick J., ed. *Drama Bibliography. A Short-Title Guide to Extended Reading in Dramatic Art for the English-Speaking Audience and Students in Theatre.* Boston, 1971.
016.7921   Z5781 H84

28.26 Lowe, Claudia J. *A Guide to Reference and Bibliography for Theatre Research.* Columbus, O., 1971.
016.792   Z5781 L87

§29. Guides

29.1 Nungezer, Edwin. *A Dictionary of Actors and of Other Persons Associated with the Public Representation of Plays in England Before 1642.* New Haven, 1929. Rpt. N.Y., 1969, 1971. St. Clair Shores, Mich., 1971.
792.0280922   PN2597 N8

29.2 Bowman, Walter P., and Robert H. Ball. *Theatre Language. A Dictionary of Terms in English of the Drama and Stage from Medieval to Modern Times.* N.Y., 1961.
792.03   PN2035 B6

29.3 Burton, Ernest J. *The Student's Guide to British Theatre and Drama.* London, 1963.
792.0942   PN2581 B87

29.4 Sharp, Harold S., and Marjorie Z. Sharp, eds. *Index to Characters in the Performing Arts.* 4 vols. N.Y. & Metuchen, N.J., 1966-69.
808.8292703   PN1579 S45

29.5 Taylor, John R. *The Penguin Dictionary of the Theatre.* Baltimore, 1966.
809.203   PN2035 T3

29.6 Hartnoll, Phyllis, ed. *The Oxford Companion to the Theatre.* 3rd ed. London, 1967. (Orig. ed. 1951.)
792.03   PN2035 H3

29.7 Band-Kuzmany, Karin R. *Glossary of the Theatre. In English, French, Italian and German.* N.Y., 1969.
792.03   PN2035 B3

29.8 *Drury's Guide. Best Plays.* 2nd ed. by James M. Salem. Metuchen, N.J., 1969. (Orig. ed. by Francis K. Drury, Washington, D.C., 1953.) Summaries of plays.
016.80882   Z5781 D4

§30. Periodicals

30.1 *Theatre Arts. A Magazine for the World Theatre.* 1916-64. 48 vols. 12/yr.
            PN2000 T45

30.2 *Drama. The Quarterly Theatre Review.* 1919- .
792.0942   PN2001 D64

30.3 *Players. The Magazine of American Theatre.* 1924- . 6/yr.

30.4 *Theatre Annual.* 1942-65. 22 vols.
792.058   PN2012 T5

30.5 *Theatre World.* N.Y., 1944- . Annual. Until 1965 *Daniel Blum's Theatre World.*
792   PN2277 N5 A17

30.6 *Theatre Notebook. Quarterly Journal of the History and Technique of the British Theatre.* 1945- .
792   PN2001 T43

30.7 *Educational Theatre Journal. Journal of the American Educational Theatre Association.* 1949- . 4/yr.
371.332505   PN3171 E38

30.8 *World Theatre.* 1950-68. 17 vols. 6/yr.
            PN2001 W6

30.9 *Plays and Players and* [since 1966] *Theatre World and Encore.* 1953- . 12/yr.

30.10 *Ohio State University Theatre Collection Bulletin. Devoted to Research in Theatre History.* 1954- . Annual.
            PN1620 O45 A3

30.11 *TDR. The Drama Review.* 1955- . 4/yr. Until 1957 *Carleton Drama Bulletin;* until 1968 *Tulane Drama Review.* *N.y.U.*
809.2   PN1601 T8

30.12 *American Society for Theatre Research Newsletter.* 1956- . 2/yr.

30.13 *Drama Critique. A Critical Review of Theatre Arts and Literature.* 1958-68. 11 vols. 3/yr.
PN1601 D55

30.14 *New Theatre Magazine.* 1959- . 3/yr.
PN2001 N485

30.15 *Theatre Survey. The American Journal of Theatre History.* 1960- . 2/yr.
PN2000 T716

30.16 *Drama Survey. A Review of Dramatic Literature and Theatrical Arts.* 1961-69. 3/yr.
PN1601 D65

30.17 *Religious Theatre.* 1964- . 2/yr.
PN1880 R4

30.18 *Stage in Canada.* 1965- . 12/yr.

30.19 *Comparative Drama.* 1967- . 4/yr.
809.2   PN1601 C66

30.20 *Yale/Theatre.* 1968- . 3/yr.

30.21 *Drama and Theatre.* 1969- . 3/yr. Succeeds *First Stage,* 1961-68.
PS634 F54

30.22 *Theatre.* New York. 1969- . Annual.
792.0973   PN2000 T33

30.23 *Concerned Theatre Japan.* 1970- . 4/yr.

30.24 *Theatre Quarterly.* 1971- .

§31. Surveys

31.1 Wynne, Arnold. *The Growth of English Drama.* Oxford, 1914. Rpt. Freeport, N.Y., 1968.
822   PR625 W8

31.2 Sayler, Oliver M. *Our American Theatre.* N.Y., 1923. Rpt. Westport, Conn., 1970; N.Y., 1971.
792.0973   PN2266 S3

31.3 O'Dell, George C. D. *Annals of the New York Stage.* 15 vols. N.Y., 1927-45. Rpt. 1970.
792.097471   PN2277 N5 O4

31.4 Coad, Oral S., and Edwin Mims. *The American Stage.* New Haven, 1929. Yale Pageant of America, 14. (E178.5 P2 v. 14.)
PN2221 C6

31.5 Malone, Andrew E. *The Irish Drama.* London & N.Y., 1929. Rpt. N.Y., 1965.
792.094183   PN2602 D82 A29

31.6 Nicoll, Allardyce. *The English Theatre. A Short History.* London, 1936. Rpt. Westport, Conn., 1970.
792.09421   PN2581 N5

31.7 Quinn, Arthur H. *A History of the American Drama from the Civil War to the Present Day.* Rev. ed. N.Y., 1936. (Orig. ed. in 2 vols., 1927.)
812.09   PS332 Q55

31.8 Robinson, Lennox, ed. *The Irish Theatre.* London, 1939. Rpt. N.Y., 1971.
822.009   PR8783 R6

31.9 Quinn, Arthur H. *A History of the American Drama from the Beginning to the Civil War.* 2nd ed. N.Y., 1943. (Orig. ed. 1923.) Rpt. 1951.
PS332 Q5

31.10 Downer, Alan S. *The British Drama. A Handbook and Brief Chronicle.* N.Y., 1950.
822.09   PR625 D55

31.11 Rossiter, Arthur P. *English Drama from Early Times to the Elizabethans. Its Background, Origins and Development.* London, 1950. Rpt. N.Y., 1959.
822.109   PR641 R6

31.12 Hughes, Glenn. *A History of the American Theatre, 1700-1950.* N.Y., 1951.
792   PN2221 H76

• Nicoll, Allardyce. *A History of English Drama 1600-1900.* 6 vols. Cambridge.

31.13   I. *Restoration Drama, 1660-1700.* 4th ed. 1952. (Orig. ed. 1923.)
822.5   PR691 N5

31.14   II. *Early Eighteenth Century Drama.* 3rd ed. 1952. (Orig. ed. 1925.)
822.509   PR711 N5

31.15 III. *Late Eighteenth Century Drama, 1750-1800.* 2nd ed. 1952. (Orig. ed. 1927.)
822.5   PR716 N5

31.16 IV. *Early Nineteenth Century Drama, 1800-1850.* 2nd ed. 1955. (Orig. ed. 1930.)
822.5

31.17 V. *Late Nineteenth Century Drama, 1850-1900.* 2nd ed. 1959. (Orig. ed. 1946.)
822.809   PR721 N46

31.18 VI. *A Short-Title Alphabetical Catalogue of Plays.* 1959.
822.5 / 016.8225

31.19 Cheney, Sheldon. *The Theatre. Three Thousand Years of Drama, Acting, and Stagecraft.* Rev. ed. N.Y., 1952. (Orig. ed. 1929.) Rpt. 1963.
792.09   PN2101 C5

31.20 Hewitt, Barnard W. *Theatre U.S.A., 1668 to 1957.* N.Y., 1959.
792.0973   PN2221 H4

31.21 Wickham, Glynne. *Early English Stages, 1300 to 1660.* 3 vols. London & N.Y., 1959-71.
792.0942   PN2587 W53

31.22 Southern, Richard. *The Seven Ages of the Theatre.* N.Y., 1961.
792.09   PN2101 S6

31.23 Nicoll, Allardyce. *British Drama. An Historical Survey from the Beginnings to the Present Time.* 5th ed. N.Y., 1963. (Orig. ed. London, 1925.)
822.09   PR625 N5

31.24 Bradbrook, Muriel C. *English Dramatic Form. A History of Its Development.* N.Y., 1965.
822.009   PR625 B68

31.25 Meserve, Walter J. *An Outline History of American Drama.* Totowa, N.J., 1965.
812.009   PS332 M4

31.26 Nicoll, Allardyce. *The Development of the Theatre. A Study of Theatrical Art from the Beginnings to the Present Day.* 5th ed. N.Y., 1966. (Orig. ed. London, 1927.)
792.09   PN2101 N5

31.27 Wilson, Garff B. *A History of American Acting.* Bloomington, Ind., 1966.
792.0922   PN2226 W5

31.28 Mitchell, Loften. *Black Drama. The Story of the American Negro in the Theatre.* N.Y., 1967.
792.0973   PS338 N4 M5

31.29 Brockett, Oscar G. *History of the Theatre.* Boston, 1968.
729.09   PN2101 B68

31.30 Edwards, Murray D., ed. *A Stage in Our Past. English-Language Theatre in Eastern Canada from the 1790's to 1914.* Toronto, 1968.
792.0971   PN2301 E3

31.31 Hewitt, Barnard W. *History of the Theatre from 1800 to the Present.* N.Y., 1970.
792.09034   PN2185 H4

31.32 Mullin, Donald C. *The Development of the Playhouse. A Survey of Theatre Architecture from the Renaissance to the Present.* Berkeley, 1970.
725.822   NA6821 M83

§32. General Studies

32.1 Thorndike, Ashley H. *Tragedy.* Boston, 1908. Rpt. as *English Tragedy,* N.Y., 1965.
PR633 T5

32.2 Craig, Edward G. *On the Art of the Theatre.* Chicago, 1911. Rpt. N.Y., 1956.
792   PN2037 C6

32.3 Archer, William. *The Old Drama and the New. An Essay in Re-Valuation.* Boston, 1923. Rpt. N.Y., 1971.
PR625 A7

32.4 Moses, Montrose J. *The American Dramatist.* New ed. Boston, 1925. (Orig. ed. 1911.) Rpt. N.Y., 1964.
812.09   PS332 M6

32.5 Thorndike, Ashley H. *English Comedy.* N.Y., 1929. Rpt. 1965.
PR631 T5

32.6 Deane, Cecil V. *Dramatic Theory and the Rhymed Heroic Play.* London, 1931. Rpt. 1967; N.Y., 1968.
822.409   PR691 D4

32.7 Granville-Barker, Harley. *On Dramatic Method.* London, 1931. Rpt. N.Y., 1956.
808.2   PN1655 G7

32.8 Nicoll, Allardyce. *The Theory of Drama.* N.Y., 1931. Rpt. 1966.
809.2   PN1631 N4

32.9 Craig, Hardin, ed. *Essays in Dramatic Literature. The Parrott Presentation Volume. By Pupils of Professor Thomas Marc Parrott*

of Princeton University, Published in His Honor. Princeton, 1935. Rpt. N.Y., 1967.
822.009   PR627 E7

32.10 Bond, Frederick W. *The Negro and the Drama. The Direct and Indirect Contribution Which the American Negro Has Made to Drama and the Legitimate Stage, with the Underlying Conditions Responsible.* Washington, D.C., 1940. Rpt. College Park, Md., 1969.
812.009   PS338 N4 B6

32.11 Isaacs, Edith J. *The Negro in the American Theatre.* N.Y., 1947. Rpt. College Park, Md., 1968.
792.0973   PN2286 I8

32.12 Prior, Moody E. *The Language of Tragedy.* N.Y., 1947. Rpt. Gloucester, Mass., 1964; Bloomington, Ind., 1966.
822.051   PR633 P7

32.13 Sper, Felix. *From Native Roots. A Panorama of Our Regional Drama.* Caldwell, Id., 1948. Rpt. Deer Park, N.Y., 1962.
812.09   PS338 N3 S6

32.14 Thompson, Alan R. *The Dry Mock. A Study of Irony in Drama.* Berkeley, 1948.
809.2   PN1680 T5

32.15 Fergusson, Francis. *The Idea of a Theatre. A Study of Ten Plays. The Art of Drama in Changing Perspective.* Princeton, 1949. Rpt. Garden City, N.Y., 1953, 1968.
808.2   PN1661 F4

32.16 Gassner, John. *Masters of the Drama.* 3rd ed. N.Y., 1954. (Orig. ed. 1940.)
809.2   PN1721 G3

32.17 Wimsatt, William K., ed. *English Stage Comedy.* English Institute Essays, 1954. N.Y., 1955.
822.09   PE1010 E5

32.18 Herrick, Marvin T. *Tragicomedy. Its Origin and Development in Italy, France, and England.* Urbana, Ill., 1955. Rpt. 1962. Illinois Studies in Lang. and Lit., 39.
809.2   PN1902 H4

32.19 Muller, Herbert J. *The Spirit of Tragedy.* N.Y., 1956.
808.2   PN1892 M7

32.20 Sherbo, Arthur. *English Sentimental Drama.* E. Lansing, Mich., 1957.
822.09   PR635 S4 S5

32.21 Mander, Raymond, and Joe Mitchenson. *The Theatres of London.* London & N.Y., 1961.
792.09421   PN2596 L6 M35

32.22 Olson, Elder. *Tragedy and the Theory of Drama.* Detroit, 1961. Rpt. 1966.
809.2　　　　PN1655 O55

32.23 Knight, George W. *The Golden Labyrinth. A Study of British Drama.* London & N.Y., 1962.
822.09　　　　PR625 K58

32.24 Nicoll, Allardyce. *The Theatre and Dramatic Theory.* N.Y., 1962.
792　　　　PN1631 N42

32.25 Bentley, Eric R. *The Life of the Drama.* N.Y., 1964.
809.2　　　　PN1631 B4

32.26 Gassner, John, ed. *Ideas in the Drama. Selected Papers from the English Institute [1963].* N.Y., 1964.
809.2　　　　PN1621 G28

32.27 Downer, Alan S., ed. *American Drama and Its Critics. A Collection of Critical Essays.* Chicago, 1965.
812.5009　　　　PS351 D59

32.28 Merchant, William M. *Creed and Drama. An Essay on Religious Drama.* London & Philadelphia, 1965.
822.0093　　　　PN1880 M4

32.29 Styan, John L. *The Dramatic Experience. A Guide to the Reading of Plays.* Cambridge, 1965.
808.2　　　　PN1701 S8

32.30 Matthews, Honor. *The Primal Curse. The Myth of Cain and Abel in the Theatre.* London & N.Y., 1967.
809.933　　　　PN57 C25 M3

32.31 Rahill, Frank. *The World of Melodrama.* University Park, Pa., 1967.
809.52　　　　PN1912 R3

32.32 Brereton, Geoffrey. *Principles of Tragedy. A Rational Examination of the Tragic Concept in Life and Literature.* Coral Gables, Fla., 1968.
809.916　　　　PN1892 B68

32.33 Calderwood, James L., and Harold E. Toliver, eds. *Perspectives on Drama.* N.Y., 1968.
809.2　　　　PN1621 C3

32.34 Patterson, Lindsay, ed. *Anthology of the American Negro in the Theatre. A Critical Approach.* International Library of Negro Life and History. 2nd ed. N.Y., 1968. (Orig. ed. 1967.)
792.0973　　　　PN2226 P3

32.35 Roston, Murray. *Biblical Drama in England from the Middle Ages to the Present Day.* Evanston, Ill., 1968.
822.0093　　　　PR635 R4 R6

32.36 Herron, Ima H. *The Small Town in American Drama.* Dallas, Tex., 1969.

812.0093   PS338 S6 H4

32.37 Coleman, Edward D. *The Jew in English Drama. An Annotated Bibliography.* (Orig. ed. 1943.) Rev. ed. together with *The Jew in Western Drama. An Essay and a Check List,* by Edgar Rosenberg. N.Y., 1970.

016.822   Z5784 J6 C6

32.38 Dawson, S. W. *Drama and the Dramatic.* The Critical Idiom, 11. London, 1970.

808.2   PN1631 D3

32.39 States, Bert O. *Irony and Drama. A Poetics.* Ithaca, N.Y., 1971.

809.291   PN1680 S7

6. Prose

§33. Style

See also §8

33.1 Saintsbury, George. *A History of English Prose Rhythm.* London, 1912. Rpt. Bloomington, Ind., 1965.
828.08   PE1561 S3

33.2 Clark, Albert C. *Prose-Rhythm in English.* Oxford, 1913.
PE1561 C5

33.3 Krapp, George P. *The Rise of English Literary Prose.* N.Y., 1915. Rpt. 1963.
828.109   PR767 K7

33.4 Paget, Violet [Vernon Lee,]. *The Handling of Words. And Other Studies in Literary Psychology.* London & N.Y., 1923. Rpt. 1927. Rpt. with Intro. by Royal A. Gettmann, Lincoln, Neb., 1968.
801.02   PN187 P3

33.5 Workman, Samuel K. *Fifteenth Century Translation as an Influence on English Prose.* Princeton, 1940. Princeton Studies in English, 18.
820.902   PR275 W6

33.6 Graves, Robert, and Alan Hodge. *The Reader over Your Shoulder.* London & N.Y., 1943.
808   PR751 G7

33.7 Williamson, George. *The Senecan Amble. A Study in Prose from Bacon to Collier.* London & Chicago, 1951. Rpt. Chicago, 1967.
820.903   PR769 W5

33.8 Baum, Paull F. *The Other Harmony of Prose. An Essay in English Prose Rhythm.* Durham, N.C., 1952.
820.1   PE1559 B3

33.9 Read, Herbert E. *English Prose Style.* Rev. ed. London, 1952. (Orig. ed. 1928.) Rpt. Boston, 1961.
808   PE1421 R35

33.10 Thomson, James A. K. *Classical Influences on English Prose.* London & N.Y., 1956. Rpt. N.Y., 1962.
820.9   PR127 T55

33.11 Martin, Harold C., ed. *Style in Prose Fiction.* English Institute Essays, 1958. N.Y., 1959.
823.09   PE1010 E5

33.12 Wilson, Frank P. *Seventeenth Century Prose. Five Lectures.* Berkeley, 1960.
820.903   PR769 W55

33.13 Brown, Huntington. *Prose Styles. Four Primary Types.* Minneapolis, 1966. Minn. Monographs in the Humanities, 1.
808   PN203 B73

33.14 Gibson, Walker. *Tough, Sweet, and Stuffy. An Essay on Modern American Prose Styles.* Bloomington, Ind., 1966. Rpt. 1970.
808.0427   PE1427 G5

33.15 Gordon, Ian A. *The Movement of English Prose.* London, 1966.
828.0809   PR751 G6

33.16 Adolph, Robert. *The Rise of Modern Prose Style.* Cambridge, Mass., 1968.
828.009   PR769 A3

33.17 Levine, George L., and William Madden, eds. *The Art of Victorian Prose.* N.Y., 1968.
828.808   PR783 L4

33.18 Webber, Joan. *The Eloquent "I." Style and Self in Seventeenth-Century Prose.* Madison, Wis., 1968.
828.40809   PR769 W4

33.19 O'Donnell, Bernard. *An Analysis of Prose Style to Determine Authorship. "The O'Ruddy" a Novel by Stephen Crane and Robert Barr.* The Hague, 1970.
813.4   PS1449 C85 O735

33.20 Fish, Stanley, ed. *Seventeenth-Century Prose. Modern Essays in Criticism.* N.Y., 1971.
828.30808   PR769 F5

§34. Diaries and Autobiography

34.1 Matthews, William. *American Diaries. An Annotated Bibliography of American Diaries Written Prior to the Year 1861.* Berkeley, 1945. Rpt. Boston, 1959. Univ. of Calif. Pubs. in English, Vol. 16.
016.920073   Z5305 U5 M3

34.2 Matthews, William. *British Diaries. An Annotated Bibliography of British Diaries Written between 1442 and 1942.* Berkeley, 1950. Rpt. Gloucester, Mass., 1967.
016.920042   Z5305 G7 M3

34.3 Matthews, William. *Canadian Diaries and Autobiographies.* Berkeley, 1950.
016.920071   Z5305 C3 M3

34.4 Matthews, William. *British Autobiographies. An Annotated Bibliography of British Autobiographies Published or Written Before 1951.* Berkeley, 1955. Rpt. Hamden, Conn., 1968.
016.920042   Z2027 A9 M3

34.5 Lillard, Richard G. *American Life in Autobiography. A Descriptive Guide.* Stanford, 1956.
016.92   Z5301 L66

34.6 Kaplan, Louis, et. al. *A Bibliography of American Autobiographies.* Madison, Wis., 1961.
016.920073   Z1224 K3

•

34.7 Ponsonby, Arthur. *English Diaries. A Review of English Diaries from the Sixteenth to the Twentieth Century with an Introduction on Diary Writing.* London, 1923. Rpt. Ann Arbor, 1971.
828.03   PR908 P6

34.8 Ponsonby, Arthur P. *More English Diaries. Further Reviews of Diaries from the Sixteenth to the Nineteenth Century with an Introduction on Diary Reading.* London, 1927.
PR908 P62

34.9 Bates, Ernest S. *Inside Out. An Introduction to Autobiography.* 2 vols. Oxford, 1936-37. Rpt. in 1 vol. N.Y., 1937.
920   CT25 B3

34.10 Shumaker, Wayne. *English Autobiography. Its Emergence, Materials, and Forms.* Berkeley, 1954.
920   CT34 G7 S5

34.11 Pascal, Roy. *Design and Truth in Autobiography.* London & Cambridge, Mass., 1960.
920.002   CT25 P37

34.12 Morris, John N. *Versions of the Self. Studies in English Autobiography from John Bunyan to John Stuart Mill.* N.Y., 1966.
828.803   CT25 M6

34.13 Delany, Paul. *British Autobiography in the Seventeenth Century.* N.Y. & London, 1969.
920.042   CT77 D4

§35. Biography

35.1 Hefling, Helen, and Jessie W. Dyde. *Index to Contemporary Biography and Criticism.* 2nd ed. Boston, 1934. (Orig. ed. 1929.)
016.92   Z5301 H46

35.2 Riches, Phyllis M. *An Analytical Bibliography of Universal Collected Biography. Comprising Books Published in the English Tongue in Great Britain and Ireland, America, and the British Dominions.* London & N.Y., 1934.
016.92   Z5301 R53

35.3 O'Neill, Edward H. *Biography by Americans, 1658-1936. A Subject Bibliography.* Philadelphia, 1939.
016.92   Z5301 O58

35.4 Dargan, Marion. *Guide to American Biography, 1607-1933.* 2 vols. Albuquerque, N.M., 1949-52.
016.920073   Z5305 U5 D32

•

35.5 Stauffer, Donald A. *English Biography Before 1700.* Cambridge, Mass., 1930. Rpt. N.Y., 1964.
920.002   CT34 G7 S7

35.6 Longaker, Mark. *English Biography in the Eighteenth Century.* Philadelphia, 1931. Rpt. N.Y., 1971.
809.93592   CT34 G7 L6

35.7 Johnson, Edgar. *One Mighty Torrent. The Drama of Biography.* N.Y., 1937. Rpt. 1955.
920   CT34 G7 J6

35.8 Stauffer, Donald A. *TheArt of Biography in Eighteenth Century England.* Princeton, 1941. *Bibliographical Supplement,* 1941. Rpt. in 2 vols. N.Y., 1970.
808.06692   CT34 G7 S67

35.9 Edel, Leon. *Literary Biography.* London, 1957. Rpt. Garden City, N.Y., 1959. The Alexander Lectures, 1955-56.
CT21 E3

35.10 Garraty, John A. *The Nature of Biography.* N.Y., 1957.
920   CT21 G3

35.11 Clifford, James L., ed. *Biography as an Art. Selected Criticism, 1560-1960.* N.Y., 1962.
920.002   CT21 C55

35.12 Altick, Richard D. *Lives and Letters. A History of Literary Biography in England and America.* N.Y., 1965.
828.08   CT31 A4

35.13 Kendall, Paul M. *The Art of Biography.* N.Y., 1965.
920.002   CT21 K4

35.14 Reed, Joseph W. *English Biography in the Early Nineteenth Century, 1801-1838.* New Haven, 1966. Yale Studies in English, 160.
920.0010942   CT81 R4

35.15 Daghlian, Philip B., ed. *Essays in Eighteenth-Century Biography.* Bloomington, Ind., 1968.
808.06692   CT21 E8

35.16 Bowen, Catherine D. *Biography. The Craft and the Calling.* Boston, 1969.
808.06692   CT21 B564

35.17 Clifford, James L. *From Puzzles to Portraits. Problems of a Literary Biographer.* Chapel Hill, N.C., 1970.
808.066   CT21 C553

§36. The Essay

36.1 MacDonald, Wilbert L. *Beginnings of the English Essay.* Toronto, 1914. Univ. of Toronto Studies: Third Ser., No. 3.
PR921 M3

36.2 Eleanore, Sister Mary. *The Literary Essay in English.* Boston, 1923.
PR921 E5

36.3 Marr, George S. *The Periodical Essayists of the Eighteenth Century. With Illustrative Extracts from the Rarer Periodicals.* N.Y., 1923. Rpt. 1970, 1971.
824.509   PR925 M3

36.4 Thompson, Elbert N. S. *The Seventeenth-Century English Essay.* Iowa City, Ia., 1926. Rpt. N.Y., 1967. Univ. of Iowa Humanistic Studies, Vol. 2, No. 3.
824.309   PR924 T5

36.5 Law, Marie H. *The English Familiar Essay in the Early Nineteenth Century. The Elements, Old and New, Which Went into Its Making, as Exemplified in the Writings of Hunt, Hazlitt and Lamb.* Philadelphia, 1934. Rpt. N.Y., 1965.
824.709   PR926 L3

§37. The Novel: Bibliographies

37.1 Griswold, William M. *A Descriptive List of Novels and Tales.* 2 vols. Cambridge, Mass., 1890-92. Rpt. of Vol. I, *Descriptive Lists of American, International, Romantic and British Novels.* N.Y., 1968.
016.808833   Z5916 G872

37.2 Baker, Ernest A. *A Guide to Historical Fiction.* New ed. London, 1914. (Orig. ed. 1907 in 2 vols.) Rpt. N.Y., 1969.
016.8088381   Z5917 H6 B2

37.3 Brown, Stephen J. *Ireland in Fiction. A Guide to Irish Novels, Tales, Romances, and Folk-Lore.* New ed. Dublin, 1919. (Orig. ed. 1916.) Rpt. N.Y., 1969, 1970.
016.823   Z2039 F4 B8

37.4 Summers, Montague. *A Gothic Bibliography.* London, 1941. Rpt. N.Y., 1964.
016.8236   Z2014 F4 S9

37.5 Kerr, Elizabeth M. *Bibliography of the Sequence Novel.* Minneapolis, 1950.
016.8   Z5917 S45 K4

37.6 Bell, Inglis F., and Donald Baird. *The English Novel, 1578-1956. A Checklist of Twentieth-Century Criticisms.* Denver, 1958.
016.82309   Z2014 F4 B4

37.7 *Cumulated Fiction Index, 1945-1960.* Ed. Gerald B. Cotton and Alan Glencross. London, 1960. Rpt. 1964.
016.80883   Z5916 C78

37.8 *Cumulated Fiction Index, 1960-1969.* Ed. Raymond F. Smith. London, 1970.
016.82391408

37.9 Spencer, Dorothy M. *Indian Fiction in English. An Annotated Bibliography.* Philadelphia, 1960.
016.823   Z3208 L5 S6

37.10 Block, Andrew. *The English Novel, 1740-1850. A Catalogue Including Prose Romances, Short Stories, and Translations of Foreign Fiction.* New ed. London, 1961. (Orig. ed. 1939.) Rpt. 1968.
016.8236   Z2014 F4 B6

37.11 Fidell, Estelle, and Esther V. Flory. *Fiction Catalogue. A List of 4,097 Works of Fiction in the English Language with Annotations.* 7th ed. N.Y., 1961. (Orig. ed. 1908.) *Supplement, 1961-1965.* Ed. E. A. Fidell. 1966.
016.823   Z5916 W74

37.12 Gerstenberger, Donna L., and George Hendrick. *The American Novel, 1789-1959. A Checklist of Twentieth-Century Criticism.* Denver, 1961.
——. *The American Novel. A Checklist of Twentieth-Century Criticism of Novels Written Since 1789.* Vol. II: *Criticism Written, 1960-1968.* Chicago, 1970.
016.81309   Z1231 F4 G4

37.13 McGarry, Daniel D., and Sarah H. White. *Historical Fiction Guide. Annotated Chronological, Geographical and Topical List of Five Thousand Selected Historical Novels.* N.Y., 1963.
016.80883   Z5917 H6 M3

37.14 Coan, Otis W., and Richard G. Lillard. *America in Fiction. An Annotated List of Novels That Interpret Aspects of Life in the United States, Canada, and Mexico.* 5th ed. Palo Alto, Calif., 1967. (Orig. ed. 1941.)
016.81300803   Z1361 C6 C6

37.15 Kearney, Elizabeth I., and Louise S. Fitzgerald. *The Continental Novel. A Checklist of Criticism in English, 1900-1966.* Metuchen, N.J., 1968.
016.80933   Z5916 K4

37.16 Van Derhoof, Jack W. *A Bibliography of Novels Related to American Frontier and Colonial History.* Troy, N.Y., 1971.
016.81303   Z1231 F4 V3

§38. The Novel: Surveys

38.1 Baker, Ernest A. *The History of the English Novel.* 10 vols. London, 1924-39. Rpt. N.Y., 1961.
823.09   PR821 B31

   38.2 Stevenson, Lionel. *Yesterday and After.* N.Y., 1967. Published as Vol. XI of Ernest A. Baker's *The History of the English Novel.*
823.9109   PR881 S7

38.3 Ford, Ford M. *The English Novel. From the Earliest Days to the Death of Joseph Conrad.* Philadelphia, 1928.
PR821 F6

38.4 Knight, Grant C. *The Novel in English.* N.Y., 1931.
823.09   PR821 K6

38.5 Lovett, Robert M., and Helen S. Hughes. *The History of the Novel in England.* Boston, 1932. Rpt. St. Clair Shores, Mich., 1971.
823.009   PR821 L7

38.6 Summers, Montague. *The Gothic Quest. A History of the Gothic Novel.* London, 1938. Rpt. N.Y., 1964.
823.609   PR830 T3 S9

38.7 Gerould, Gordon H. *The Patterns of English and American Fiction. A History.* Boston, 1942. Rpt. N.Y., 1966.
823.009   PR821 G4

38.8 Wagenknecht, Edward C. *Cavalcade of the English Novel from Elizabeth to George VI.* N.Y., 1943. Rpt. with supp. bibliographies, 1954.
823.09   PR821 W25

38.9 Church, Richard. *The Growth of the English Novel.* London, 1951. Rpt. N.Y., 1961.
823   PR821 C45

38.10 Allen, Walter E. *The English Novel. A Short Critical History.* N.Y., 1954. Rpt. 1958.
823.09   PR821 A4

38.11 Stevenson, Lionel. *The English Novel. A Panorama.* Boston, 1960.
823.09   PR821 S7

38.12 Neill, S. Diana. *A Short History of the English Novel.* Rev. ed. London & N.Y., 1964. (Orig. ed. 1951.)
823.09   PR821 N4

38.13 Kettle, Arnold. *An Introduction to the English Novel.* 2 vols. 2nd ed. London, 1967; N.Y., 1968. (Orig. ed. London, 1951-53.)
823.009   PR821 K42

38.14 Argyle, Barry. *An Introduction to the Australian Novel, 1830-1930.* Oxford, 1971.

•

38.15 Quinn, Arthur H. *American Fiction. An Historical and Critical Survey.* N.Y., 1936.
813.09   PS371 Q5

38.16 Van Doren, Carl C. *The American Novel, 1789-1939.* Rev. ed. 1940. (Orig. ed. 1921.)
813.09   PS371 V3

38.17 Cowie, Alexander. *The Rise of the American Novel.* N.Y., 1948. Rpt. 1951.
813.09   PS371 C73

38.18 Wagenknecht, Edward C. *Cavalcade of the American Novel. From the Birth of the Nation to the Middle of the Twentieth Century.* N.Y., 1952.
813.09   PS371 W3

38.19 Chase, Richard V. *The American Novel and Its Tradition.* Garden City, N.Y., 1957.
813.09   PS371 C5

§39. The Novel: General Studies

39.1 *Novel. A Forum on Fiction.* 1967- . 3/yr.

39.2 *Studies in the Novel.* 1969- . 4/yr.
809.3305   PN3311 S82

39.3 *Count Dracula Society Quarterly.* 1970- .

•

39.4 Birkhead, Edith. *The Tale of Terror. A Study of the Gothic Romance.* London, 1921. Rpt. N.Y., 1963.
823.093   PN3435 B5

39.5 Forster, Edward M. *Aspects of the Novel.* N.Y., 1927. Rpt. 1954.
PN3353 F6

39.6 Muir, Edwin. *The Structure of the Novel.* London, 1928. Rpt. 1954, 1957; N.Y. 1963, 1969.
808.833   PN3353 M8

39.7 Lubbock, Percy. *The Craft of Fiction.* Rev. format. N.Y., 1929. (Orig. ed. 1921.) Rpt. 1947, 1957.
808.3   PN3355 L8

39.8 Edgar, Pelham. *The Art of the Novel from 1700 to the Present Time.* N.Y., 1933. Rpt. 1965.
823.03   PN3365 E4

39.9 James, Henry. *The Art of the Novel. Critical Prefaces.* Intro. Richard P. Blackmur. N.Y., 1934. Rpt. 1950.
813.46   PS2112 A3

39.10 Fox, Ralph W. *The Novel and the People.* 2nd ed. London, 1944. (Orig. ed. London & N.Y., 1937.)
808.3   PN3344 F6

39.11 Liddell, Robert. *A Treatise on the Novel.* London, 1947. Rpt. 1949, 1953, 1958. Also in *Robert Liddell on the Novel.* Ed. Wayne C. Booth. Chicago, 1969.
808.33   PN3353 L48

39.12 James, Henry. *The Art of Fiction and Other Essays.* Intr. Morris Roberts. N.Y., 1948.
808.3   PN3499 J25

39.13 Howe, Susanne. *Novels of Empire.* N.Y., 1949. Rpt. 1971.
809.3   PN3448 I5 H6

39.14 Brown, Edward K. *Rhythm in the Novel.* The Alexander Lectures, 1949-50. Toronto, 1950. Rpt. 1963.
808.3   PN3383 R5 B7

39.15 Mendilow, Adam A. *Time and the Novel*. London, 1952. Rpt. N.Y., 1965.
808.3   PN3355 M4

39.16 Liddell, Robert. *Some Principles of Fiction*. London, 1953. Rpt. in *Robert Liddell on the Novel*. Ed. Wayne C. Booth. Chicago, 1969.
808.33   PN3353 L49

39.17 Schorer, Mark, ed. *Society and Self in the Novel*. English Institute Essays, 1955. N.Y., 1956.
808.3   PE1010 E5

39.18 Allott, Miriam, ed. *Novelists on the Novel*. N.Y., 1959.
808.3   PN3321 A4

39.19 Brooks, Cleanth, and Robert Penn Warren, eds. *Understanding Fiction*. 2nd ed. N.Y., 1959. (Orig. ed. 1943.)
808.3   PN3335 B7

39.20 Krieger, Murray. *The Tragic Vision. Variations on a Theme in Literary Interpretation*. N.Y., 1960. Rpt. Chicago, 1966.
809.3   PN3491 K7

39.21 Booth, Wayne C. *The Rhetoric of Fiction*. Chicago, 1961.
808.3   PN3451 B6

39.22 Alter, Robert. *Rogue's Progress. Studies in the Picaresque Novel*. Cambridge, Mass., 1964. Harvard Studies in Comp. Lit., 26.
803.3   PN3428 A4

39.23 Beebe, Maurice. *Ivory Towers and Sacred Founts. The Artist as Hero in Fiction from Goethe to Joyce*. N.Y., 1964.
809.3   PN3491 B4

39.24 Hardy, Barbara. *The Appropriate Form. An Essay on the Novel*. London, 1964.
809.3   PN3335 H3

39.25 Pritchett, Victor S. *The Living Novel and Later Appreciations*. Rev. ed. N.Y., 1964. (Orig. ed., *The Living Novel*, London, 1946.)
823.09   PN3324 P7

39.26 Harvey, William J. *Character and the Novel*. Ithaca, N.Y. & London, 1965.
809.33   PN218 H3

39.27 Walcutt, Charles C. *Man's Changing Mask. Modes and Methods of Characterization in Fiction*. Minneapolis, 1966.
808.3   PN218 W3

39.28 Kermode, John Frank. *The Sense of an Ending. Studies in the Theory of Fiction*. N.Y., 1967.
801   PN45 K44

39.29 Calderwood, James L., and Harold E. Toliver, eds. *Perspectives on Fiction.* N.Y., 1968.
809.3   PN3354 C27

39.30 Miller, Joseph Hillis, ed. *Aspects of Narrative. Selected Papers from the English Institute* [1969-70]. N.Y., 1971.
809.923   PN3321 E5

§40. The English Novel

40.1 Shepperson, Archibald B. *The Novel in Motley. A History of the Burlesque Novel in English.* Cambridge, Mass., 1936. Rpt. N.Y., 1967.
823.0091   PR830 B8 S5

40.2 Van Ghent, Dorothy B. *The English Novel. Form and Function.* N.Y., 1953.
823.09   PR821 V3

40.3 Tillyard, Eustace M. W. *The Epic Strain in the English Novel.* London & Fair Lawn, N.J., 1958.
823.09   PR830 E6 T5

40.4 Rosenberg, Edgar. *From Shylock to Svengali. Jewish Stereotypes in English Fiction.* Stanford, 1960.
823.093   PR151 J5 R6

40.5 Shapiro, Charles, ed. *Twelve Original Essays on Great English Novels.* Detroit, 1960.
820.9   PR823 S5

40.6 Lodge, David. *Language of Fiction. Essays in Criticism and Verbal Analysis of the English Novel.* N.Y. & London, 1966.
823.009   PR821 L6

40.7 Hoyt, Charles A., ed. *Minor British Novelists.* Carbondale, Ill., 1967.
823.009   PR823 H6

40.8 Mack, Maynard, and Ian Gregor, eds. *Imagined Worlds. Essays on Some English Novels and Novelists in Honour of John Butt.* London, 1968.
823.009   PR823 I5

40.9 Pearce, Roy H., ed. *Experience in the Novel. Selected Papers from the English Institute* [*1967*]. N.Y., 1968.
823.009   PR823 E5

40.10 Mews, Hazel. *Frail Vessels. Woman's Role in Women's Novels from Fanny Burney to George Eliot.* London, 1969.
823.7093   PR830 W6 M4

§41. The American Novel

41.1 Taylor, Walter F. *The Economic Novel in America*. Chapel Hill, N.C. 1942. Rpt. N.Y., 1969.
813.4093   PS374 S7 T35

41.2 Gloster, Hugh M. *Negro Voices in American Fiction*. Chapel Hill, N.C. 1948. Rpt. N.Y., 1965.
813.509   PS374 N4 G5

41.3 Leisy, Ernest E. *The American Historical Novel*. Norman, Okla., 1950. Rpt. 1969.
813.09   PS374 H5 L4

41.4 Shapiro, Charles, ed. *Twelve Original Essays on Great American Novels*. Detroit, 1958.
813.04   PS371 S45

41.5 Bewley, Marius. *The Eccentric Design. Form in the Classic American Novel*. N.Y., 1959. Rpt. 1963.
813.09   PS371 B4

41.6 Folsom, James K. *The American Western Novel*. New Haven, 1961.
813.0874   PS374 W4 F6

41.7 Rubin, Louis D., and John R. Moore, eds. *The Idea of an American Novel*. N.Y., 1961.
813.09   PS371 R8

41.8 Lyons, John O. *The College Novel in America*. Carbondale, Ill., 1962.
813.09   PS374 U52 L9

41.9 Auchincloss, Louis. *Pioneers and Caretakers. A Study of 9 American Women Novelists*. Minneapolis, 1965.
813.09   PS151 A8

41.10 Bone, Robert A. *The Negro Novel in America*. Rev. ed. New Haven, 1965. (Orig. ed. 1958.) Yale Pubs. in Amer. Studies, 3.
813.509   PS153 N5 B6

41.11 Stegner, Wallace E., ed. *The American Novel. From James Fenimore Cooper to William Faulkner*. N.Y., 1965.
813.03   PS371 S73

41.12 Fiedler, Leslie A. *Love and Death in the American Novel*. Rev. ed. N.Y., 1966. (Orig. ed. 1960.)
813.03   PS374 L6 F5

41.13 Weimer, David R. *The City as Metaphor*. N.Y., 1966.
810.93   PS374 C5 W4

41.14 Hemenway, Robert, ed. *The Black Novelist.* Columbus, O.,
1970.
813.009   PS374 N4 H4

41.15 Miller, Wayne C. *An Armed America, Its Face in Fiction. A
History of the American Military Novel.* N.Y., 1970.
813.0093   PS374 M5 M5

41.16 Dickinson, Arthur T. *American Historical Fiction.* 3rd ed. Metuchen, N.J., 1971. (Orig. ed. 1958.)
016.81303   PS374 H5 D5

41.17 Hauck, Richard B. *A Cheerful Nihilism. Confidence and "The
Absurd" in American Humorous Fiction.* Bloomington, Ind., 1971.
813.00917   PS430 H27

41.18 Starke, Catherine J. *Black Portraiture in American Fiction.
Stock Characters, Archetypes, and Individuals.* N.Y., 1971.
810.9352   PS374 N4 S8

§42. The Short Story

42.1 Cook, Dorothy E., and Isabel S. Monro. *Short Story Index. An
Index to 60,000 Stories in 4320 Collections.* N.Y., 1953. Four *Supplements, 1950-1968,* 1956-69.
016.80883   Z5917 S5 C6

42.2 Thurston, Jarvis A., et al. *Short Fiction Criticism. A Checklist of
Interpretations Since 1925 of Stories and Novelettes (American, British, Continental), 1800-1958.* Denver, 1960.
016.80931   Z5917 S5 T5

42.3 Walker, Warren S. *Twentieth-Century Short Story Explication.
Interpretations, 1900-1966 Inclusive, of Short Fiction Since 1800.*
2nd ed. Hamden, Conn., 1968. (Orig. ed. 1961.) *Supplement, 1967-
1969,* 1970.
016.808831   Z5917 S5 W33

•

42.4 *Studies in Short Fiction.* 1963-   . 4/yr. Annual bibliography.
PN3311 S8

•

42.5 Pattee, Fred Lewis. *The Development of the American Short Story. An Historical Survey.* N.Y., 1923. Rpt. 1966.
813.01   PS374 S5 P3

42.6 West, Ray B. *The Short Story in America, 1900-1950.* Chicago,
1952. Rpt. Freeport, N.Y., 1968.
813.509   PS374 S5 W4

42.7 Ross, Danforth R. *The American Short Story.* Univ. of Minn. Pamphlets on Amer. Lit., 14. Minneapolis, 1961.
813.09   PS374 S5 R6

42.8 Wright, Austin McG. *The American Short Story in the Twenties.* Chicago, 1961.
813.5209   PS379 W7

42.9 O'Connor, Frank [Michael O'Donovan]. *The Lonely Voice. A Study of the Short Story.* London & Cleveland, 1963.
809.31   PN3373 O36

42.10 Beachcroft, Thomas O. *The English Short Story.* 2 vols. London & N.Y., 1964. Writers and Their Work, 168-69.
823.2   PR14 B5

42.11 Peden, William H. *The American Short Story. Front line in the National Defense of Literature.* Boston, 1964.
813.509   PS374 S5 P4

42.12 Beachcroft, Thomas O. *The Modest Art. A Survey of the Short Story in English.* London & N.Y., 1968.
823.01   PR829 B42

§43. The Mystery or Detective Story

43.1 *Baker Street Journal. An Irregular Quarterly of Sherlockiana.* 1946- .
823.91   PR4623 A17

43.2 *Sherlock Holmes Journal.* 1952- . 2/yr.
PR4623 A24

43.3 *Armchair Detective. A Quarterly Journal Devoted to the Appreciation of Mystery, Detective and Suspense Fiction.* 1967- .

•

43.4 Symons, Julian. *The Detective Story in Britain.* London, 1962. Writers and Their work, 145.
823.91   PR830 D4 S9

43.5 Haycraft, Howard. *Murder for Pleasure. The Life and Times of the Detective Story.* New ed. N.Y., 1968. (Orig. ed. 1941.)
808.3   PN3448 D4 H3

43.6 Hagen, Ordean A. *Who Done It? A Guide to Detective, Mystery and Suspense Fiction.* N.Y., 1969.
016.80883872   Z5917 D5 H3

43.7 Barzun, Jacques, and Wendell H. Taylor. *A Catalogue of Crime.* N.Y., 1971.
016.80880353   Z5917 D5 B37

43.8 Watson, Colin. *Snobbery with Violence.* London, 1971.
823.0872   PR830 D4 W3

§44. Science Fiction

44.1 Gove, Philip B. *The Imaginary Voyage in Prose Fiction. A History of Its Criticism and a Guide for Its Study, with an Annotated Check List of 215 Imaginary Voyages from 1700 to 1800.* N.Y., 1941. Rpt. London, 1961. Columbia Univ. Studies in English and Comp. Lit., 152.
809.3   PN3432 G6

44.2 Bleiler, Everett F., ed. *The Checklist of Fantastic Literature. A Bibliography of Fantasy, Weird, and Science Fiction Books Published in the English Language.* Chicago, 1948.
016.8083   Z5917 F3 B55

44.3 Day, Donald B. *Index to the Science-Fiction Magazines, 1926-1950.* Portland, Ore., 1952.
016.5   Z5917 S36 D3

44.4 Clarke, Ignatius F. *The Tale of the Future from the Beginning to the Present Day. A Check-List of those Satires, Ideal States, Imaginary Wars and Invasions, Political Warnings and Forecasts, Interplanetary Voyages and Scientific Romances—All Located in an Imaginary Future Period—That Have Been Published in the United Kingdom between 1644 and 1960.* London, 1961.
016.823   Z6207 P7 C5

44.5 Strauss, Erwin S., ed. *The MIT Science Fiction Society's Index to Science-Fiction Magazines, 1951-1965.* Cambridge, Mass., 1966.

44.6 Siemon, Frederick. *Science Fiction Story Index, 1950-1968.* Chicago, 1971.
016.8230876   Z5917 S36 S5

•

44.7 *Extrapolation. The Newsletter of the MLA Seminar on Science Fiction.* 1959- . 2/yr.

44.8 *Riverside Quarterly.* 1964- . Supersedes *Inside*, 1962-63, and *Inside Science Fiction*, 1957-63.

•

44.9 Bailey, James O. *Pilgrims Through Space and Time. Trends and Patterns in Scientific and Utopian Fiction.* N.Y., 1947.
808.3   PN3383 S4 B3

44.10 Bretnor, Reginald, ed. *Modern Science Fiction. Its Meaning and Its Future.* N.Y., 1953.
808.3   PN3383 S4 B7

82 / *Prose*

44.11 Gerber, Richard. *Utopian Fantasy. A Study of English Utopian Fiction Since the End of the Nineteenth Century.* London, 1955.
823.9109   PR888 U7 G4

44.12 Green, Roger L. *Into Other Worlds. Space-Flight in Fiction, from Lucian to Lewis.* London, 1958.
808.3   PN3448 S45 G67

44.13 Amis, Kingsley. *New Maps of Hell. A Survey of Science Fiction.* N.Y., 1960.
823.093   PR830 S35 A4

44.14 Moskowitz, Samuel. *Explorers of the Infinite. Shapers of Science Fiction.* Cleveland, 1963. Rpt. Los Angeles, 1971.
809.3   PN3448 S45 M65

44.15 Davenport, Basil, et al. *The Science Fiction Novel. Imagination and Social Criticism.* 2nd ed. Chicago, 1964. (Orig. ed. 1959.)
809.3   PN3448 S45 S35

44.16 Franklin, Howard Bruce. *Future Perfect. American Science Fiction of the Nineteenth Century.* N.Y., 1966.
813.0876   PN3448 S45 F7

44.17 Moskowitz, Samuel. *Seekers of Tomorrow. Masters of Modern Science Fiction.* Cleveland, 1966. Rpt. Los Angeles, 1971.
809.387   PN3448 S45 M66

44.18 Knight, Damon F. *In Search of Wonder. Essays on Modern Science Fiction.* 2nd ed. Chicago, 1967. (Orig. ed. 1956.)
813.509   PS374 S35 K5

44.19 Blish, James [William Atheling, Jr., pseud.]. *More Issues at Hand. Critical Studies in Contemporary Science Fiction.* Chicago, 1970.
823.0876   PN3448 S45 B47

44.20 Philmus, Robert M. *Into the Unknown. The Evolution of Science Fiction from Francis Godwin to H. G. Wells.* Berkeley, 1970.
823.076   PR830 S35 P5

44.21 Rose, Lois, and Stephen Rose. *The Shattered Ring. Science Fiction and the Quest for Meaning.* Richmond, Va., 1970.
809.3876   PN3448 S45 R6

44.22 Clareson, Thomas D., ed. *SF: The Other Side of Realism. Essays on Modern Fantasy and Science Fiction.* Bowling Green, O., 1971.
809.3876   PN3448 S45 C5

44.23 Wollheim, Donald A. *The Universe Makers. Science Fiction Today.* N.Y., 1971.
823.0876   PN3448 S45 W57

7. The Medieval Period

§45. Bibliographies and Periodicals

45.1 Tucker, Lena L., and Allen R. Benham. *A Bibliography of Fifteenth Century Literature. With Special Reference to the History of English Culture.* Seattle, 1928. Univ. of Washington Pubs. in Lang. and Lit., Vol. 2, No. 3.
Z2012 T89

45.2 Heusinkveld, Arthur H., and Edwin J. Bashe. *A Bibliographical Guide to Old English. A Selective Bibliography of the Language, Literature, and History of the Anglo-Saxons.* Iowa City, 1931. Rpt. Folcroft, Pa., 1969. Univ. of Iowa Humanistic Studies, Vol. 4, No. 5.
016.429   Z2012 A1 H5

45.3 Farrar, Clarissa P., and Austin P. Evans. *Bibliography of English Translations from Medieval Sources.* N.Y., 1946. Records of Civilization: Sources and Studies, 39.
016.8   Z6517 F3

45.4 Bonser, Wilfrid. *An Anglo-Saxon and Celtic Bibliography, 450-1087.* 2 vols. Oxford & Berkeley, 1957.
016.94201   Z2017 B6

45.5 Zesmer, David M. *Guide to English Literature from Beowulf Through Chaucer and Medieval Drama.* With Bibliographies by Stanley B. Greenfield. N.Y., 1961. College Outline Series, 53.
820.9   PR166 Z4

45.6 Fisher, John H., ed. *The Medieval Literature of Western Europe. A Review of Research, Mainly 1930-1960.* N.Y., 1966. MLA Revolving Fund Series, 22.
809.02   PN671 F5

45.7 Matthews, William., ed. *Old and Middle English Literature.* Goldentree Bibliographies. N.Y., 1968.
016.8209001   Z2012 M32

45.8 Robinson, Fred C. *Old English Literature. A Select Bibliography.*
Toronto, 1970. Toronto Med. Bibliographies, 3.
016.829   Z2012 R6

•

45.9 Rouse, Richard H. *Serial Bibliographies for Medieval Studies.*
Berkeley, 1969.
016.016914031   Z6203 R66

•

45.10 *Neuphilologische Mitteilungen.* Helsinki. 1899- . 4/yr. Annual
"Research in Progress," 1964- .
405   PB10 N415

45.11 *Progress of Medieval and Renaissance Studies in the United
States and Canada.* 1923-60. 2/yr.
Z6203 P96

45.12 *Speculum. A Journal of Mediaeval Studies.* 1925- . 4/yr with
bibliography of Amer. periodical literature, 1959- .
PN661 S6

45.13 *Cahiers de Civilisation Médiévale: Xe-XIIe Siècles.* 1958- . 4/yr
with bibliographies.
CB3 C3

45.14 *Quarterly Check List of Medievalia. An International Index of
Current Books, Monographs, Brochures and Separates.* 1958- .
Z6203 Q34

45.15 *International Guide to Medieval Studies. A Quarterly Index to
Periodical Literature.* 1961- .
Z6203 I6

45.16 *International Medieval Bibliography.* 1968 (for 1967)- . Annual.
016.914031   Z6203 I63

•

45.17 *Le Moyen Âge. Revue d'histoire et de philologie.* 1888- . 4/yr.
D111 M9

45.18 *Arthuriana. A Review of Mediaeval Studies.* 1928-30. 2 vols.
PB1 A6

45.19 *Medium Aevum. Journal of the Society for the Study of
Mediaeval Languages and Literature.* 1932- . 3/yr.
405   PB1 M4

45.20 *Mediaeval Studies.* 1939- . Annual.
940.104   D111 M44

45.21 *Medievalia et Humanistica. Studies in Medieval and Renaissance Culture.* 1943-66. New Series 1970- . Annual.
940.105   D111 M5

45.22 *Annuale Mediaevale.* 1960- .
940.105   D111 A55

45.23 *Medieval and Renaissance Studies.* Proceedings of the South-eastern Institute of Medieval and Renaissance Studies. 1966- . Annual.
914.031   CB361 M42

45.24 *Journal of Medieval and Renaissance Studies.* 1971- . 4/yr.

•

45.25 Wells, John E. *A Manual of the Writings in Middle English, 1050-1400.* New Haven, 1916. *Supplements.* 9 vols. 1919-51.
PR255 W4

The following work in progress is an expanded new edition.

45.26 Severs, Jonathan B. *A Manual of the Writings in Middle English, 1050-1500.* Hamden, Conn., 1967- .
820.9001   PR255 S4

§46. Surveys

46.1 Chadwick, Hector M. *The Heroic Age.* Cambridge, 1912. Rpt. 1926, 1967.
831.9001   PN1303 C6

46.2 Ker, William P. *English Literature. Medieval.* London, 1912. Rpt. London & N.Y., 1932, and as *Medieval English Literature,* London, 1962, 1969.
820.9   PR255 K4

46.3 Benham, Allen R. *English Literature from Widsith to the Death of Chaucer. A Source Book.* New Haven, 1916. Rpt. N.Y., 1968; Freeport, N.Y., 1970.
820.9001   PR255 B4

46.4 Baldwin, Charles S. *Three Medieval Centuries of Literature in England, 1100-1400.* Boston, 1932. Rpt. N.Y., 1968.
820.9001   PR255 B3

46.5 Coulton, George G. *Chaucer and His England.* 7th ed. London, 1946. (Orig. ed. 1908.) Rpt. with new biblio., N.Y., 1963.
821.1   PR1905 C58

46.6 Kane, George. *Middle English Literature. A Critical Study of the Romances, the Religious Lyrics, Piers Plowman.* London, 1951. Rpt. London & N.Y., 1970.
820.8001   PR255 K35

46.7 Jackson, William T. H. *The Literature of the Middle Ages.* N.Y., 1960.
809.02   PN671 J3

46.8 Greenfield, Stanley B. *A Critical History of Old English Literature.* N.Y., 1965.
829.09   PR173 G7

46.9 Ackerman, Robert W. *Backgrounds to Medieval English Literature.* N.Y., 1966.
820.9001   PR255 A3

46.10 Anderson, George K. *The Literature of the Anglo-Saxons.* Rev. ed. Princeton, 1966. (Orig. ed. 1949. Rpt. N.Y., 1962.)
829   PR173 A5

46.11 Wilson, Richard M. *Early Middle English Literature.* 3rd ed. London, 1968.
820.903   PR1502 M4

46.12 Wilson, Richard M. *The Lost Literature of Medieval England.* 2nd ed. London & N.Y., 1970. (Orig. ed. London, 1952. Rpt. N.Y., 1969.)
820.9001   PR255 W5

§47. General Studies

47.1 Ker, William P. *Epic and Romance. Essays on Medieval Literature.* 2nd ed. London, 1908. (Orig. ed. 1896.) Rpt. N.Y., 1957.
809.02   PN671 K4

47.2 Mosher, Joseph A. *The Exemplum in the Early Religious and Didactic Literature of England.* N.Y., 1911. Rpt. 1966.
BV4208 G7 M6

47.3 Chaytor, Henry J. *The Troubadours and England.* Cambridge, 1923.
PR355 T7 C5

47.4 Holzknecht, Karl J. *Literary Patronage in the Middle Ages.* Philadelphia, 1923. Rpt. N.Y., 1966.
809.02   PN682 P3 H6

47.5 Owst, Gerald R. *Preaching in Medieval England. An Introduction to Sermon Manuscripts of the Period, c. 1350-1450.* Cambridge, 1926. Rpt. N.Y., 1965.
251.00942   BV4208 G7 O8

47.6 Patch, Howard R. *The Goddess Fortuna in Mediaeval Literature.* Cambridge, Mass., 1927. Rpt. N.Y., 1967.
809.933   PN687 F55 P3

47.7 Lewis, Clive S. *The Allegory of Love. A Study in Medieval Tradition.* Corrected ed. London, 1938. (Orig. ed. 1936.) Rpt. 1958.
809   PN688 L4

47.8 Utley, Francis L. *The Crooked Rib. An Analytical Index to the Argument About Women in English and Scots Literature to the End of the Year 1568.* Columbus, O., 1944. Rpt. N.Y., 1970. Contr. to Lang. and Lit. of OSU, 10.
Z2014 W8 U8

47.9 Chaytor, Henry J. *From Script to Print. An Introduction to Medieval Vernacular Literature.* Cambridge, 1945. Rpt. 1950.
809.02   PN671 C5

47.10 Denomy, Alexander J. *The Heresy of Courtly Love.* N.Y., 1947.
177.6   GT2620 D4

47.11 Sisam, Kenneth. *Studies in the History of Old English Literature.* Oxford, 1953.
829.09   PR181 S5

47.12 Everett, Dorothy. *Essays on Middle English Literature.* Ed. Patricia Kean. London, 1955.
PR255 E9

47.13 Peter, John D. *Complaint and Satire in Early English Literature.* Oxford, 1956.
820.903   PR931 P4

47.14 Schlauch, Margaret. *English Medieval Literature and Its Social Foundations.* Warsaw, 1956. Rpt. London, 1967; St. Clair Shores, Mich. & N.Y., 1971.
820.9   PR173 S33

47.15 Whitelock, Dorothy. *The Audience of Beowulf.* Corrected ed. London, 1958. (Orig. ed. 1951.)
829.3   PR1587 A8 W5

✓47.16 Leach, MacEdward, ed. *Studies in Medieval Literature in Honor of Professor Albert Croll Baugh.* Philadelphia, 1961.
809.02   PR251 P45   *festschrift*

47.17 Owst, Gerald R. *Literature and Pulpit in Medieval England. A Neglected Chapter in the History of English Letters and of the English People.* 2nd ed. N.Y., 1961. (Orig. ed. Cambridge, 1933.)
820.902   PR275 O8

47.18 Utley, Francis L., ed. *The Forward Movement of the Fourteenth Century.* Columbus, O., 1961.
901.903   CB365 U8

✓47.19 Davis, Norman, and Charles L. Wrenn, eds. *English and Medieval Studies Presented to J. R. R. Tolkien on the Occasion of His Seventieth Birthday.* London, 1962.
821.0902   PE26 T6

✓47.20 Greenfield, Stanley B., ed. *Studies in Old English Literature in Honor of Arthur G. Brodeur.* Eugene, Ore., 1963.
829.109   PR176 G7

√**47.21** Bessinger, Jess B., and Robert P. Creed, eds. *Franciplegius. Medieval and Linguistic Studies in Honor of Francis P. Magoun, Jr.* N.Y., 1965.
829.082   PN681 B4

47.22 Morrell, Minnie C. *A Manual of Old English Biblical Materials.* Knoxville, Tenn., 1965.
220.5   BS132 M6

47.23 Vasta, Edward, ed. *Middle English Survey. Critical Essays.* Notre Dame, Ind., 1965.
820.9001   PR251 V3

47.24 Wrenn, Charles L. *A Study of Old English Literature.* London, 1967.
829   PR173 W75

47.25 Stevens, Martin, and Jerome Mandel, eds. *Old English Literature. Twenty-Two Analytical Essays.* Lincoln, Neb., 1968.
829.009   PR176 S7

√**47.26** *Medieval Literature and Civilization. Studies in Memory of G. N. Garmonsway.* Ed. Derek A. Pearsall and Ronald A. Waldron. London, 1969.
809.02   PN681 M4

47.27 Bethurum, Dorothy, ed. *Critical Approaches to Medieval Literature. Selected Papers from the English Institute, 1958-59.* N.Y., 1970.
809.02   PN681 B4

47.28 Cameron, Angus, et al., eds. *Computers and Old English Concordances.* Toronto, 1970.
829.03   PR171 C6

47.29 Loomis, Roger S. *Studies in Medieval Literature. A Memorial Collection of Essays.* N.Y., 1970.
820.9001   PN681 L63

√**47.30** *Medieval Literature and Folklore Studies. Essays in Honor of Francis Lee Utley.* Ed. Jerome Mandel and Bruce A. Rosenberg. New Brunswick, N.J., 1970.
809.02   PN681 M42

47.31 Wimsatt, James I. *Allegory and Mirror. Tradition and Structure in Middle English Literature.* N.Y., 1970.
821.109   PR275 A4 W5

47.32 Gatch, Milton M. *Loyalties and Traditions. Man and His World in Old English Literature.* N.Y., 1971.
829   PR173 G3

47.33 Gradon, Pamela. *Form and Style in Early English Literature.* London, 1971.
820.9001   PR173 G67

§48. Language

48.1 Stratmann, Francis H. *A Middle-English Dictionary. Containing Words Used by English Writers from the Twelfth to the Fifteenth Century.* New ed. by Henry Bradley. Oxford, 1891. (Orig. ed. 1867.)
PE679 S7

48.2 Kurath, Hans, and Sherman M. Kuhn, eds. *Middle English Dictionary.* Ann Arbor, 1952- .
427.02   PE679 M54

48.3 Chambers, Raymond W., and Marjorie Daunt, eds. *A Book of London English, 1384-1425.* Oxford, 1967.
427.1   PE1963 C5

48.4 Clark, John W. *Early English. A Study of Old and Middle English.* Rev. ed. London, 1967. (Orig. ed. 1957.)
427   PE124 C5

48.5 Hieatt, Constance B. *Essentials of Old English. Readings with Keyed Grammar and Vocabulary.* N.Y., 1968.
429.8242   PE135 H57

48.6 Meritt, Herbert D. *Some of the Hardest Glosses in Old English.* Stanford, 1968.
429.3   PE274 M42

48.7 Mitchell, Bruce C. *A Guide to Old English.* 2nd ed. Oxford & N.Y., 1968. (Orig. ed. 1965.)
429.5   PE131 M5

48.8 Cottle, Basil. *The Triumph of English, 1350-1400.* London & N.Y., 1969.
820.9001 / 914.20337   PE1075 C66 / DA185 C65

48.9 Frey, Leonard H. *An Introduction to Early English Grammar.* N.Y., 1970.
425   PE1101 F7

✓**48.10** *Philological Essays. Studies in Old and Middle English Language and Literature, in Honour of Herbert Dean Meritt.* Ed. James L. Rosier. The Hague, 1970.
429.17   PE26 M4

48.11 Kispert, Robert J. *Old English. An Introduction.* N.Y., 1971.
429.82421   PE135 K45

§49. The Metrical Romance and Arthurian Literature

49.1 Modern Language Association. *A Bibliography of Critical Arthurian Literature, 1922-1935.* Ed. John J. Parry with Margaret Schlauch. 2 vols. N.Y., 1931-36.
016.39822   Z8045 M69

•

49.2 *Modern Language Quarterly.* 1940- . Extends coverage 1936-39 with annual bibliographies until 1963.
405   PB1 M642

49.3 International Arthurian Society. *Bibliographical Bulletin.* Paris. 1949- . Annual.
Z8045 I5

•

49.4 Ackerman, Robert W. *An Index of the Arthurian Names in Middle English.* Stanford, 1952. Rpt. N.Y., 1967. Stanford Univ. Pubs. in Lang. and Lit., 10.
398.22   PE1660 A23

49.5 Bordman, Gerald. *Motif-Index of the English Metrical Romances.* Helsinki, 1963. Folklore Fellows Communications, 190.
GR1 F55 no. 190

•

49.6 Maynadier, Howard G. *The Arthur of the English Poets.* Boston, 1907. Rpt. N.Y., 1969.
821.1   PN686 A7 M3

49.7 Loomis, Roger S. *Celtic Myth and Arthurian Romance.* N.Y., 1927. Rpt. 1967.
891.6   PN685 L6

49.8 Taylor, Albert B. *An Introduction to Medieval Romance.* London, 1930. Rpt. N.Y., 1969.
809.385   PN671 T27

49.9 Starr, Nathan C. *King Arthur Today. The Arthurian Legend in English and American Literature, 1901-1953.* Gainesville, Fla., 1954.
820.904   PR479 A7 S7

49.10 Loomis, Roger S., ed. *Arthurian Literature in the Middle Ages. A Collaborative History.* Oxford, 1959.
809.93   PN57 A6 L6

49.11 Hibbard, Laura A. [Loomis]. *Mediaeval Romance in England. A Study of the Sources and Analogues of the Non-Cyclic Metrical Romances.* New ed. N.Y., 1960. (Orig. ed. 1924.)
823.109   PR321 L6

49.12 Barber, Richard W. *Arthur of Albion. An Introduction to the Arthurian Literature and Legends of England.* London & N.Y., 1961. Rpt. N.Y., 1971.
820.92   PN57 A6 B3

49.13 Loomis, Roger S. *The Development of Arthurian Romance.* London, 1963. Rpt. N.Y., 1970.
809.93   PN685 L62

49.14 Cosman, Madeleine P. *The Education of the Hero in Arthurian Romance.* Chapel Hill, N.C., 1968.
809.933   PN685 C6

49.15 Mehl, Dieter. *The Middle English Romances of the Thirteenth and Fourteenth Centuries.* London & N.Y., 1969. (Rev. of German ed., Heidelberg, 1967.)
821.109   PR321 M413

49.16 Ashe, Geoffrey. *Camelot and the Vision of Albion.* London, 1971.
398.22   DA152.5 A7 A79

49.17 Owen, Douglas D. R. *Arthurian Romance. Seven Essays.* London & N.Y., 1971.
398.220942   PN685 O9

§50. Poetry

50.1 Brown, Carleton, and Rossell H. Robbins. *The Index of Middle English Verse.* N.Y., 1943. *Supplement.* Ed. R. H. Robbins and John L. Cutler. Lexington, Ky., 1965.
016.8211   Z2012 B86

• *The Anglo-Saxon Poetic Records. A Collective Edition.* 6 vols. N.Y., 1931-53.
PR1502 A7

50.2 I. *The Junius Manuscript.* Ed. George P. Krapp.

50.3 II. *The Vercelli Book.* Ed. George P. Krapp.
829.1   PR1495 A1

50.4 III. *The Exeter Book.* Ed. George P. Krapp and Elliott V. Dobbie.
829.082   PR1490 A1

50.5 IV. *The Beowulf Manuscript: Beowulf and Judith.* Ed. Elliott V. Dobbie.
829.3   PR1580 D6

50.6 V. *The Paris Psalter and the Meters of Boethius.* Ed. George P. Krapp.

50.7 VI. *The Anglo-Saxon Minor Poems.* Ed. Elliott V. Dobbie.
829.1   PR1502 D6

•

50.8 Williams, Blanch C. *Gnomic Poetry in Anglo-Saxon.* N.Y., 1914. Rpt. 1966. Columbia Univ. Studies in English and Comp. Lit.
PR215 W4

50.9 Lawrence, William W. *Beowulf and Epic Tradition.* Cambridge, Mass., 1928. Rpt. N.Y., 1961.
829.3   PR1585 L3

50.10 Oakden, James P. *Alliterative Poetry in Middle English.* 2 vols. Manchester, Eng., 1930-35. Rpt. in 1 vol. Hamden, Conn., 1968.
426.0902   PE659 A6 O3

50.11 Haber, Tom B. *A Comparative Study of "Beowulf" and the "Aeneid."* Princeton, 1931. Rpt. N.Y., 1968.
829.3   PR1585 H2

50.12 Bartlett, Adeline C. *The Larger Rhetorical Patterns in Anglo-Saxon Poetry.* N.Y., 1935. Rpt. 1966. Columbia Univ. Studies in English and Comp. Lit., 122.
829.109   PR203 B3

50.13 Kennedy, Charles W. *The Earliest English Poetry. A Critical Survey of the Poetry Written Before the Norman Conquest, with Illustrative Translations.* London, 1943. Rpt. 1948, 1963; Totowa, N.J., 1971.
829.109   PR201 K4

50.14 Moore, Arthur K. *The Secular Lyric in Middle English.* Lexington, Ky., 1951. Rpt. Westport, Conn., 1970.
821.04   PR354 M6

50.15 Lehmann, Winfred P. *The Alliteration of Old Saxon Poetry.* Oslo, 1953.
439.26   PF3995 L4

50.16 Lehmann, Winfred P. *The Development of Germanic Verse Form.* Austin, Tex., 1956. Rpt. N.Y., 1971.
436   PD505 L4

50.17 Speirs, John H. *Medieval English Poetry. The Non-Chaucerian Tradition.* London, 1957.
821.109   PR311 S7

50.18 Bliss, Alan J. *The Metre of Beowulf.* Oxford, 1958. Rpt. N.Y., 1962.
829.3   PR1588 B6

50.19 Chambers, Raymond W. *Beowulf. An Introduction to the Study of the Poem with a Discussion of the Stories of Offa and Finn.* 3rd ed. with Supplement by Charles L. Wrenn. Cambridge, 1959. (Orig. ed. 1921.)
829.3   PR1585 C5

50.20 Huppé, Bernard F. *Doctrine and Poetry. Augustine's Influence on Old English Poetry.* Albany, N.Y., 1959.
829.109   PR182 H8

50.21 Bessinger, Jess B. *A Short Dictionary of Anglo-Saxon Poetry. In a Normalized Early West-Saxon Orthography.* Toronto, 1960. Rpt. 1961.
829.103   PE279 B4

50.22 Bliss, Alan J. *An Introduction to Old English Metre.* Oxford, 1962.
829.1   PE253 B5

50.23 Pope, John C. *The Rhythm of Beowulf. An Interpretation of the Normal and Hypermetric Verse-Forms in Old English Poetry.* Rev. ed. New Haven, 1966. (Orig. ed. 1942.)
829.3   PR1588 P6

50.24 Creed, Robert P., ed. *Old English Poetry. Fifteen Essays.* Providence, R.I., 1967.
829.109   PR201 C7

50.25 Bessinger, Jess B., and Stanley J. Kahrl, eds. *Essential Articles for the Study of Old English Poetry.* Hamden, Conn., 1968.
829.109   PR176 B4

50.26 Fry, Donald K., ed. *The Beowulf Poet. A Collection of Critical Essays.* Englewood Cliffs, N.J., 1968.
829.3   PR1585 F7

50.27 Isaacs, Neil D. *Structural Principles in Old English Poetry.* Knoxville, Tenn., 1968.
829.1   PR201 I8

50.28 Woolf, Rosemary. *The English Religious Lyric in the Middle Ages.* Oxford, 1968.
821.109   PR311 W6

50.29 Oliver, Raymond. *Poems Without Names. The English Lyric, 1200-1500.* Berkeley, 1970.
821.109   PR351 O5

§51. Drama and Theater

51.1 Stratman, Carl J. *Bibliography of Medieval Drama.* Berkeley, 1954.
016.80882   Z5782 A2 S8

•

51.2 Chambers, Edmund K. *The Mediaeval Stage.* 2 vols. Oxford, 1903. Rpt. 1925.
792.09401   PN2152 C4

51.3 Mackenzie, William R. *The English Moralities from the Point of View of Allegory.* Boston, 1914. Rpt. 1970; N.Y., 1966, 1969, 1970. Harvard Studies in English, 2.
822.051   PR643 M7 M3

51.4 Pollard, Alfred W. *English Miracle Plays, Moralities, and Interludes. Specimens of the Pre-Elizabethan Drama.* 8th ed. Oxford, 1927. Rpt. 1961.
822.10822   PR1260 P7

51.5 Young, Karl. *The Drama of the Medieval Church.* 2 vols. N.Y., 1933. Rpt. 1951.
792.1   PN1751 Y6

51.6 Gardiner, Harold C. *Mysteries' End. An Investigation of the Last Days of the Medieval Religious Stage.* New Haven, 1946. Rpt. Hamden, Conn., 1967. Yale Studies in English, 103.
822.109   PR641 G3

51.7 Williams, Arnold. *The Characterization of Pilate in the Towneley Plays.* E. Lansing, Mich., 1950.
822.13   PR644 T6 W5

51.8 Craig, Hardin. *English Religious Drama of the Middle Ages.* Oxford, 1955. Rpt. 1960.
822.109   PR641 C7

51.9 Salter, Frederick M. *Medieval Drama in Chester.* Toronto, 1955. Rpt. N.Y., 1968.
822.051   PR644 C4 S3

51.10 Southern, Richard. *The Medieval Theatre in the Round. A Study of the Staging of "The Castle of Perseverance" and Related Matters.* London, 1957.
792   PN2587 S6

51.11 Prosser, Eleanor A. *Drama and Religion in the English Mystery Plays. A Re-evaluation.* Stanford, 1961. Stanford Studies in Lang. and Lit., 23.
822.1093   PR643 M8 P7

51.12 Williams, Arnold. *The Drama of Medieval England.* E. Lansing, Mich., 1961.
822.109   PR641 W55

51.13 Anderson, Mary D. *Drama and Imagery in English Medieval Churches.* Cambridge, 1963.
246.1   PR641 A7

51.14 Hardison, Osborne B. *Christian Rite and Christian Drama in the Middle Ages. Essays in the Origin and Early History of Modern Drama.* Baltimore, 1965.
809.251   BX1970 H28

8. The Renaissance

§52. Bibliographies and Periodicals

52.1 Scott, Mary A. *Elizabethan Translations from the Italian.* Rev. ed. Boston, 1916. (Orig. ed. 1895-99 in *PMLA*.) Rpt. N.Y., 1969.
016.85   Z2354 T7 S3

52.2 Williams, Franklin B. *Index of Dedications and Commendatory Verses in English Books Before 1641.* London, 1962.
655   PN171 D4 W55

52.3 Lievsay, John L., ed. *The Sixteenth Century. Skelton Through Hooker.* Goldentree Bibliographies. N.Y., 1968.
016.8209002   Z2012 L5

•

52.4 *Studies in Philology.* 1906-   . 5/yr. Annual Renaissance bibliography since 1918.
P25 S8

52.5 *Bibliothèque d'Humanisme et Renaissance.* 1941-   . 3/yr. Annual bibliography 1958-65.
901   CB361 B5

52.6 *SCN. Seventeenth-Century News. Including "The Neo-Latin News."* 1942-   . 4/yr.
PR1 S47

52.7 *Renaissance Quarterly.* 1948-   . Until 1966 *Renaissance News.*
901   CB361 R45

52.8 *Studies in the Renaissance.* 1954-   . Annual.
940.21   D223 S8

52.9 *Quarterly Check-List of Renaissance Studies.* 1959-   .
Z6207 R4 Q34

52.10 *Bibliographie Internationale d'Humanisme et de la Renaissance.* 1966-   . Annual.
Z6207 R4 B5

§53. Surveys and General Studies

53.1 Schelling, Felix E. *English Literature During the Lifetime of Shakespeare.* Rev. ed. N.Y., 1927. (Orig. ed. 1910.)
820.9003   PR421 S35

53.2 Dunn, Esther C. *The Literature of Shakespeare's England.* N.Y., 1936. Rpt. 1969.
820.9003   PR651 D8

53.3 Wilson, Frank P. *Elizabethan and Jacobean.* London, 1945.
820.903   PR421 W5

53.4 Muir, Kenneth. *An Introduction to Elizabethan Literature.* N.Y., 1967.
820.9003   PR424 M8

53.5 Wedgwood, Cicely V. *Seventeenth-Century English Literature.* 2nd ed. London & N.Y., 1970. (Orig. ed. 1950.)
820.9004   PR431 W4

•

53.6 Clark, Donald L. *Rhetoric and Poetry in the Renaissance. A Study of Rhetorical Terms in English Renaissance Literary Criticism.* N.Y., 1922. Rpt. 1963.
821.309   PN1035 C5

53.7 Grierson, Herbert J. C. *Cross Currents in English Literature of the Seventeenth Century. Or, the World, the Flesh and the Spirit, Their Actions and Reactions.* London, 1929. Rpt. 1948; N.Y., 1958.
820.903   PR431 G7

53.8 Matthiessen, Francis O. *Translation. An Elizabethan Art.* Cambridge, Mass., 1931. Rpt. N.Y., 1965.
828.309   PR428 T7 M3

53.9 Eliot, T[homas] S. *Elizabethan Essays.* London, 1934. Rpt. 1942; N.Y., 1969.
822.304   PR653 E6

53.10 Willey, Basil. *The Seventeenth Century Background. Studies in the Thought of the Age in Relation to Poetry and Religion.* London, 1934. Rpt. 1941; N.Y. 1941, 1953.
192   B1131 W5

53.11 White, Harold O. *Plagiarism and Imitation During the English Renaissance. A Study in Critical Distinctions.* Cambridge, Mass., 1935. Harvard Studies in English, 12. Rpt. N.Y., 1965.
820.9003   PR418 P6 W5

53.12 Wright, Louis B. *Middle-Class Culture in Elizabethan England.* Chapel Hill, N.C., 1935. Rpt. Ithaca, N.Y., 1958.
820.903   PR421 W7

53.13 Craig, Hardin. *The Enchanted Glass. The Elizabethan Mind in Literature.* N.Y., 1936. Rpt. 1950.
820.903   PR421 C67

53.14 Mills, Laurens J. *One Soul in Bodies Twain. Friendship in Tudor Literature and Drama.* Bloomington, Ind., 1937.
820.9   PR429 F7 M5

53.15 Haller, William. *The Rise of Puritanism. Or, the Way to the New Jerusalem as Set Forth in Pulpit and Press from Thomas Cartwright to John Lilburne and John Milton, 1570-1643.* N.Y., 1938. Rpt. 1957.
285.942   BX9334 H3

53.16 *Seventeenth Century Studies Presented to Sir Herbert Grierson.* Oxford, 1938. Rpt. N.Y., 1967.
809.032   PN741 S4

53.17 Allen, Don C. *The Star-Crossed Renaissance. The Quarrel About Astrology and Its Influence in England.* Durham, N.C., 1941. Rpt. N.Y., 1966.
133.50903   BF1679 A4

53.18 Tillyard, Eustace M. W. *The Elizabethan World Picture.* London, 1943: N.Y., 1944. Rpt. N.Y., 1959; Harmondsworth, Eng., 1966.
820.903   PR428 P5 T5

53.19 Knights, Lionel C. *Explorations. Essays in Criticism, Mainly on the Literature of the Seventeenth Century.* London, 1946. Rpt. 1951; N.Y., 1964.
820.9   PR433 K5

53.20 Harris, Victor. *All Coherence Gone. A Study of the Seventeenth Century Controversy over Disorder and Decay in the Universe.* Chicago, 1949. Rpt. London, 1966.
236   BT875 H32

53.21 Southern, Alfred C. *Elizabethan Recusant Prose, 1559-1582. A Historical and Critical Account of the Books of the Catholic Refugees Printed and Published Abroad and at Secret Presses in England Together with an Annotated Bibliography of the Same.* London, 1950.
820.903   PR428 C3 S6

53.22 Babb, Lawrence. *The Elizabethan Malady. A Study of Melancholia in English Literature from 1580 to 1642.* E. Lansing, Mich., 1951.
820.903   PR658 M37 B3

53.23 Jones, Richard F., et al. *The Seventeenth Century. Studies in the History of English Thought and Literature from Bacon to Pope.* Stanford, 1951. Rpt. 1969.
820.903   PR433 J6

53.24 Kelso, Ruth. *Doctrine for the Lady of the Renaissance.* Urbana, Ill., 1956.
396   HQ1148 K4

53.25 Campbell, Lily B. *Divine Poetry and Drama in Sixteenth-Century England.* Berkeley, 1959. Rpt. N.Y., 1971.
PR419 R4 C3

53.26 *Elizabethan and Jacobean Studies. Presented to Frank Percy Wilson in Honour of His Seventieth Birthday.* Oxford, 1959. Rpt. 1969.
820.9003   PR423 E5

53.27 Kernan, Alvin B. *The Cankered Muse. Satire of the English Renaissance.* New Haven, 1959. Yale Studies in English, 142.
827.309   PR933 K4

53.28 Craig, Hardin. *New Lamps for Old.* Oxford, 1960.
800   BD161 C67

53.29 Hardison, Osborne B. *The Enduring Monument. A Study of the Idea of Praise in Renaissance Literary Theory and Practice.* Chapel Hill, N.C., 1962.
809.03   PN88 H34

53.30 McNeir, Waldo F., ed. *Studies in English Renaissance Literature.* Baton Rouge, La., 1962.
821.309   PR423 M3

53.31 Hamilton, Kenneth G. *The Two Harmonies. Poetry and Prose in the Seventeenth Century.* Oxford, 1963.
821.0903   PR541 H3

53.32 Allen, Don C. *Doubt's Boundless Sea. Skepticism and Faith in the Renaissance.* Baltimore, 1964.
273.0903   CB361 A48

53.33 Tayler, Edward W. *Nature and Art in Renaissance Literature.* N.Y., 1964.
809.93   PN48 T3

53.34 Bush, Douglas. *Prefaces to Renaissance Literature.* Cambridge, Mass. & N.Y., 1965.
820.9   PR413 B8

53.35 Sheavyn, Phoebe A. *The Literary Profession in the Elizabethan Age.* 2nd ed. London & N.Y., 1967. (Orig. ed. Manchester, Eng., 1909.)
820.23   PR428 A8 S5

53.36 Levin, Harry T. *The Myth of the Golden Age in the Renaissance.* Bloomington, Ind., 1969.
809.933   PN721 L4

53.37 Murrin, Michael. *The Veil of Allegory. Some Notes Toward a Theory of Allegorical Rhetoric in the English Renaissance.* Chicago, 1969.
821.3   PR535 A4 M8

53.38 Allen, Don C. *Mysteriously Meant. The Rediscovery of Pagan Symbolism and Allegorical Interpretation in the Renaissance.* Baltimore, 1970.
809.9337   PA57 A4

53.39 Cole, Howard C. *A Quest of Inquiries. Some Contexts of Tudor Literature.* N.Y., 1971.

§54. Poetry

54.1 Case, Arthur E. *A Bibliography of English Poetical Miscellanies, 1521-1750.* Oxford, 1935.
016.8210822   Z2014 P7 C3

54.2 Spencer, Theodore, and Mark Van Doren. *Studies in Metaphysical Poetry. Two Essays and a Bibliography.* N.Y., 1939. Rpt. Pt. Washington, N.Y., 1964.
016.821409   Z2014 P7 S6

54.3 Berry, Lloyd E., ed. *A Bibliography of Studies in Metaphysical Poetry, 1939-1960.* Madison, Wis., 1964.
016.821409   Z2014 P7 B4

54.4 Frank, Joseph. *Hobbled Pegasus. A Descriptive Bibliography of Minor English Poetry, 1641-1660.* Albuquerque, N.M., 1968.
016.821408   Z2014 P7 F7

•

54.5 Berdan, John M. *Early Tudor Poetry, 1485-1547. Studies in Tudor Literature.* N.Y., 1920. Rpt. 1931; Hamden, Conn., 1961, 1968.
821.209   PR521 B4

54.6 Pearson, Lu E. *Elizabethan Love Conventions.* Berkeley, 1933. Rpt. N.Y., 1967.
821.309   PR535 L7 P4

54.7 Leishman, James B. *The Metaphysical Poets. Donne, Herbert, Vaughan, Traherne.* Oxford, 1934. Rpt. N.Y., 1963.
821.309   PR543 L4

54.8 White, Helen C. *The Metaphysical Poets. A Study in Religious Experience.* N.Y., 1936. Rpt. 1962.
821.309   PR549 R4 W5

54.9 John, Lisle C. *The Elizabethan Sonnet Sequences. Studies in Conventional Conceits.* N.Y., 1938. Rpt. 1964. Columbia Univ. Studies in English and Comp. Lit., 133.
821.309   PR539 S7 J6

54.10 Sharp, Robert L. *From Donne to Dryden. The Revolt Against Metaphysical Poetry.* Chapel Hill, N.C., 1940.
821.309   PR541 S5

54.11 Rubel, Veré L. *Poetic Diction in the English Renaissance. From Skelton Through Spenser.* N.Y., 1941. Rpt. 1966. MLA Revolving Fund Series, 12.
821.209   PR525 L3 R82

54.12 Tuve, Rosemond. *Elizabethan and Metaphysical Imagery. Renaissance Poetic and Twentieth-Century Critics.* Chicago, 1947.
821.309   PR535 F5 T8

54.13 Mahood, Molly M. *Poetry and Humanism.* London & New Haven, 1950. Rpt. Pt. Washington, N.Y., 1967; N.Y., 1970.
821.30931   PR549 R4 M3

54.14 Nicolson, Marjorie H. *The Breaking of the Circle. Studies in the Effect of the "New Science" upon Seventeenth-Century Poetry.* Evanston, Ill., 1950.
821.309   PR545 S3 N5

54.15 Wallerstein, Ruth C. *Studies in Seventeenth-Century Poetic.* Madison, Wis., 1950.
821.409   PR529 E4 W3

54.16 Zocca, Louis R. *Elizabethan Narrative Poetry.* New Brunswick, N.J., 1950. Rpt. N.Y., 1970.
821.309   PR535 N3 Z6

54.17 Ing, Catherine M. *Elizabethan Lyrics. A Study in the Development of English Metres and Their Relation to Poetic Effect.* London, 1951. Rpt. N.Y., 1969.
821.309   PR525 V4 I5

54.18 Danby, John F. *Poets on Fortune's Hill. Studies in Sidney, Shakespeare, Beaumont and Fletcher.* London, 1952. Rpt. Pt. Washington, N.Y., 1966. British rpt. title *Elizabethan and Jacobean Poets,* 1964.
821.309   PR535 S6 D3

54.19 Smith, Hallett D. *Elizabethan Poetry. A Study in Conventions, Meanings, and Expression.* Cambridge, Mass., 1952.
821.309   PR531 S6

54.20 Cruttwell, Patrick. *The Shakespearean Moment and Its Place in the Poetry of the Seventeenth Century.* London, 1954. Rpt. N.Y., 1960.
821.309   PR541 C7

54.21 Lever, Julius W. *The Elizabethan Love Sonnet.* London, 1956.
Rpt. N.Y., 1968.
821.309   PR539 S7 L4

54.22 Mason, Harold A. *Humanism and Poetry in the Early Tudor
Period. An Essay.* London, 1959.
821.2091   PR418 H8 M3

54.23 *Elizabethan Poetry.* Stratford-upon-Avon Studies, 2. London &
N.Y., 1960.
821.309   PR531 E4

54.24 Skelton, Robin. *Cavalier Poets.* London, 1960. Writers and Their
Work, 117.
821.4   PR541 S55

54.25 Wedgwood, Cicely V. *Poetry and Politics Under the Stuarts.*
Cambridge, 1960. Rpt. Ann Arbor, 1964.
821.3093   PR545 P6 W4

54.26 Alvarez, Alfred. *The School of Donne.* London & N.Y., 1961.
Rpt. N.Y., 1967.
821.3   PR541 A5 A7

54.27 Williamson, George. *The Proper Wit of Poetry.* Chicago & London, 1961.
821.07   PR541 W53

54.28 Martz, Louis L. *The Poetry of Meditation. A Study of English
Religious Literature of the Seventeenth Century.* Rev. ed. New
Haven, 1962. (Orig. ed. 1954.) Yale Studies in English, 125.
821.309   PR549 R4 M3

54.29 Bennett, Joan. *Five Metaphysical Poets. Donne, Herbert,
Vaughan, Crashaw, Marvell.* 3rd ed. Cambridge, 1964. (Orig. ed.
Four Metaphysical Poets, 1934.)
821.409   PR543 B4

54.30 Richmond, Hugh M. *The School of Love. The Evolution of the
Stuart Love Lyric.* London & Princeton, 1964.
809.93   PR548 L6 R5

54.31 Hunter, Jim. *The Metaphysical Poets.* London, 1965.
821.409   PR541 H8

54.32 Stewart, Stanley. *The Enclosed Garden. The Tradition and the
Image in Seventeenth-Century Poetry.* Madison, Wis., 1966.
821.40915   PR541 S8

54.33 Alpers, Paul J., ed. *Elizabethan Poetry. Modern Essays in Criticism.* N.Y., 1967.
821.309   PR533 A65

54.34 Evans, Maurice. *English Poetry in the Sixteenth Century.*
2nd ed. London & N.Y., 1967. (Orig. ed. London, 1955.)
821.209   PR521 E9

54.35 Peterson, Douglas L. *The English Lyric from Wyatt to Donne. A History of the Plain and Eloquent Styles.* Princeton, 1967.
821.009   PR529 L8 P4

54.36 Williamson, George. *Six Metaphysical Poets. A Reader's Guide.* N.Y., 1967.
821.009   PR541 W54

54.37 Allen, Don C. *Image and Meaning. Metaphoric Traditions in Renaissance Poetry.* 2nd ed. Baltimore, 1968. (Orig. ed. 1960.)
821.009   PR531 A4

54.38 Kermode, John Frank, ed. *The Metaphysical Poets. Key Essays on Metaphysical Poetry and the Major Metaphysical Poets.* Greenwich, Conn., 1969.
821.4   PR543 K44

54.39 Williamson, George. *Seventeenth Century Contexts.* Rev. ed. Chicago, 1969. (Orig. ed. London, 1960.)
821.309   PR543 W5

54.40 Fowler, Alastair. *Triumphal Forms. Structural Patterns in Elizabethan Poetry.* Cambridge, 1970.
821.309   PR535 S9 F6

54.41 Grundy, Joan. *The Spenserian Poets. A Study in Elizabethan and Jacobean Poetry.* N.Y., 1970.
821.309   PR534 G7

54.42 Keast, William R., ed. *Seventeenth-Century English Poetry. Modern Essays in Criticism.* Rev. ed. N.Y., 1971. (Orig. ed. 1962.)
821.309   PR543 K4

54.43 Miner, Earl, ed. *Seventeenth Century Imagery. Essays on the Use of Figurative Language from Donne to Farquhar.* Berkeley, 1971.

§55. Drama and Theater

55.1 Ribner, Irving, ed. *Tudor and Stuart Drama.* Goldentree Bibliographies. N.Y., 1966.
016.8223   Z2014 D7 R5

55.2 *Renaissance Drama.* 1955-   . Annual. Until 1963 *Research Opportunities in Renaissance Drama.*
809.20902

•

55.3 Fleay, Frederick G. *A Chronicle History of the London Stage, 1559-1642.* London, 1890. Rpt. N.Y., 1964.
792.09421   PN2589 F5

55.4 Fleay, Frederick G. *A Biographical Chronicle of the English Drama, 1559-1642.* 2 vols. London, 1891. Rpt. N.Y., 1969.
822.309   PR651 F5

55.5 Greg, Walter W. *Pastoral Poetry and Pastoral Drama. A Literary Inquiry, with Special Reference to the Pre-Restoration Stage in England.* London, 1906. Rpt. N.Y., 1959.
821.309   PR509 P3 G3

55.6 Murray, John T. *English Dramatic Companies, 1558-1642.* 2 vols. Boston, 1910. Rpt. N.Y., 1963.
792.0942   PN2589 M8

55.7 Brooke, Charles F. Tucker. *The Tudor Drama. A History of English National Drama to the Retirement of Shakespeare.* Boston, 1911. Rpt. Hamden, Conn., 1964, 1970.
822.309   PR651 B7

55.8 Boas, Frederick S. *University Drama in the Tudor Age.* Oxford, 1914. Rpt. N.Y., 1966.
822.309   PR649 U6 B6

55.9 Creizenach, Wilhelm. *The English Drama in the Age of Shakespeare.* Trans. Cécile Hugon. London, 1916. (Orig. German ed. 1904.) Rpt. N.Y., 1967, 1969.
822.309   PR651 C7

55.10 Adams, Joseph Quincy. *Shakespearean Playhouses. A History of English Theatres from the Beginnings to the Restoration.* Boston, 1917. Rpt. Gloucester, Mass., 1960.
792.09421   PN2596 L6 A55

55.11 Campbell, Lily B. *Scenes and Machines on the English Stage During the Renaissance. A Classical Revival.* Cambridge, 1923. Rpt. N.Y., 1960.
792.025   PN2590 S7 C3

55.12 Chambers, Edmund K. *The Elizabethan Stage* [1558-1616]. 4 vols. Oxford, 1923.
792.0942   PN2589 C4

    55.13 White, Beatrice. *An Index to "The Elizabethan Stage"* . . . Oxford, 1934. Rpt. N.Y., 1964.
           PR2894 C442

55.14 Reed, Arthur W. *Early Tudor Drama. Medwall, the Rastells, Heywood, and the More Circle.* London, 1926. Rpt. N.Y., 1969.
822.209   PR646 R45

55.15 Baldwin, Thomas W. *The Organization and Personnel of the Shakespearean Company.* Princeton, 1927. Rpt. N.Y., 1961.
792.0942   PR3095 B3

55.16 Lawrence, William J. *The Physical Condition of the Elizabethan Public Playhouse.* Cambridge, Mass., 1927. Rpt. N.Y., 1968.
792.09   PN2589 L35

55.17 Greg, Walter W. *Dramatic Documents from the Elizabethan Playhouses. Stage Plots, Actors' Parts, Prompt Books.* 2 vols. Oxford, 1931. Rpt. 1969.
792.0942   PN2589 G74

55.18 Boas, Frederick S. *An Introduction to Tudor Drama.* Oxford, 1933.
822.209   PR646 B6

55.19 Bradbrook, Muriel C. *Themes and Conventions of Elizabethan Tragedy.* Cambridge, 1935.
822.309   PR658 T7 B7

55.20 Sharpe, Robert B. *The Real War of the Theatres. Shakespeare's Fellows in Rivalry with the Admiral's Men, 1594-1603. Repertoires, Devices, and Types.* Boston, 1935. Rpt. N.Y., 1966. MLA Monograph Series, 5.
792.09421   PN2596 L6 S48

55.21 Farnham, Willard. *The Medieval Heritage of Elizabethan Tragedy.* Berkeley, 1936. Rpt. with corrections, Oxford, 1956.
                    PR658 T7 F3

55.22 Knights, Lionel C. *Drama and Society in the Age of Jonson.* London, 1937. Rpt. 1951, 1957; N.Y., 1968.
822.3   PR655 K62

55.23 Nicoll, Allardyce. *Stuart Masques and the Renaissance Stage.* N.Y., 1938. Rpt. 1963.
792.02   PR658 M3 N5

55.24 Bentley, Gerald E. *The Jacobean and Caroline Stage.* Oxford, 1941-68. 7 vols.
792.0942   PN2592 B4

55.25 Harbage, Alfred. *Shakespeare's Audience.* N.Y., 1941.
822.33   PR3091 H36

55.26 Bowden, William R. *The English Dramatic Lyric, 1603-42. A Study in Stuart Dramatic Technique.* New Haven, 1951. Rpt. Hamden, Conn., 1969. Yale Studies in English, 118.
821.309   PR509 L8 B68

55.27 Doran, Madeleine. *Endeavors of Art. A Study of Form in Elizabethan Drama.* Madison, Wis., 1954.
822.309   PR651 D67

55.28 Bradbrook, Muriel C. *The Growth and Structure of Elizabethan Comedy.* London, 1955.
822.309   PR658 C6 B7

55.29 Craik, Thomas W. *The Tudor Interlude. Stage, Costume, and Acting.* Leicester, Eng., 1958. Rpt. 1967.
822.309   PN2589 C7

55.30 *Jacobean Theatre.* Stratford-upon-Avon Studies, 1. London & N.Y., 1960.
792.0942   PR651 J3

55.31 Ornstein, Robert. *The Moral Vision of Jacobean Tragedy.* Madison, Wis., 1960.
822.309   PR658 T707

55.32 Adams, John C. *The Globe Playhouse. Its Design and Equipment.* 2nd ed. N.Y., 1961. (Orig. ed. Cambridge, Mass., 1942.)
792.094216   PR2920 A38

55.33 Kaufmann, Ralph J., ed. *Elizabethan Drama. Modern Essays in Criticism.* N.Y., 1961.
822.309   PR653 K3

55.34 Bevington, David M. *From "Mankind" to Marlowe. Growth of Structure in the Popular Drama of Tudor England.* Cambridge, Mass., 1962.
822.209   PR646 B4

55.35 Ribner, Irving. *Jacobean Tragedy. The Quest for Moral Order.* N.Y., 1962.
822.309   PR658 T7 R5

55.36 Ellis-Fermor, Una M. *The Jacobean Drama. An Interpretation.* 5th ed. London, 1965. (Orig. ed. 1936.)
822.309   PR651 E5

55.37 Ribner, Irving. *The English History Play in the Age of Shakespeare.* Rev. ed. N.Y., 1965. (Orig. ed. Princeton, 1957.)
822.3093   PR658 H5 R5

55.38 *Elizabethan Theatre.* Stratford-upon-Avon Studies, 9. London & N.Y., 1966.
822.309   PR653 E66

55.39 Bentley, Gerald E., ed. *The Seventeenth-Century Stage. A Collection of Critical Essays.* Chicago, 1968.
792.09032   PN2592 B43

55.40 Bevington, David M. *Tudor Drama and Politics. A Critical Approach to Topical Meaning.* Cambridge, Mass., 1968.
822.3093   PR649 P6 B4

55.41 Gibbons, Brian. *Jacobean City Comedy. A Study of Satiric Plays by Jonson, Marston, and Middleton.* Cambridge, Mass. & London, 1968.
822.309   PR651 G5

• International Conference on Elizabethan Theatre. University of Waterloo, Canada.

55.42 *The Elizabethan Theatre.* 1st Conf., 1968. Ed. David Galloway. Hamden, Conn., 1970.

55.43 *The Elizabethan Theatre, II.* 2nd Conf., 1969. Ed. David Galloway. Hamden, Conn., 1970.
792.0942   PN2589 I5

55.44 Long, John H., ed. *Music in English Renaissance Drama.* Lexington, Ky., 1968.
780.942   ML286.2 L65

55.45 Rabkin, Norman, ed. *Reinterpretations of Elizabethan Drama. Selected Papers from the English Institute* [*1968*]. N.Y., 1969.
822.3   PR653 R4

55.46 *Drama of the Renaissance. Essays for Leicester Bradner.* Ed. Elmer M. Blistein. Providence, R.I., 1970.
809.2   PN1785 D7

55.47 Feldman, Sylvia D. *The Morality-Patterned Comedy of the Renaissance.* The Hague, 1971.
822.052   PR646 F4

55.48 King, Thomas J. *Shakespearean Staging, 1599-1642.* Cambridge, Mass., 1971.
792.025   PN2590 S7 K5

55.49 Levin, Richard. *The Multiple Plot in English Renaissance Drama.* Chicago, 1971.
822.309   PR658 P6 L4

9. The Restoration and Eighteenth Century

§56. Bibliographies, Periodicals, Surveys

56.1 Tobin, James E. *Eighteenth Century English Literature and Its Cultural Background. A Bibliography.* N.Y., 1939. Rpt. 1967.
016.8209006   Z2013 T62

56.2 *Philological Quarterly. A Journal Devoted to Scholarly Investigation of the Classical and Modern Languages and Literatures.* 1922- Annual bibliographies "Engl. Lit., 1660-1800"; "The Romantic Movement," 1950-64.
PI P55

56.3 *English Literature, 1660-1800. A Bibliography of Modern Studies Compiled for "Philological Quarterly."* Ed. Ronald S. Crane et al. 4 vols. Princeton, 1950-62.
016.82   Z2011 E6

56.4 Bond, Donald F., ed. *The Age of Dryden.* Goldentree Bibliographies. N.Y., 1970.
016.8209004   Z2012 B74

•

56.5 *Johnsonian News Letter.* 1940- . 4/yr.
PR1 J64

56.6 *Scriblerian. A Newsjournal Devoted to Pope, Swift, and Their Circle.* 1968- . 2/yr.
820.900505   PR445 S3

56.7 *Eighteenth-Century Studies. An Interdisciplinary Journal.* 1967- 4/yr.

•

56.8 Elton, Oliver. *A Survey of English Literature, 1730-1780.* 2 vols. London & N.Y., 1928. Rpt. 1963.
820.9   PR441 E6

56.9 Turberville, Arthur S., ed. *Johnson's England. An Account of the Life and Manners of His Age.* 2 vols. Oxford, 1933. Rpt. 1952.
914.2   DA485 T77

56.10 McKillop, Alan D. *English Literature from Dryden to Burns.* N.Y., 1948.
820.9   PR404 M3

56.11 Butt, John. *The Augustan Age.* 3rd ed. London, 1965. (Orig. ed. 1950.)
820.903   PR441 B8

56.12 Greene, Donald J. *The Age of Exuberance. Backgrounds to Eighteenth-Century English Literature.* N.Y., 1970.
820.9   DA380 G7

56.13 Williams, Kathleen, ed. *Backgrounds to Eighteenth-Century Literature.* Scranton, Pa., 1971.
820.9005   PR442 W5

§57. General Studies

57.1 Stephen, Leslie. *History of English Thought in the Eighteenth Century.* 3rd ed. 2 vols. London, 1902. (Orig. ed. 1876.) Rpt. with Preface by Crane Brinton, N.Y., 1962.
192   B1301 S8

57.2 Stephen, Leslie. *English Literature and Society in the Eighteenth Century.* London, 1904. Rpt. N.Y., 1963.
820.9   PR443 S8

57.3 Tinker, Chauncey B. *The Salon and English Letters. Chapters on the Interrelations of Literature and Society in the Age of Johnson.* N.Y., 1915. Rpt. 1967.
820.9006   PR448 S3 T5

57.4 Saintsbury, George. *The Peace of the Augustans. A Survey of Eighteenth Century Literature as a Place of Rest and Refreshment.* London, 1916. Rpt. 1946; N.Y., 1970.
820.9005   PR441 S3

57.5 Tinker, Chauncey B. *Nature's Simple Plan. A Phase of Radical Thought in the Mid-Eighteenth Century.* Princeton, 1922. Rpt. N.Y., 1964.
901.9   CB411 T5

57.6 Whitney, Lois. *Primitivism and the Idea of Progress in English Popular Literature of the Eighteenth Century.* Baltimore, 1934. Rpt. N.Y., 1965.
820.93   PR448 P7 W5

57.7 Monk, Samuel H. *The Sublime. A Study of Critical Theories in Eighteenth-Century England.* N.Y., 1935. Rpt. Ann Arbor, 1960.
111.85   BH301 S7 M6

57.8 Maclean, Kenneth. *John Locke and English Literature of the Eighteenth Century.* New Haven, 1936. Rpt. 1962.
151   B1294 M2

57.9 Watkins, Walter B. C. *Perilous Balance. The Tragic Genius of Swift, Johnson, and Sterne.* Princeton, 1939. Rpt. Cambridge, Mass., 1960.
820.4   PR442 W35

57.10 Willey, Basil. *The Eighteenth Century Background.* London, 1940. Rpt. 1961; N.Y., 1961; Boston, 1966.
192   B1301 W5

57.11 Bate, Walter J. *From Classic to Romantic. Premises of Taste in Eighteenth-Century England.* Cambridge, Mass., 1946. Rpt. N.Y., 1961.
701.17   BH221 G7 B36

57.12 Wasserman, Earl R. *Elizabethan Poetry in the Eighteenth Century.* Urbana, Ill., 1947. Illinois Studies in Lang. and Lit., Vol. 32, Nos. 2, 3.
821.309   PR535 C7 W3

57.13 Wilson, John H. *The Court Wits of the Restoration. An Introduction.* Princeton, 1948. Rpt. N.Y., 1967; London, 1968.
820.9004   PR437 W54

57.14 Clifford, James L., and Louis A. Landa, eds. *Pope and His Contemporaries. Essays Presented to George Sherburn.* N.Y., 1949.
820.4   PR442 C6

57.15 *The Age of Johnson. Essays Presented to Chauncey Brewster Tinker.* Ed. Frederick W. Hilles. New Haven, 1949. Rpt. 1964.
820.903   PR442 T5

57.16 Moore, Cecil A. *Backgrounds of English Literature, 1700-1760.* Minneapolis, 1953. Rpt. N.Y., 1969.
820.9005   PR442 M6

57.17 Hipple, Walter J. *The Beautiful, the Sublime, and the Picturesque in Eighteenth-Century British Aesthetic Theory.* Carbondale, Ill., 1957.
701.17   BH221 G72 H5

57.18 Clifford, James L., ed. *Eighteenth Century English Literature. Modern Essays in Criticism.* N.Y., 1959.
820.903   PR442 C58

57.19 Wasserman, Earl R. *The Subtler Language. Critical Readings of Neo-Classic and Romantic Poems.* Baltimore, 1959. Rpt. 1968.
821.0903   PR503 W35

57.20 Schilling, Bernard N. *Essential Articles for the Study of English Augustan Backgrounds.* Hamden, Conn., 1961.
820.903   PR437 S35

57.21 Tillotson, Geoffrey. *Augustan Studies.* London, 1961.
820.903   PR442 T47

57.22 Camden, Charles C., ed. *Restoration and Eighteenth-Century Literature. Essays in Honor of Alan Dugald McKillop.* Chicago, 1963.
820.903   PR442 C3

57.23 Lillywhite, Bryant. *London Coffee Houses. A Reference Book of Coffee Houses of the Seventeenth, Eighteenth, and Nineteenth Centuries.* London, 1963.
394   TX910 E5 L5

57.24 Price, Martin. *To the Palace of Wisdom. Studies in Order and Energy from Dryden to Blake.* Garden City, N.Y., 1964. Rpt. Carbondale, Ill., 1970.
820.903   PR441 P7

57.25 Fussell, Paul. *The Rhetorical World of Augustan Humanism. Ethics and Imagery from Swift to Burke.* Oxford, 1965. Rpt. 1970.
820.9005   PR561 F8

57.26 Sutherland, William O. S. *The Art of the Satirist. Essays on the Satire of Augustan England.* Austin, Tex., 1965.
827.009   PR935 S8

57.27 Wasserman, Earl R., ed. *Aspects of the Eighteenth Century.* Baltimore, 1965.
901.933   CB411 W3

57.28 Gay, Peter. *The Enlightenment. An Interpretation. The Rise of Modern Paganism. The Science of Freedom.* 2 vols. N.Y., 1966-69.
190   B802 G3

57.29 Anderson, Howard P., and John S. Shea, eds. *Studies in Criticism and Aesthetics, 1660-1800. Essays in Honor of Samuel Holt Monk.* Minneapolis, 1967.
700.8   PR73 A5

57.30 *Essays in English Literature of the Classical Period Presented to Dougald MacMillan.* Ed. Daniel W. Patterson and Albrecht B. Strauss. Chapel Hill, N.C., 1967. *Studies in Philology,* Extra Series, 4.
820.9   P25 S82

57.31 Johnson, James W. *The Formation of English Neo-Classical Thought.* Princeton, 1967.
820.9   PR441 J6

57.32 Trawick, Leonard M., ed. *Backgrounds of Romanticism. English Philosophical Prose of the Eighteenth Century.* Bloomington, Ind., 1967.
192.09033   B1300 T7

57.33 Tucker, Susie I. *Protean Shape. A Study in Eighteenth-Century Vocabulary and Usage.* London, 1967.
424.1   PE1083 T8

57.34 Bronson, Bertrand H. *Facets of the Enlightenment. Studies in English Literature and Its Contexts.* Berkeley, 1968.
820.9006   PR442 B7

57.35 *Studies in the Eighteenth Century. Papers Presented at the David Nicol Smith Memorial Seminar, Canberra, 1966.* Ed. Robert F. Brissenden. Toronto, 1969.
820.9005   PR442 D3

57.36 *Augustan Milieu. Essays Presented to Louis A. Landa.* Ed. Henry K. Miller et al. Oxford, 1970.
820.9005   PR442 A9

57.37 Bond, William H., ed. *Eighteenth-Century Studies in Honor of Donald F. Hyde.* N.Y., 1970.
820.9006   PR442 E4

57.38 *Proceedings of the Modern Language Association Neoclassicism Conferences, 1967-1968.* Ed. Paul J. Korshin. N.Y., 1970.
820.9005   PR445 P7

§58. Poetry

58.1 Bond, Richmond P. *English Burlesque Poetry, 1700-1750.* Cambridge, Mass., 1932. Rpt. N.Y., 1964.
821.509   PR559 B8 B6

58.2 Aubin, Robert A. *Topographical Poetry in Eighteenth Century England.* N.Y., 1936. Rpt. 1966. MLA Revolving Fund Series, 6.
PR555 P6 A8

58.3 Nicolson, Marjorie H. *Newton Demands the Muse. Newton's "Opticks" and the Eighteenth Century Poets.* Princeton, 1946.
821.509   PR565 O6 N5

58.4 Fitzgerald, Margaret M. *First Follow Nature. Primitivism in English Poetry, 1725-1750.* N.Y., 1947.
821.509   PR568 P7 F5

58.5 Sutherland, James R. *A Preface to Eighteenth Century Poetry.* London, 1948. Corrected rpt. 1958, 1963.
821.509   PR551 S8

58.6 Arthos, John. *The Language of Natural Description in Eighteenth Century Poetry.* Ann Arbor, 1949. Rpt. N.Y., 1966. Univ. of Mich. Pubs.: Lang. and Lit. Ser., 24.
821.5093   PR555 L3 A7

58.7 Congleton, James E. *Theories of Pastoral Poetry in England, 1684-1798.* Gainesville, Fla., 1952. Rpt. N.Y., 1968.
821.409   PR509 P3 C6

58.8 Jack, Ian R. *Augustan Satire. Intention and Idiom in English Poetry, 1660-1750.* London, 1952. Rpt. 1967.
821.409   PR565 L3 J3

58.9 Chapin, Chester F. *Personification in Eighteenth-Century English Poetry.* N.Y., 1955. Rpt. 1967.
821.0093   PR555 P4 C5

58.10 Hagstrum, Jean H. *The Sister Arts. The Tradition of Literary Pictorialism and English Poetry from Dryden to Gray.* Chicago, 1958.
821.09   PR445 H3

58.11 Spacks, Patricia. *The Insistence of Horror. Aspects of the Supernatural in Eighteenth-Century Poetry.* Cambridge, Mass., 1962.
809.93   PR555 S8 S65

58.12 Tillotson, Geoffrey. *Augustan Poetic Diction.* London, 1964.
821.509   PR442 T48

58.13 Pinto, Vivian De S. *The Restoration Court Poets.* London, 1965. Writers and Their Work, 186.
821.409   PR561 P5

58.14 Jones, William P. *The Rhetoric of Sciences. A Study of Scientific Ideas and Imagery in Eighteenth-Century Poetry.* Berkeley, 1966.
821.5093   PR555 S3 J6

58.15 Stone, P. W. K. *The Art of Poetry, 1750-1820. Theories of Poetic Composition and Style in the Late Neo-Classic and Early Romantic Periods.* London & N.Y., 1967.
821.609   PR575 P6 S7

58.16 Trickett, Rachel. *The Honest Muse. A Study in Augustan Verse.* Oxford, 1967.
821.4   PR437 T7

§59. Drama and Theater

59.1 MacMillan Dougald. *Drury Lane Calendar, 1747-1776. Compiled from the Playbills and Edited with an Introduction.* Oxford, 1938.
792.094212 PN2596 L7 D6

59.2 *The London Stage, 1660-1800. A Calendar of Plays, Entertainments and Afterpieces Together with Casts, Box-Receipts and Contemporary Comment.* 11 vols. Carbondale, Ill., 1960-68.
792.09421 PN2592 L6

59.3 *Restoration and 18th Century Theatre Research.* 1962- . 2/yr. Annual bibliography.

59.4 Stratman, Carl J., ed. *Restoration and 18th Century Theatre Research Bibliography, 1961-1968.* Comp. Edmund Napieralski and Jean E. Westbrook. Troy, N.Y., 1969.
016.822509 Z2014 D7 S853

59.5 Stratman, Carl J., et al. *Restoration and Eighteenth Century Theatre Research. A Bibliographical Guide, 1900-1968.* Carbondale, Ill., 1971.
016.822509 Z2014 D7 S854

●

59.6 Genest, John, ed. *Some Account of the English Stage from the Restoration in 1660 to 1830.* 10 vols. Bath, Eng., 1832. Rpt. N.Y., 1965.
792.0942 PN2581 G4

59.7 Palmer, John L. *The Comedy of Manners.* London, 1913. Rpt. N.Y., 1962.
822.409 PR691 P3

59.8 Dobrée, Bonamy. *Restoration Comedy, 1660-1720.* Oxford, 1925.
PR691 D6

59.9 Hotson, John L. *The Commonwealth and Restoration Stage.* Cambridge, Mass., 1928. Rpt. N.Y., 1962.
792.094212 PN2592 H6

59.10 Dobrée, Bonamy. *Restoration Tragedy, 1660-1720.* Oxford, 1929. Rpt. 1954.
822.09 PR698 T7 D6

59.11 Lynch, James J. *Box, Pit, and Gallery. Stage and Society in Johnson's London.* Berkeley, 1953. Rpt. N.Y., 1970.
792.09421 PN2596 L6 L9

59.12 Pedicord, Harry W. *The Theatrical Public in the Time of Garrick.* N.Y., 1954. Rpt. Carbondale, Ill., 1966.
792 PN2596 L6 P4

59.13 Holland, Norman N. *The First Modern Comedies. The Significance of Etherege, Wycherley, and Congreve.* Cambridge, Mass., 1959. Rpt. Bloomington, Ind., 1967.
822.409   PR3432 H6

59.14 Loftis, John C. *Comedy and Society from Congreve to Fielding.* Stanford, 1959. Stanford Studies in Lang. and Lit., 19.
822.509   PR714 S6 L6

59.15 Loftis, John C. *The Politics of Drama in Augustan England.* Oxford, 1963.
822.509   PR714 P6 L6

59.16 Singh, Sarup. *The Theory of Drama in the Restoration Period.* Bombay, 1963.
PR691 S5

59.17 Wilson, John H. *A Preface to Restoration Drama.* Boston, 1965. Text ed. 1968.
792.0942   PN2592 W52

59.18 *Restoration Theatre.* Stratford-upon-Avon Studies, 6. London & N.Y., 1965.
822.409   PR693 R4

59.19 Cunningham, John E. *Restoration Drama.* London, 1966.
822.409   PR691 C8

59.20 Loftis, John C., ed. *Restoration Drama. Modern Essays in Criticism.* N.Y., 1966.
822.409   PR693 L6

59.21 Miner, Earl Roy, ed. *Restoration Dramatists. A Collection of Critical Essays.* Englewood Cliffs, N.J., 1966.
822.409   PR693 M5

59.22 Rothstein, Eric. *Restoration Tragedy. Form and the Process of Change.* Madison, Wis., 1967.
822.051   PR691 R6

59.23 Birdsall, Virginia O. *Wild Civility. The English Comic Spirit on the Restoration Stage.* Bloomington, Ind., 1970.
822.052   PR698 C6 B5

59.24 Hughes, Leo. *The Drama's Patrons. A Study of the Eighteenth-Century London Audience.* Austin, Tex., 1971.
792   PN2596 L6 H8

59.25 Schneider, Ben R. *The Ethos of Restoration Comedy.* Urbana, Ill., 1971.
822.052   PR691 S3

§60. Prose Fiction Before 1800

60.1 Esdaile, Arundell. *A List of English Tales and Prose Romances Printed Before 1740*. London, 1912. Rpt. N.Y., 1971.
016.823085   Z2014 F4 E8

60.2 O'Dell, Sterg. *A Chronological List of Prose Fiction in English Printed in England and Other Countries, 1475-1640*. Cambridge, Mass., 1954. Rpt. N.Y., 1969.
Z5916 O32

60.3 McBurney, William H. *A Check List of English Prose Fiction, 1700-1739*. Cambridge, Mass., 1960.
016.8235   Z2014 F4 M3

60.4 McBurney, William H., and Charlene M. Taylor. *English Prose Fiction, 1700-1800, in the University of Illinois Library*. Urbana, 1965.
016.8235   Z2014 F4 M33

60.5 Mish, Charles C. *English Prose Fiction 1600-1700. A Chronological Checklist*. 2nd ed. Charlottesville, Va., 1967. (Orig. ed. 1952.)
016.8233   Z2014 F4 M57

60.6 Bonheim, Helmut W. *The English Novel Before Richardson. A Checklist of Texts and Criticism to 1970*. Metuchen, N.J., 1971.
016.82303   Z2014 F4 B65

•

60.7 Tompkins, Joyce M. S. *The Popular Novel in England, 1770-1800*. London, 1932. Rpt. Lincoln, Neb., 1961; London, 1969.
823.609   PR851 T6

60.8 Wright, Walter F. *Sensibility in English Prose Fiction, 1760-1814. A Reinterpretation*. Urbana, Ill., 1937. Rpt. N.Y., 1972. Illinois Studies in Lang. and Lit., Vol. 22, Nos. 3-4.
823.03   PR858 S45 W7

60.9 Black, Frank G. *The Epistolary Novel in the Late Eighteenth Century. A Descriptive and Bibliographical Study*. Eugene, 1940. Univ. of Oregon Monographs, Studies in Lit. and Philology, 2.
823.609   PN3495 B5

60.10 Taylor, John T. *Early Opposition to the English Novel. The Popular Reaction from 1760 to 1830*. N.Y., 1943.
823.509   PR851 T3

60.11 Foster, James R. *History of the Pre-Romantic Novel in England*. N.Y., 1949. Rpt. 1966. MLA Monograph Series, 17.
823.609   PR858 R6 F6

60.12 McKillop, Alan D. *The Early Masters of English Fiction.* Lawrence, Kan., 1956.
823.509   PR851 M33

60.13 Watt, Ian P. *The Rise of the Novel. Studies in Defoe, Richardson, and Fielding.* London & Berkeley, 1957.
823.5   PR851 W3

60.14 Mayo, Robert D. *The English Novel in the Magazines, 1740-1815. With a Catálogue of 1375 Magazine Novels and Novelettes.* Evanston, Ill., 1962.
823.09   PR851 M37

60.15 Schlauch, Margaret. *Antecedents of the English Novel, 1400-1600 (from Chaucer to Deloney).* Warsaw, 1963.
823.2   PR833 S3

60.16 Spector, Robert D., ed. *Essays on the English Eighteenth-Century Novel.* Bloomington, Ind., 1965.
823.509   PR853 S6

60.17 Day, Robert A. *Told in Letters. Epistolary Fiction Before Richardson.* Ann Arbor, 1966.
823.009   PR821 D3

60.18 Donovan, Robert A. *The Shaping Vision. Imagination in the English Novel from Defoe to Dickens.* Ithaca, N.Y., 1966.
823.009   PR851 D6

60.19 Paulson, Ronald. *Satire and the Novel in Eighteenth-Century England.* New Haven, 1967.
823.609   PR858 S3 P3

60.20 Sherbo, Arthur. *Studies in the Eighteenth Century English Novel.* E. Lansing, Mich., 1969.
823.509   PR823 S55

60.21 Preston, John. *The Created Self. The Reader's Role in Eighteenth-Century Fiction.* London & N.Y., 1970.
823.03   PR851 P7

60.22 Williams, Ioan M., ed. *Novel and Romance, 1700-1800. A Documentary Record.* N.Y., 1970.
823.7   PR852 W5

10. The Nineteenth Century

§61. Romantic Period: Bibliographies, Periodicals, Surveys

61.1 Bernbaum, Ernest. *Guide Through the Romantic Movement.* 2nd ed. N.Y., 1949. (Orig. ed. 1930.)
820.903   PR447 B55

61.2 *ELH. Journal of English Literary History.* 1934-   . 4/yr. Romantic Movement annual bibliography, 1937-50. (See *Philological Quarterly.*)
820.8   PR1 E5

61.3 *English Language Notes.* 1963-   . 4/yr. Romantic Movement annual bibliography since 1965.
        PE1 E53

61.4 *Keats-Shelley Journal. Keats, Shelley, Byron, Hunt, and Their Circles.* 1952-   . Annual. Bibliography.
        PR5 K4

61.5 Green, David B., and Edwin G. Wilson, eds. *Keats, Shelley, Byron, Hunt, and Their Circles. A Bibliography. July 1, 1950–June 30, 1962.* Lincoln, Neb., 1964.
016.821709   Z2013 K4

61.6 *Studies in Romanticism.* 1961-   . 4/yr. Succeeds *Boston University Studies in English,* 1955-61, 5 vols.
820.5   PR1 B6

61.7 Houtchens, Carolyn W., and Lawrence H. Houtchens, eds. *The English Romantic Poets and Essayists. A Review of Research and Criticism.* Rev. ed. N.Y., 1966. (Orig. ed. 1957.) MLA Revolving Fund Series, 20.
820.903   ·   PR590 H6

61.8 Fogle, Richard H. *Romantic Poets and Prose Writers.* Goldentree Bibliographies. N.Y., 1967.
016.8208008   Z2013 F6

•

61.9 Elton, Oliver. *A Survey of English Literature, 1780-1830.* 2 vols. London & N.Y., 1912. Rpt. 1920, 1948, 1963.
820.9   PR451 E5

§62. Romantic Period: General Studies

62.1 Fairchild, Hoxie N. *The Noble Savage. A Study in Romantic Naturalism.* N.Y., 1928. Rpt. 1961.
820.93   PR146 F3

62.2 Fairchild, Hoxie N. *The Romantic Quest.* N.Y., 1931. Rpt. 1965.
821.7093   PR457 F3

62.3 Davis, Herbert J., et al., eds. *Nineteenth-Century Studies. Dedicated by His Colleagues . . . to Clark Sutherland Northup.* Ithaca, N.Y., 1940. Rpt., N.Y., 1968.
820.9   PR453 D3

62.4 Dykes, Eva B. *The Negro in English Romantic Thought. Or, a Study of Sympathy for the Oppressed.* Washington, D.C., 1942.
820.903   PR447 D9

62.5 *Essays Mainly on the Nineteenth Century. Presented to Sir Humphrey Milford.* London, 1948. Rpt. Freeport, N.Y., 1970.
820.9008   PR463 E8

62.6 James, David G. *The Romantic Comedy.* London, 1948.
820.903   PR457 J3

62.7 Brailsford, Henry N. *Shelley, Godwin, and Their Circle.* 2nd ed. Oxford, 1951. (Orig. ed. 1913.) Rpt. Hamden, Conn., 1969.
820.9007   PR5433 B74

62.8 Praz, Mario. *The Romantic Agony.* 2nd ed. Trans. Angus Davidson. London, 1951. (Orig. Ital. ed. 1930.) Rpt. N.Y., 1956; London, 1960. Re-issued with Foreword by John Frank Kermode, London & N.Y., 1970.
809.034   PR755 P713

62.9 Abrams, Meyer H. *The Mirror and the Lamp. Romantic Theory and the Critical Tradition.* N.Y., 1953. Rpt. 1965, 1971.
801   PN769 R7 A2

62.10 Brand, Charles P. *Italy and the English Romantics. The Italianate Fashion in Early Nineteenth-Century England.* Cambridge, 1957.
327.450942   DG499 G7 B7

62.11 Kermode, John Frank. *Romantic Image.* London, 1957. Rpt. N.Y., 1959, 1963, 1964.
821.9109   PN1111 K4

62.12 Chiari, Joseph. *Realism and Imagination.* London, 1960. Rpt. with new Preface, N.Y., 1970.
701.15   N66 C47

62.13 Hough, Graham G. *Image and Experience. Studies in a Literary Revolution.* London, 1960. Rpt. Lincoln, Neb., 1964.
820.9   PR453 H58

62.14 Peckham, Morse. *Beyond the Tragic Vision. The Quest for Identity in the Nineteenth Century.* N.Y., 1962.
171.3   B803 P4

62.15 Frye, Northrop, ed. *Romanticism Reconsidered. Selected Papers from the English Institute* [1962]. N.Y., 1963.
809.91   PN751 F7

62.16 Rodway, Allan E. *The Romantic Conflict.* London, 1963.
821.6   PR571 R6

62.17 Jones, Howard M. *History and the Contemporary. Essays in Nineteenth-Century Literature.* Madison, Wis., 1964.
810.903   PS201 J58

62.18 Hilles, Frederick W., and Harold Bloom, eds. *From Sensibility to Romanticism. Essays Presented to Frederick A. Pottle.* N.Y., 1965.
821.09   PR571 H5

62.19 Wellek, René. *Confrontations. Studies in the Intellectual and Literary Relations Between Germany, England, and the United States During the Nineteenth Century.* Princeton, 1965.
809.91   B803 W37

62.20 Frye, Northrop. *A Study of English Romanticism.* N.Y., 1968.
820.914   PR447 F7

62.21 Kroeber, Karl. *Backgrounds to British Romantic Literature.* San Francisco, 1968.
914.03253   PR447 K7

62.22 Harris, Ronald W. *Romanticism and the Social Order, 1780-1830.* London, 1969.
001.20942   PR447 H3

62.23 Hayden, John O. *The Romantic Reviewers, 1802-1824.* Chicago & London, 1969.
801.950942   PR457 H3

62.24 Furst, Lilian R. *Romanticism in Perspective. A Comparative Study of Aspects of the Romantic Movement in England.* N.Y., 1970.
809.033   PN603 F8

62.25 Gleckner, Robert F., and Gerald E. Enscoe, eds. *Romanticism. Points of View.* 2nd ed. Englewood Cliffs, N.J., 1970. (Orig. ed. 1962.)
820.914   PR146 G5

62.26 Peckham, Morse. *The Triumph of Romanticism. Collected Essays.* Columbia, S.C., 1970.
808.914   PN603 P4

62.27 Abrams, Meyer H. *Natural Supernaturalism. Tradition and Revolution in Romantic Literature.* N.Y., 1971.
809.914   PN603 A3

62.28 Elledge, W. Paul, and Richard L. Hoffman, eds. *Romantic and Victorian. Studies in Memory of William H. Marshall.* New Brunswick, N.J., 1971.
820.9007   PR14 R6

62.29 Knight, George W. *Neglected Powers. Essays on Nineteenth and Twentieth Century Literature.* N.Y., 1971.
821.009   PR584 K54

62.30 Sutherland, Donald. *On Romanticism.* N.Y., 1971.
701.1   NX600 R6 S9

§63. Victorian Period: Bibliographies, Periodicals, Surveys

63.1 Ehrsam, Theodore G., et al., eds. *Bibliographies of Twelve Victorian Authors.* N.Y., 1936. Rpt. 1968.
016.09008   Z2013 E33

   63.2 See also Joseph G. Fucilla, "Bibliographies of Twelve Victorian Authors: A Supplement," *Modern Philology,* 37 (1939), 89-96.

63.3 Fredeman, William E. *Pre-Raphaelitism. A Bibliocritical Study.* Cambridge, Mass., 1965.
016.70942   Z5948 P9 F7

63.4 Buckley, Jerome H., ed. *Victorian Poets and Prose Writers.* Goldentree Bibliographies. N.Y., 1966.
016.8209008   Z2013 B8

63.5 Altholz, Josef L. *Victorian England, 1837-1901.* Bibliographical Handbook. Cambridge, 1970.
016.91420381   Z2019 A56

63.6 Madden, Lionel. *How to Find Out About the Victorian Period. A Guide to Sources of Information.* N.Y., 1970.
016.9142038   Z2019 M34

●

63.7 *Modern Philology. A Journal Devoted to Research in Medieval and Modern Literature.* 1903- . 4/yr. Annual Victorian bibliography, 1932-57.
PB1 M7

✓**63.8** *Victorian Studies. A Quarterly Journal of the Humanities, Arts, and Sciences.* 1958- . Annual bibliography.

63.9 Templeman, William D., ed. *Bibliographies of Studies in Victorian Literature for the Thirteen Years 1932-1944.* Urbana, Ill., 1945. Rpt. N.Y., 1971.
016.82   Z2013 T4

63.10 Wright, Austin, ed. *Bibliographies of Studies in Victorian Literature for the Ten Years 1945-1954.* Urbana, Ill., 1956. Rpt. N.Y., 1971.
016.82   Z2013 W77

63.11 Slack, Robert C., ed. *Bibliographies of Studies in Victorian Literature for the Ten Years 1955-1964.* Urbana, Ill., 1967.
016.8209008   Z2013 B59

63.12 *Victorian Newsletter.* 1955- . 2/yr.

63.13 *Victorian Periodicals Newsletter.* 1968- . Irreg.

•

63.14 Walker, Hugh. *The Literature of the Victorian Era.* Cambridge, 1910. Rpt. 1921.
PR461 W3

63.15 Elton, Oliver. *A Survey of English Literature, 1830-1880.* 2 vols. London & N.Y., 1920. Rpt. 1963.
820.903   PR451 E53

63.16 Cooke, John D., and Lionel Stevenson. *English Literature of the Victorian Period.* N.Y., 1949. Rpt. 1971.
820.90098   PR461 C6

63.17 Parrott, Thomas M., and Robert B. Martin. *A Companion to Victorian Literature.* N.Y., 1955.
820.903   PR461 P3

63.18 Schneewind, Jerome B. *Backgrounds of English Victorian Literature.* N.Y., 1970.
914.20381   DA550 S33

§64. Victorian Period: General Studies

64.1 Granville-Barker, Harley, ed. *The Eighteen-Seventies. Essays by Fellows of the Royal Society of Literature.* N.Y. & Cambridge, 1929.
PR463 R75

64.2 Welby, Thomas E. *The Victorian Romantics, 1850-70. The Early Work of Dante Gabriel Rossetti, William Morris, Burne-Jones, Swinburne, Simeon Solomon, and Their Associates.* London, 1929. Rpt. Hamden, Conn., 1966.
821.60914   PR466 W4

64.3 De La Mare, Walter, ed. *The Eighteen-Eighties. Essays by Fellows of the Royal Society of Literature.* Cambridge, 1930. Rpt. St. Clair Shores, Mich., 1971.
820.9008   PR463 R76

64.4 Drinkwater, John, ed. *The Eighteen-Sixties. Essays by Fellows of the Royal Society of Literature.* N.Y. & Cambridge, 1932.
820.4   PR463 R74

64.5 Cunliffe, John W. *Leaders of the Victorian Revolution.* N.Y., 1934. Rpt. 1963; Pt. Washington, N.Y., 1969.
820.9008   PR461 C83

64.6 Routh, Harold V. *Towards the Twentieth Century. Essays in the Spiritual History of the Nineteenth.* Cambridge & N.Y., 1937. Rpt. Freeport, N.Y., 1969.
820.93   PR451 R72

64.7 Hough, Graham G. *The Last Romantics.* London, 1947. Rpt. London & N.Y., 1961.
820.903   PR468 R6 H6

64.8 Willey, Basil. *Nineteenth Century Studies. Coleridge to Matthew Arnold.* N.Y., 1949. Rpt. 1964, 1966.
192   B1561 W5

64.9 Baker, Joseph E., ed. *The Reinterpretation of Victorian Literature.* Princeton, 1950. Rpt. N.Y., 1962.
820.903   PR463 B7

64.10 Shine, Hill, ed. *Booker Memorial Studies. Eight Essays on Victorian Literature in Memory of John Manning Booker, 1881-1948.* Chapel Hill, N.C., 1950. Rpt. N.Y., 1969.
820.9008   PR463 B6

64.11 Somervell, David C. *English Thought in the Nineteenth Century.* 6th ed. London, 1950. Rpt. 1962.
DA533 S65

64.12 Buckley, Jerome H. *The Victorian Temper. A Study in Literary Culture.* Cambridge, Mass., 1951. Rpt. 1969, 1970; N.Y., 1964.
820.90098   PR461 B75

64.13 Holloway, John. *The Victorian Sage. Studies in Argument.* London, 1953. Rpt. Hamden. Conn., 1962; N.Y., 1965.
820.809   PR463 H6

64.14 Willey, Basil. *More Nineteenth Century Studies. A Group of Honest Doubters.* London & N.Y., 1956.
192   B1561 W5

64.15 Houghton, Walter E. *The Victorian Frame of Mind, 1830-1870.* New Haven, 1957. Rpt. 1963.
942.081   DA533 H85

64.16 Appleman, Philip, et al., eds. *1859. Entering an Age of Crisis.* Bloomington, Ind., 1959.
942.08   DA560 A75

64.17 Moers, Ellen. *The Dandy. Brummell to Beerbohm.* N.Y. & London, 1960.
809.93   CT9985 M6

64.18 Wright, Austin, ed. *Victorian Literature. Modern Essays in Criticism.* N.Y., 1961.
820.903   PR463 W7

64.19 Miller, Joseph Hillis. *The Disappearance of God. Five Nineteenth-Century Writers.* Cambridge, Mass., 1963.
820.993   PR469 R4 M5

64.20 Cockshut, Anthony O. J. *The Unbelievers. English Agnostic Thought, 1840-1890.* London, 1964.
209.42   BR477 C7

64.21 Charlesworth, Barbara. *Dark Passages. The Decadent Consciousness in Victorian Literature.* Madison, Wis., 1965.
820.9   PR469 D4 C4

64.22 Tillotson, Geoffrey, and Kathleen Tillotson. *Mid-Victorian Studies.* London, 1965.
820.9008   PR463 T52

64.23 Adams, Robert M. *Nil. Episodes in the Literary Conquest of Void During the Nineteenth Century.* N.Y., 1966.
809.933   PN761 A3

64.24 Buckley, Jerome H. *The Triumph of Time. A Study of the Victorian Concepts of Time, History, Progress, and Decadence.* Cambridge, Mass., 1966.
820.9008   PR731 B8

64.25 Anderson, Warren D., and Thomas D. Clareson, eds. *Victorian Essays, a Symposium. Essays on the Occasion of the Centennial of the College of Wooster, in Honor of Emeritus Professor Waldo H. Dunn.* Kent, O., 1967.
820.9008   PR463 C64

64.26 Preyer, Robert O., ed. *Victorian Literature. Selected Essays.* N.Y., 1967.
820.9   PR461 P7

64.27 Himmelfarb, Gertrude. *Victorian Minds.* N.Y., 1968.
942.081   DA533 H55

64.28 Hunt, John D. *The Pre-Raphaelite Imagination, 1848-1900.* London, 1968.
820.9008   PR466 H8

64.29 De Laura, David J. *Hebrew and Hellene in Victorian England. Newman, Arnold, and Pater.* Austin, Tex., 1969.
001.20942   PR461 D4

64.30 Miyoshi, Masao. *The Divided Self. A Perspective on the Literature of the Victorians.* N.Y., 1969.
820.9008   PR461 M55

64.31 Altick, Richard D. *Victorian Studies in Scarlet. Murders and Manners in the Age of Victoria.* N.Y., 1970.
364.15230942   HV6535 G4 A68

64.32 Chapman, Raymond. *Faith and Revolt. Studies in the Literary Influence of the Oxford Movement.* London, 1970.
283.42   BX5100 C47

64.33 Goldfarb, Russell M. *Sexual Repression and Victorian Literature.* Lewisburg, Pa., 1970.
820.93   PR469 S4 G6

64.34 Langbaum, Robert W. *The Modern Spirit. Essays on the Continuity of Nineteenth- and Twentieth-Century Literature.* N.Y., 1970.
820.809   PR99 L32

64.35 Lansbury, Coral M. *Arcady in Australia. The Evocation of Australia in Nineteenth-Century English Literature.* Melbourne, 1970.

64.36 Peckham, Morse. *Victorian Revolutionaries. Speculations on Some Heroes of a Culture Crisis.* N.Y., 1970.
001.2   CB417 P38

64.37 Lucas, John, ed. *Literature and Politics in the Nineteenth Century.* London, 1971.
820.9008   PR469 P6 L8

§65. The Literature of the United States and Canada Before 1900: Surveys, Periodicals, General Studies

65.1 Tyler, Moses C. *A History of American Literature, 1607-1765.* 2 vols. N.Y., 1878. Rpt. in 1 vol., Fwd, by Howard M. Jones, Ithaca, N.Y., 1949; abr. ed. Chicago, 1967.
810.9   PS185 T8

65.2 Tyler, Moses C. *The Literary History of the American Revolution, 1763-1783.* 2 vols. N.Y., 1897. (Abr. ed. by Archie H. Jones. Chicago, 1967.) Rpt. 1957, 1970.
810.9001   PS193 T9

65.3 Baker, Ray P. *A History of English-Canadian Literature to the Confederation. Its Relation to the Literature of Great Britain and the United States.* Cambridge, Mass., 1920. Rpt. N.Y., 1968.
810.9002   PR9111 B3

65.4 Canby, Henry S. *Classic Americans. A Study of Eminent American Writers from Irving to Whitman with an Introductory Survey of the Colonial Background of Our National Literature.* N.Y., 1931. Rpt. 1959.
928.1   PS88 C35

65.5 Pattee, Fred L. *The First Century of American Literature, 1770-1870.* N.Y., 1935. Rpt., 1966.
810.9   PS88 P35

● Brooks, Van Wyck. *Makers and Finders. A History of the Writer in America, 1800-1915.*

   65.6 I. *The World of Washington Irving.* Philadelphia, 1944. Rpt. 1945.
810.903   PS208 B7

   65.7 II. *The Flowering of New England, 1815-1865.* New ed. 1940. (Orig. ed. 1936.) Rpt. 1952.
810.903   PS243 B7

   65.8 III. *The Times of Melville and Whitman.* N.Y., 1947. Rpt. 1953.
810.903   PS201 B7

   65.9 IV. *New England: Indian Summer, 1865-1915.* N.Y., 1940.
810.903   PS243 B72

   65.10 V. *The Confident Years, 1885-1915.* N.Y., 1952.
810.903   PS214 B7

65.11 Nye, Russel B. *American Literary History, 1607-1830.* N.Y., 1970.
810.9001   PS88 N9

●

65.12 *Emerson Society Quarterly. Journal of the American Renaissance.* 1955- .
PS1629 E6

65.13 *Early American Literature.* 1966- . 3/yr. Until 1969 *EAL Newsletter.*

65.14 *American Literary Realism, 1870-1910.* 1967- . 4/yr.

65.15 *American Transcendental Quarterly. Journal of New England Writers.* 1969- .

●

65.16 Perry, Bliss. *The American Spirit in Literature. A Chronicle of Great Interpreters.* New Haven, 1918. Rpt. 1921.
PS88 P4

65.17 Rusk, Ralph L. *The Literature of the Middle Western Frontier.* 2 vols. N.Y., 1925. Rpt. 1962.
810.977   PS273 R8

65.18 Schneider, Herbert W. *The Puritan Mind.* N.Y., 1930. Rpt. Ann Arbor, 1958.
285.9   BX9321 S4

65.19 Gohdes, Clarence L. *The Periodicals of American Transcendentalism.* Durham, N.C., 1931. Rpt. N.Y., 1971.
141.30973   B905 G65

65.20 Loggins, Vernon. *The Negro Author. His Development in America to 1900.* N.Y., 1931. Rpt. Pt. Washington, N.Y., 1964.
810.9   PS153 N5 L65

65.21 Matthiessen, Francis O. *American Renaissance. Art and Expression in the Age of Emerson and Whitman.* N.Y., 1941. Rpt. 1968.
810.903   PS201 M3

65.22 Gohdes, Clarence L. *American Literature in Nineteenth Century England.* N.Y., 1944. Rpt. Carbondale, Ill., 1963.
810.903   PS159 G8 G6

65.23 Murdock, Kenneth B. *Literature and Theology in Colonial New England.* Cambridge, Mass., 1949. Rpt. N.Y., 1963; Westport, Conn., 1970.
810.9001   PS195 R4 M8

65.24 Vail, Robert W. G. *The Voice of the Old Frontier.* Philadelphia, 1949. Rpt. N.Y., 1970.
016.9173032   Z1249 F9 V3

65.25 Knight, Grant C. *The Critical Period in American Literature.* Chapel Hill, N.C., 1951.
810.903   PS214 K6

65.26 Stafford, John. *The Literary Criticism of "Young America." A Study in the Relationship of Politics and Literature, 1837-1850.* Berkeley, 1952. Rpt. N.Y., 1967. Univ. of Calif. Pubs.: English Studies, 3.
801.9   PN99 U5 S7

65.27 Hubbell, Jay B. *The South in American Literature, 1607-1900.* Durham, N.C., 1954.
810.9   PS261 H78

65.28 Lewis, Richard W. B. *The American Adam. Innocence, Tragedy, and Tradition in the Nineteenth Century.* Chicago, 1955. Rpt. 1959.
810.902   PS201 L4

65.29 Moore, Arthur K. *The Frontier Mind. A Cultural Analysis of the Kentucky Frontiersman.* Lexington, Ky., 1957.
917.69   F454 M65

65.30 Spencer, Benjamin T. *The Quest for Nationality. An American Literary Campaign.* Syracuse, N.Y., 1957.
810.903   PS88 S58

65.31 Bode, Carl. *The Anatomy of American Popular Culture, 1840-1861.* Berkeley, 1959.
917.3   E169.1 B657

65.32 Nye, Russel B. *The Cultural Life of the New Nation, 1776-1830.* N.Y., 1960. Rpt. 1963.
973.3   E169.1 N9

65.33 Jones, Howard M. *O Strange New World. American Culture, the Formative Years.* N.Y., 1964.
917.3   E169.1 J644

65.34 Berthoff, Warner. *The Ferment of Realism. American Literature, 1884-1919.* N.Y., 1965.
810.912   PS214 B4

65.35 Fussell, Edwin S. *Frontier. American Literature and the American West.* Princeton, 1965.
810.93   PS169 W4 F8

65.36 Hall, Wade H. *The Smiling Phoenix. Southern Humor from 1865 to 1914.* Gainesville, Fla., 1965.
817.40975   PS437 H32

65.37 Pizer, Donald. *Realism and Naturalism in Nineteenth-Century American Literature.* Carbondale, Ill., 1966.
810.912   PS214 P5

65.38 Ziff, Larzer. *The American 1890's. Life and Times of a Lost Generation.* N.Y., 1966.
810.9004   PS214 Z5

65.39 Martin, Jay. *Harvests of Change. American Literature, 1865-1914.* N.Y., 1967.
810.9004   PS214 M35

65.40 Spiller, Robert E., ed. *The American Literary Revolution, 1783-1837.* N.Y. & Garden City, N.Y., 1967.
810.900208   PS375 S65

65.41 Charvat, William. *The Profession of Authorship in America, 1800-1870. The Papers of William Charvat.* Ed. Matthew J. Bruccoli. Columbus, O., 1968.
810.9   PS88 C47

65.42 Guttenberg, Antoine C. V. *Early Canadian Art and Literature.* Vaduz, Liechtenstein, 1969.

65.43 Kolb, Harold H. *The Illusion of Life. American Realism as a Literary Form.* Charlottesville, Va., 1969.
810.9004   PS214 K63

65.44 Morgan, Howard W. *The Gilded Age. A Reappraisal.* Rev. ed. Syracuse, N.Y., 1970. (Orig. ed. 1963.)
917.303   E169.1 M79

65.45 *Fifteen American Authors Before 1900. Bibliographic Essays on Research and Criticism.* Ed. Robert A. Rees and Earl N. Harbert. Madison, Wis., 1971.

65.46 Yellin, Jean F. *The Intricate Knot. The Negro in American Literature, 1776-1863.* N.Y., 1971.

§66. British Poetry

66.1 Raysor, Thomas M. *The English Romantic Poets. A Review of Research.* Rev. ed. N.Y., 1956. (Orig. ed. 1950.) Rpt. 1966.
016.8217   PR590 R3

66.2 Faverty, Frederic E. *The Victorian Poets. A Guide to Research.* 2nd ed. Cambridge, Mass., 1968. (Orig. ed. 1956.)
821.809   PR593 F3

•

66.3 *Victorian Poetry. A Critical Journal of Victorian Literature.* 1963- . 4/yr.
PR500 V5

•

66.4 Stevenson, Lionel. *Darwin Among the Poets.* Chicago, 1932. Rpt. N.Y., 1963.
821.8093   PR508 E8 S7

66.5 Sherwood, Margaret. *Undercurrents of Influence in English Romantic Poetry.* Cambridge, Mass., 1934. Rpt. Freeport, N.Y., 1968; N.Y., 1971.
821.00914   PR571 S5

66.6 Beach, Joseph W. *The Concept of Nature in Nineteenth Century Poetry.* N.Y., 1936. Rpt., 1956, 1966.
821.7093   PR585 N3 B4

66.7 Knight, George W. *The Starlit Dome. Studies in the Poetry of Vision.* London, 1941. Corrected rpt. N.Y., 1960. Rpt. 1971.
821.709   PR590 K5

66.8 Miles, Josephine. *Pathetic Fallacy in the Nineteenth Century.* Berkeley, 1942. Rpt. with New Pref. N.Y., 1965. Univ. of Calif. Publications in English, Vol. 12, No. 2.
821.709   PR468 N3 M5

66.9 Bowra, Cecil M. *The Romantic Imagination.* Cambridge, Mass., 1949. Rpt. London & N.Y., 1961.
821.709   PR590 B6

66.10 Warren, Alba H. *English Poetic Theory, 1825-1865.* Princeton, 1950. Princeton Studies in English, 29.
801.951   PN1031 W27

66.11 Johnson, Edward D. H. *The Alien Vision of Victorian Poetry. Sources of the Poetic Imagination in Tennyson, Browning, and Arnold.* Princeton, 1952. Rpt. Hamden, Conn., 1963. Princeton Studies in English, 34.
821.809   PR593 J6

66.12 Hough, Graham G. *The Romantic Poets.* 2nd ed. London, 1957. (Orig. ed. 1953.) Rpt. N.Y., 1964.
821.709   PR590 H57

66.13 Thorpe, Clarence D., et al., eds. *The Major English Romantic Poets. A Symposium in Reappraisal.* Carbondale, Ill., 1957.
821.709   PR590 T5

66.14 Foakes, Reginald A. *The Romantic Assertion. A Study in the Language of Nineteenth Century Poetry.* New Haven, 1958. Rpt. Folcroft, Pa., 1969; London & N.Y., 1971.
821.709   PR585 L3 F6

66.15 Perkins, David. *The Quest for Permanence. The Symbolism of Wordsworth, Shelley, and Keats.* Cambridge, Mass., 1959.
821.7091   PR5892 P5 P4

66.16 Abrams, Meyer H., ed. *English Romantic Poets. Modern Essays in Criticism.* N.Y., 1960.
821.709   PR590 A2

66.17 Kroeber, Karl. *Romantic Narrative Art.* Madison, Wis., 1960.
821.709   PR590 K7

66.18 Matthews, John P. *Tradition in Exile. A Comparative Study of Social Influences on the Development of Australian and Canadian Poetry in the Nineteenth Century.* Toronto, 1962.
PR9469 M3

66.19 Piper, Herbert W. *The Active Universe. Pantheism and the Concept of Imagination in the English Romantic Poets.* London, 1962.
821.809   PR590 P5

66.20 Bostetter, Edward E. *The Romantic Ventriloquists. Wordsworth, Coleridge, Keats, Shelley, Byron.* Seattle, 1963.
821.709   PR590 B58

66.21 Wilkie, Brian. *Romantic Poets and Epic Tradition.* Madison, Wis., 1965.
821.709   PR590 W4

66.22 Evans, Benjamin Ifor. *English Poetry in the Later Nineteenth Century.* 2nd ed. N.Y., 1966. (Orig. ed. London, 1933.)
821.809   PR591 E8

66.23 Power, Patrick C. *The Story of Anglo-Irish Poetry (1800-1922).*
Cork, 1967.
821   PR8765 P63

66.24 Ball, Patricia M. *The Central Self. A Study in Romantic and
Victorian Imagination.* London, 1968.
821.709   PR590 B25

66.25 Armstrong, Isobel, ed. *The Major Victorian Poets. Reconsidera-
tions.* London & Lincoln, Neb., 1969.
821.809   PR593 M3

66.26 Woodring, Carl R. *Politics in English Romantic Poetry.*
Cambridge, Mass., 1970.
821.709   PR590 W57

66.27 Bloom, Harold. *The Visionary Company. A Reading of English
Romantic Poetry.* Rev. ed. Ithaca, N.Y., 1971. (Orig. ed. 1961.)
821.709   PR590 B39

§67. American Poetry

67.1 Wegelin, Oscar. *Early American Poetry. A Compilation of the
Titles of Volumes of Verse and Broadsides by Writers Born or Residing in North America North of the Mexican Border.* 2nd ed.
2 vols. in 1. N.Y., 1930. (Orig. ed. 1903-7.)
016.81   Z1231 P7 W4

67.2 Stoddard, Roger E. *A Catalogue of Books and Pamphlets
Unrecorded in Oscar Wegelin's Early American Poetry, 1650-1820.*
Providence, R.I., 1969.

67.3 Porter, Dorothy B. *North American Negro Poets. A Bibliographical Checklist of Their Writings, 1760-1944.* Hattiesburg, Miss., 1945.
Rpt. N.Y., 1969. New ed. in prep.
016.811   Z1361 N39 P6

•

67.4 Stedman, Edmund C. *Poets of America.* Boston, 1885. Rpt. N.Y.,
1970; St. Clair Shores, Mich., 1971.
811.309   PS303 S7

67.5 Jantz, Harold S. *The First Century of New England Verse.*
Worcester, Mass., 1944. Rpt. N.Y., 1962.
811.109   PS312 J3

67.6 Arms, George W. *The Fields Were Green. A New View of Bryant, Whittier, Holmes, Lowell, and Longfellow.* Stanford, 1953.
811.3082   PS541 A8

67.7 Kindilien, Carlin T. *American Poetry in the Eighteen Nineties. A Study of American Verse, 1890-1899, Based upon the Volumes from That Period Contained in the Harris Collection of American Poetry and Plays in the Brown University Library.* Providence, R.I., 1956.
811.409   PS321 K5

67.8 Bigelow, Gordon E. *Rhetoric and American Poetry of the Early National Period.* Gainesville, Fla., 1960. Univ. of Fla. Mono., Humanities, 4.
811.209   PS314 B5

67.9 Kramer, Aaron. *The Prophetic Tradition in American Poetry, 1835-1900.* Rutherford, N.J., 1968.
811.304   PS201 K7

§68. Drama and Theater: British

68.1 Watson, Ernest B. *Sheridan to Robertson. A Study of the Nineteenth-Century London Stage.* Cambridge, Mass., 1926. Rpt. N.Y., 1963.
792.09421   PN2596 L6 W3

68.2 Reynolds, Ernest. *Early Victorian Drama (1830-1870).* Cambridge, 1936. Rpt. N.Y., 1965.
822.809   PR731 R4

68.3 Rowell, George. *The Victorian Theatre. A Survey.* London, 1956.
792.0942   PN2594 R65

68.4 Booth, Michael R. *English Melodrama.* London, 1965.
822.709   PR728 M4 B6

68.5 Fletcher, Richard M. *English Romantic Drama, 1795-1843. A Critical History.* N.Y., 1966.
822.709   PR716 F55

68.6 Southern, Richard. *The Victorian Theatre. A Pictorial Survey.* N.Y., 1970.
792.0942   PN2594 S6

68.7 *Essays on Nineteenth-Century British Theatre. The Proceedings of a Symposium, Sponsored by the Manchester University Department of Drama.* Ed. Kenneth Richards and Peter Thomson. London, 1971.
792.0942   PR723 E8

§69. Drama and Theater: United States and Canada

69.1 Wegelin, Oscar. *Early American Plays, 1714-1830. Being a Compilation of the Titles of Plays by American Authors Published and*

Performed in America Previous to 1830. 2nd ed. N.Y., 1905. (Orig. ed. 1900.) Rpt. 1968, 1970.
016.8121   Z1231 D7 W4

69.2 Hill, Frank P. *American Plays Printed 1714-1830. A Bibliographical Record.* Stanford, 1934. Rpt. N.Y., 1968.
016.812   Z1231 D7 H6

69.3 U.S. Copyright Office. *Dramatic Compositions Copyrighted in the United States, 1870-1916.* 2 vols. Ed. Mary W. Davis et al. Washington, D.C., 1918. Rpt. N.Y., 1970 [?].
Z5781 U55

•

69.4 Brown, Thomas A. *History of the American Stage. Containing Biographical Sketches of Nearly Every Member of the Profession That Has Appeared on the American Stage, 1733 to 1870.* N.Y., 1870. Rpt. 1969.
790.20922   PN2285 B75

69.5 Seilhamer, George O. *History of the American Theater [1749-1797].* 3 vols. Philadelphia, 1888-91. Rpt. N.Y., 1968, 1969; Grosse Pt., Mich., 1968.
792.0973   PN2221 S4

69.6 Brown, Thomas A. *History of the New York Stage from the First Performance in 1732 to 1901.* 3 vols. N.Y., 1903. Rpt. 1964.
792.097471   PN2277 N5 B7

69.7 Hornblow, Arthur. *A History of the Theatre in America from Its Beginnings to the Present Time.* 2 vols. Philadelphia, 1919. Rpt. N.Y., 1965.
792.0973   PN2221 H6

69.8 Hodge, Francis. *Yankee Theatre. The Image of America on the Stage, 1825-1850.* Austin, Tex., 1964.
792.20973   PN2248 H6

69.9 Dormon, James H. *Theater in the Ante Bellum South, 1815-1861.* Chapel Hill, N.C., 1967.
792.0975   PN2248 D6

69.10 Nolan, Paul T., ed. *Provincial Drama in America, 1870-1916. A Casebook of Primary Materials.* Metuchen, N.J., 1967.
812.409   PS345 N6

69.11 Grimstead, David. *Melodrama Unveiled. American Theater and Culture, 1800-1850.* Chicago, 1968.
792.20973   PN1918 U5 G7

69.12 McNamara, Brooks. *The American Playhouse in the Eighteenth Century.* London & Cambridge, Mass., 1969.
725.822   NA6830 M3

§70. Fiction: British

70.1 National Book League, London. *Victorian Fiction. An Exhibition of Original Editions . . . Arranged by John Carter with the Collaboration of Michael Sadleir.* Cambridge, 1947.
016.8238   Z2014 F4 N3

70.2 Sadleir, Michael. *Nineteenth Century Fiction. A Bibliographical Record Based on His Own Collection.* 2 vols. London, 1951. Rpt. N.Y., 1969.
016.8238   Z2014 F4 S16

70.3 Stevenson, Lionel, ed. *Victorian Fiction. A Guide to Research.* Cambridge, Mass., 1964.
823.809   PR873 S8

•

70.4 *Nineteenth-Century Fiction.* 1945-   . 4/yr. Until 1949 *Trollopian.*
823.809   PR873 T76

•

70.5 Weygandt, Cornelius. *A Century of the English Novel. Being a Consideration of the Place in English Literature of the Long Story. Together with an Estimate of Its Writers from the Heyday of Scott to the Death of Conrad.* N.Y., 1925. Rpt. Freeport, N.Y., 1968.
823.009   PR821 W4

70.6 Myers, Walter L. *The Later Realism. A Study of Characterization in the British Novel.* Chicago, 1927.
PR830 R4 M8

70.7 Henkin, Leo J. *Darwinism in the English Novel, 1860-1910. The Impact of Evolution on Victorian Fiction.* N.Y., 1940. Rpt. 1963.
823.8093   PR878 E9 H4

70.8 Leavis, Frank R. *The Great Tradition. George Eliot, Henry James, Joseph Conrad.* London & N.Y., 1948. Rpt. N.Y., 1963.
823.809   PR873 L4

70.9 Tillotson, Kathleen M. *Novels of the Eighteen-Forties.* London, 1954. Rpt. N.Y., 1961.
823.809   PR871 T5

70.10 Praz, Mario. *The Hero in Eclipse in Victorian Fiction.* Trans. Angus Davidson. London, 1956. (Orig. Italian ed. 1952.) Rpt. 1969.
823.8093   PR872 P712

70.11 Cecil, David. *Victorian Novelists. Essays in Revaluation.* Rpt. with New Foreword. Chicago, 1958. (Orig. title *Early Victorian Novelists,* London, 1934.)
823.809   PR873 C4

70.12 Rathburn, Robert C., and Martin Steinmann, eds. *From Jane Austen to Joseph Conrad. Essays Collected in Memory of James T. Hillhouse.* Minneapolis, 1958. Rpt. 1967.
823.804   PR863 R3

70.13 Flanagan, Thomas J. *The Irish Novelists, 1800-1850.* N.Y., 1959.
823.709   PR8801 F55

70.14 Stang, Richard. *The Theory of the Novel in England, 1850-1870.* London & N.Y., 1959.
823.809   PR871 S8

70.15 Maison, Margaret M. *Search Your Soul, Eustace. A Survey of the Religious Novel in the Victorian Age.* London, 1961. American title *The Victorian Vision,* N.Y., 1962.
823.809   PR878 R4 M3

70.16 Hollingsworth, Keith. *The Newgate Novel, 1830-1847. Bulwer, Ainsworth, Dickens, and Thackeray.* Detroit, 1963.
823.8093   PR868 C7 H6

70.17 James, Louis. *Fiction for the Working Man, 1830-1850. A Study of the Literature Produced for the Working Classes in Early Victorian Urban England.* N.Y., 1963.
823.809   PR878 L3 J3

70.18 Ray, Gordon N. *Bibliographical Resources for the Study of Nineteenth Century English Fiction.* Los Angeles, 1964.
Z2014 F4 R36

70.19 Graham, George K. *English Criticism of the Novel, 1865-1900.* Oxford, 1965.
823.8   PR871 G7

70.20 Colby, Robert A. *Fiction with a Purpose. Major and Minor Nineteenth-Century Novels.* Bloomington, Ind., 1967.
823.709   PR861 C6

70.21 Marshall, William H. *The World of the Victorian Novel.* South Brunswick, N.J., 1967.
823.809   PR861 M3

70.22 Miller, Joseph Hillis. *The Form of Victorian Fiction. Thackeray, Dickens, Trollope, George Eliot, Meredith, and Hardy.* Notre Dame, Ind., 1968.
823.8092   PR873 M5

70.23 Colby, Vineta. *The Singular Anomaly. Women Novelists of the Nineteenth Century.* London & N.Y., 1970.
823.809   PR115 C6

70.24 Griest, Guinevere L. *Mudie's Circulating Library and the Victorian Novel.* Bloomington, Ind., 1970.
027.2421   Z792 M84 G7

70.25 Williams, Raymond. *The English Novel. From Dickens to Lawrence.* London & N.Y., 1970.
823.809   PR871 W5

70.26 Fleishman, Avrom. *The Historical Novel. Walter Scott to Virginia Woolf.* Baltimore, 1971.
823.081   PR868 H5 F5

70.27 Watt, Ian P., ed. *The Victorian Novel. Modern Essays in Criticism.* N.Y., 1971.
823.03   PR873 W3

§71. Fiction: The United States and Canada Before 1900

71.1 Wegelin, Oscar. *Early American Fiction, 1774-1830. A Compilation of the Titles of Works of Fiction, by Writers Born or Residing in North America, North of the Mexican Border and Printed Previous to 1831.* 3rd ed. N.Y., 1929. (Orig. ed. 1902.)
Z1231 F4 W4

71.2 Whiteman, Maxwell. *A Century of Fiction by American Negroes, 1853-1952. A Descriptive Bibliography.* Philadelphia, 1955. Rpt., 1968.
016.8134   Z1361 N39 W5

71.3 Holman, C. Hugh, ed. *The American Novel Through Henry James.* Goldentree Bibliographies. N.Y., 1966.
016.813   Z1231 F4 H64

71.4 Wright, Lyle. *American Fiction, 1774-1850. A Contribution Towards a Bibliography.* 2nd ed. San Marino, Calif., 1969. (Orig. ed. 1939.)
016.8132   Z1231 F4 W9

71.5 ——. . . . *1851-1875.* . . . Rpt. with additions, 1965. (Orig. ed. 1957.)
016.8133   Z1231 F4 W92

71.6 ——. . . . *1876-1900.* . . . 1966.
016.8134   Z1231 F4 W93

71.7 Eichelberger, Clayton L., et al., eds. *A Guide to Critical Reviews of United States Fiction, 1870-1910.* Metuchen, N.J., 1971.
016.813409   Z1225 E35

•

71.8 Brown, Herbert R. *The Sentimental Novel in America, 1789-1860.* Durham, N.C., 1940. Rpt. N.Y., 1959.
813.209   PS377 B7

71.9 Åhnebrink, Lars. *The Beginnings of Naturalism in American Fiction. A Study of the Works of Hamlin Garland, Stephen Crane,*

and Frank Norris with Special Reference to Some European Influences, 1891-1903. Cambridge, 1950. Rpt. N.Y., 1961.
813.409   PS371 A2

71.10 Johannsen, Albert. *The House of Beadle and Adams and Its Dime and Nickel Novels. The Story of a Vanished Literature.* 3 vols. Norman, Okla., 1950-62.
655.4747   Z1231 F4 J68

71.11 Lively, Robert A. *Fiction Fights the Civil War. An Unfinished Chapter in the Literary History of the American People.* Chapel Hill, N.C., 1957.
813.409   PS374 H5 L5

71.12 Gaston, Edwin W. *The Early Novel of the Southwest.* Albuquerque, N.M., 1961.
813.09   PS277 G3

71.13 Hoffman, Daniel G. *Form and Fable in American Fiction.* N.Y., 1961.
813.309   PS377 H6

71.14 Kaul, Ajodhia N. *The American Vision. Actual and Ideal Society in Nineteenth-Century Fiction.* New Haven, 1963. Rpt. 1970. Yale Pubs. in Amer. Studies, 7.
813.309   PS374 S7 K3

71.15 Maxwell, Desmond E. S. *American Fiction. The Intellectual Background.* London & N.Y., 1963.
813.09   PS371 M3

71.16 Falk, Robert P. *The Victorian Mode in American Fiction, 1865-1885.* E. Lansing, Mich., 1965.
813.409   PS377 F3

71.17 Porte, Joel. *The Romance in America. Studies in Cooper, Poe, Hawthorne, Melville and James.* Middletown, Conn., 1969.
813.309   PS377 P6

71.18 Petter, Henri. *The Early American Novel.* Columbus, O., 1971.
813.209   PS375 P4

11. The Modern Period

§72. The Age of Transition

72.1 *English Literature in Transition, 1880-1920.* 1957- . 4/yr. Until 1961 *English Fiction in Transition, 1880-1920.*
PR1 E55

●

72.2 Ryan, William P. *The Irish Literary Revival. Its History, Pioneers and Possibilities.* London, 1894. Rpt. N.Y., 1970.
820.9   PR8750 R8

72.3 Kennedy, John M. *English Literature, 1880-1905.* London, 1912.
PR471 K4

72.4 Jackson, Holbrook. *The Eighteen-Nineties. A Review of Art and Ideas at the Close of the Nineteenth Century.* London, 1913. Rpt. 1931; Harmondsworth, Eng., 1939; N.Y., 1922, 1966; St. Clair Shores, Mich., 1971.
820.903   PR461 J2

72.5 Boyd, Ernest A. *The Contemporary Drama of Ireland.* Boston, 1917. Rpt. 1924, 1928.
PR8789 B6

72.6 Morris, Lloyd R. *The Celtic Dawn. A Survey of the Renascence in Ireland, 1889-1916.* N.Y., 1917. Rpt. 1970.
820.9008   PR8750 M6

72.7 Sherman, Stuart P. *On Contemporary Literature.* N.Y., 1917. Rpt. 1931; N.Y., 1970; Freeport, N.Y., 1971.
809   PN710 S48

72.8 Burdett, Osbert. *The Beardsley Period. An Essay in Perspective.* London & N.Y., 1925. Rpt. 1969.
820.9008   PR461 B8

72.9 Le Gallienne, Richard. *The Romantic '90s.* N.Y., 1925.
PR462 L4

72.10 Williams, Harold H. *Modern English Writers. Being a Study of Imaginative Literature, 1890-1914.* 3rd ed. London, 1925. (Orig. ed. 1918.) Rpt. in 2 vols. Pt. Washington, N.Y., 1970.
820.9008   PR471 W5

72.11 Wilson, Edmund. *Axel's Castle. A Study in the Imaginative Literature of 1870-1930.* N.Y., 1931.
809   PN771 W55

72.12 Elwin, Malcolm. *Old Gods Falling.* London & N.Y., 1939. Rpt. Freeport, N.Y. & N.Y., 1971.
820.9008/823.03   PR463 E54

72.13 Hicks, Granville. *Figures of Transition. A Study of British Literature at the End of the Nineteenth Century.* N.Y., 1939. Rpt. Westport, Conn., 1969.
820.9008   PR461 H5

72.14 Frierson, William C. *The English Novel in Transition, 1885-1940.* Norman, Okla., 1942. Rpt. N.Y., 1965.
823.809   PR881 F8

72.15 Kavanagh, Peter. *The Story of the Abbey Theatre. From Its Origins in 1899 to the Present.* N.Y., 1950.
792   PN2602 D82 A27

72.16 Swinnerton, Frank A. *The Georgian Literary Scene, 1910-1935. A Panorama.* 6th ed. London & N.Y., 1950. (Orig. ed. *The Georgian Scene. A Literary Panorama,* N.Y., 1934.)
820.904   PR471 S8

72.17 Wilson, Albert E. *Edwardian Theatre.* London, 1951.
792   PN2595 W55

72.18 Johnstone, John K. *The Bloomsbury Group. A Study of E. M. Forster, Lytton Strachey, Virginia Woolf, and Their Circle.* London, 1954. Rpt. N.Y., 1963.
820.904   PR471 J6

72.19 Tindall, William York. *Forces in Modern British Literature, 1885-1956.* Rev. ed. N.Y., 1956. (Orig. ed. . . . *1885-1946,* N.Y., 1947. Rpt. Freeport, N.Y., 1970.)
820.900912   PR471 T5

72.20 Blunden, Edmund C. *War Poets, 1914-1918.* London, 1958. Writers and Their Work, 100.
821.9109   PR604 B6

72.21 Howarth, Herbert. *The Irish Writers, 1880-1940. Literature Under Parnell's Star.* London, 1958.
820.93   PR8753 H6

72.22 Ellmann, Richard, ed. *Edwardians and Late Victorians.* English Institute Essays, 1959. N.Y., 1960.
820.903   PE1010 E5

72.23 Cox, Charles B. *The Free Spirit. A Study of Liberal Humanism in the Novels of George Eliot, Henry James, E. M. Forster, Virginia Woolf, and Angus Wilson.* London, 1963.
823.91209   PR830 H8 C6

72.24 Ellis-Fermor, Una. *The Irish Dramatic Movement.* 2nd ed. London, 1964. (Orig. ed. 1939.) Rpt. 1967.
822   PR8789 E6

72.25 Johnston, John H. *English Poetry of the First World War. A Study in the Evolution of Lyric and Narrative Form.* Princeton, 1964.
821.91209   PR605 E8 J58

72.26 Stead, Christian K. *The New Poetic. Yeats to Eliot.* London, 1964. Rpt. N.Y., 1966; Harmondsworth, Eng., 1967.
821.91209   PR604 S7

72.27 Bergonzi, Bernard. *Heroes' Twilight. A Study of the Literature of the Great War.* London, 1965.
820.900912   PR478 E8 B4

72.28 Pinto, Vivian de S. *Crisis in English Poetry, 1880-1940.* 4th ed. London, 1965. (Orig. ed. 1951.)
821.809   PR601 P57

72.29 Ross, Robert H. *The Georgian Revolt, 1910-1922. Rise and Fall of a Poetic Ideal.* Carbondale, Ill., 1965.
821.91209   PR601 R65

72.30 Balakian, Anna E. *The Symbolist Movement. A Critical Appraisal.* N.Y., 1967.
809.1915   PN56 S9 B3

72.31 Hogan, Robert G. *After the Irish Renaissance. A Critical History of the Irish Drama Since "The Plough and the Stars."* Minneapolis, 1967.
822   PR8789 H6

72.32 Sandison, Alan. *The Wheel of Empire. A Study of the Imperial Idea in Some Late Nineteenth and Early Twentieth-Century Fiction.* N.Y. & London, 1967.
823.91   PR781 S2

72.33 Thompson, William I. *The Imagination of an Insurrection, Dublin, Easter, 1916. A Study of an Ideological Movement.* N.Y., 1967.
941.59   DA962 T45

72.34 Bell, Quentin. *Bloomsbury.* London, 1968.
820.900912   PR471 B4

72.35 Boyd, Ernest A. *Ireland's Literary Renaissance.* 3rd ed. N.Y., 1968. (Orig. ed. 1916.)
820   PR8750 B6

72.36 Hynes, Samuel L. *The Edwardian Turn of Mind.* Princeton, 1968.
914.20382   DA570 H9

72.37 Lester, John A. *Journey Through Despair, 1880-1914. Transformations in British Literary Culture.* Princeton, 1968.
820.9008   PR471 L4

72.38 Clarke, Austin. *The Celtic Twilight and the Nineties.* Dublin, 1969.
820.9008   PR461 C57

72.39 Greenberger, Allen J. *The British Image of India. A Study in the Literature of Imperialism, 1880-1960.* London & N.Y., 1969.
820.9   PR830 I6 G7

72.40 Chapple, John A. V. *Documentary and Imaginative Literature, 1880-1920.* London & N.Y., 1970.
820.9008   PR461 C48

72.41 Nelson, James G. *The Early Nineties. A View from the Bodley Head.* Cambridge, Mass., 1971.
070.50942   Z325 B7 N4

72.42 O'Driscoll, Robert, ed. *Theatre and Nationalism in Twentieth-Century Ireland.* Toronto, 1971.
822.9109   PR8789 T5

72.43 Stanford, Derek. *Critics of the Nineties.* London & N.Y., 1971.
809.034   PN99 C72 S8

§73. Bibliographies, Periodicals, Surveys

73.1 Cutler, Bradley D., and Villa Stiles, eds. *Modern British Authors. Their First Editions.* N.Y., 1930.
016.82   Z2014 F5 C9

73.2 Jones, Howard M., and Richard M. Ludwig. *Guide to American Literature and Its Background Since 1890.* 3rd ed. Cambridge, Mass., 1964. (Orig. ed. 1953.)
016.81   Z1225 J65

73.3 Gibian, George. *Soviet Russian Literature in English. A Selective Bibliography of Soviet Russian Literary Works in English and of Articles and Books in English About Soviet Russian Literature.* Ithaca, N.Y., 1967. Cornell Res. Papers in International Studies, 6.
016.8917   Z2504 T8 G5

73.4 Temple, Ruth Z., and Martin Tucker, eds. *Twentieth Century British Literature. A Reference Guide and Bibliography.* N.Y., 1968.
016.82090091   Z2013.3 T4

73.5 *Fifteen Modern American Authors. A Survey of Research and Criticism.* Ed. Jackson R. Bryer, Durham. N.C., 1969.
810.900502   PS221 F45

73.6 Jones, Brynmor. *A Bibliography of Anglo-Welsh Literature, 1900-1965.* Swansea, 1970.
016.8209009

●

73.7 *Twentieth Century Literature. A Scholarly and Critical Journal.* 1955- . 4/yr with bibliographies.
809.04   PN2 T8

73.8 *Studies in the 20th Century. A Scholarly and Critical Journal.* 1968- . 2/yr.
NX1 S85

73.9 *Journal of Modern Literature.* 1970- . 5/yr.
809.04   PN2 J6

●

73.10 Cunliffe, John W. *English Literature During the Last Half Century.* 2nd ed. N.Y., 1923. (Orig. ed. 1919.) Rpt. Freeport, N.Y., 1971.
820.9008   PR461 C8

73.11 Green, Elizabeth A. *The Negro in Contemporary American Literature. An Outline for Individual and Group Study.* Chapel Hill, N.C., 1928. Rpt. College Park, Md., 1968.
810.93   PS153 N5 G7

73.12 Millett, Fred B. *Contemporary British Literature.* 3rd ed. based on ed. by John M. Manly and Edith Rickert. N.Y., 1935. Rpt. 1948, 1969.
820.904   PR471 M5

73.13 Green, Henry M. *Australian Literature, 1900-1950.* Melbourne, 1951. Rpt. 1963.
828.9999409   PR9453 G7

73.14 Brodbeck, May, et al., *American Non-Fiction, 1900-1950.* Chicago, 1952. Rpt. Westport, Conn., 1970.
818.508   PS369 B7

73.15 Longaker, Mark, and Edwin C. Bolles. *Contemporary English Literature.* N.Y., 1953.
820.904   PR85 L7

73.16 Collins, Arthur S. *English Literature of the Twentieth Century.* 4th ed. London, 1960. (Orig. ed. 1951.)
820.904   PR471 C63

73.17 Eastwood, Wilfred, and John T. Good. *Signposts. A Guide to Modern English Literature.* Cambridge, 1960.
016.82   PR474 E3

73.18 Spiller, Robert E., ed. *A Time of Harvest. American Literature, 1910-1960.* N.Y., 1962.
810.904   PS221 S66

73.19 Curley, Dorothy N., et al., eds. *A Library of Literary Criticism: Modern American Literature.* 4th ed. 3 vols. N.Y., 1969. (Orig. ed. 1960.)
810.9005   PS221 C8

73.20 Richardson, Kenneth R., and R. Clive Willis, eds. *Twentieth Century Writing. A Reader's Guide to Contemporary Literature.* London, 1969.
809.04   PN771 R5

73.21 Robson, William W. *Modern English Literature.* London & N.Y., 1970.
820.900912   PR471 R6

73.22 Ward, Alfred C. *Longman Companion to Twentieth Century Literature in English.* London, 1970.
820.90091   PN771 W28

§74. General Studies

74.1 Hansen, Harry. *Midwest Portraits. A Book of Memories and Friendships.* N.Y., 1923.
PS273 H3

74.2 Pattee, Fred L. *The New American Literature, 1890-1930.* N.Y., 1930. Rpt. 1968.
810.9   PS221 P3

74.3 Ransom, John C., et al. *I'll Take My Stand. The South and the Agrarian Tradition, by Twelve Southerners.* N.Y. & London, 1930. Rpt. N.Y., 1962.
917.5   F209 I37

74.4 Hicks, Granville. *The Great Tradition. An Interpretation of American Literature Since the Civil War.* Rev. ed. N.Y., 1935. (Orig. ed. 1933.) Rpt. 1967.
810.9004   PS214 H5

74.5 Spender, Stephen. *The Destructive Element. A Study of Modern Writers and Beliefs.* London, 1935. Rpt. Philadelphia, 1953.
820.4   PR471 S7

74.6 Brook, Donald. *Writers' Gallery. Biographical Sketches of Britain's Greatest Writers and Their Views on Reconstruction [of Society].* London, 1944. Rpt. Pt. Washington, N.Y., 1970.
820.900912   PR473 B77

74.7 Gurko, Leo. *The Angry Decade.* N.Y., 1947. Rpt. 1968.
973.916   E741 G8

74.8 Evans, Benjamin Ifor. *English Literature Between the Wars.*
London, 1948.
820.904   PR478 I5 E9

74.9 Commager, Henry S. *The American Mind. An Interpretation of
American Thought and Character Since the 1880's.* New Haven,
1950. Rpt. N.Y., 1970.
917.3   E169.1 C673

74.10 Routh, Harold V. *English Literature and Ideas in the Twentieth
Century. An Inquiry into Present Difficulties and Future Prospects.*
3rd ed. London, 1950. (Orig. ed. 1946.) Rpt. N.Y., 1970.
820.90091   PR471 R6

74.11 Aldridge, John W. *After the Lost Generation. A Critical Study
of the Writers of Two Wars.* N.Y., 1951. Rpt., 1958; Freeport, N.Y.,
1971.
813.03   PS379 A5

74.12 Isaacs, Jacob. *An Assessment of Twentieth-Century Literature.
Six Lectures Delivered in the B.B.C. Third Programme.* London,
1951. Rpt. Pt. Washington, N.Y., 1968.
809.04   PN771 I8

74.13 Ransom, John C., ed. *The Kenyon Critics. Studies in Modern
Literature from "The Kenyon Review."* Cleveland, 1951. Rpt. Pt.
Washington, N.Y., 1967.
809.04   PN771 K4

74.14 Wilson, Edmund. *The Shores of Light. A Literary Chronicle of
the Twenties and Thirties.* N.Y., 1952.
804   PS221 W56

74.15 Gurko, Leo. *Heroes, Highbrows, and the Popular Mind.* Indianapolis, Ind., 1953. Rpt. Freeport, N.Y., 1971.
917.30392   E169.1 G955

74.16 Rubin, Louis D., and Robert D. Jacobs, eds. *Southern Renascence. The Literature of the Modern South.* Baltimore, 1953. Rpt.
1966.
810.9   PS261 R67

74.17 Cowley, Malcolm. *The Literary Situation.* N.Y., 1954.
810.904   PS221 C67

74.18 Knight, Grant C. *The Strenuous Age in American Literature.*
Chapel Hill, N.C., 1954. Rpt. N.Y., 1970.
810.90054   PS221 K6

74.19 Taylor, Estella R. *The Modern Irish Writers. Cross Currents of
Criticism.* Lawrence, Kan., 1954. Rpt. N.Y., 1969.
820.904   PR8753 T3

74.20 Lynn, Kenneth S. *The Dream of Success. A Study of the Modern American Imagination.* Boston, 1955.
813.509   PS379 L9

74.21 Walcutt, Charles C. *American Literary Naturalism, a Divided Stream.* Minneapolis, 1956.
813.509   PS379 W28

74.22 Times Literary Supplement. *American Writing Today. Its Independence and Vigor.* Ed. Allan Angoff. N.Y., 1957. First appeared in *TLS*, Sept. 17, 1954. Rpt. Freeport, N.Y., 1971.
810.900952   PS221 T5

74.23 Geismar, Maxwell. *American Moderns. From Rebellion to Conformity.* N.Y., 1958.
813.509   PS379 G35

74.24 Heiney, Donald W. *Recent American Literature.* Great Neck, N.Y., 1958.
810.904   PS221 H38

74.25 Ross, Malcolm, ed. *The Arts in Canada. A Stock-Taking at Mid-Century.* Toronto, 1958.
709.71   N6545 R57

74.26 Cowan, Louise. *The Fugitive Group. A Literary History.* Baton Rouge, La., 1959. Rpt. 1968.
810.975   PS261 C6

• *Writers at Work. The Paris Review Interviews.*
    74.27 *First Series.* Ed. with Intro. by Malcolm Cowley. N.Y., 1959.
029.6/808.06   PN453 P3
    74.28 *Second Series.* Intro. Van Wyck Brooks. N.Y., 1963.
808.6   PN453 P3
    74.29 *Third Series.* Intro. Alfred Kazin. N.Y., 1967.
808.856   PN453 W73

74.30 Thorp, Willard. *American Writing in the Twentieth Century.* Cambridge, Mass., 1960.
810.904   PS221 T48

74.31 Times Literary Supplement. *The American Imagination. A Critical Survey of the Arts.* ed. Alan Pryce-Jones. N.Y., 1960. First appeared in *TLS*, Nov. 6, 1959.
917.3   E169.1 T56

74.32 Aaron, Daniel. *Writers on the Left. Episodes in American Literary Communism.* N.Y., 1961. Rpt. 1969.
810.904   PS228 C6 A2

• *Approaches to the Study of Twentieth-Century Literature.* Proceedings of the Conference in the Study of Twentieth-Century Literature. Michigan State University, E. Lansing, Mich.

74.33 *First Session,* 1961. Ed. Hazard Adams et al.

74.34 *Second Session,* 1962. Ed. Sam Baskett.

74.35 *Third Session,* 1963. Ed. Carl Hartman.
  PN68 C6

74.36 Frohock, Wilbur M. *Strangers to This Ground. Cultural Diversity in Contemporary American Writing.* Dallas, Tex., 1961.
810.904   PS221 F7

74.37 Mander, John. *The Writer and Commitment.* London, 1961.
820.904   PR471 M27

74.38 Times Literary Supplement. *The British Imagination. A Critical Survey from the TLS* [*Sept. 9, 1960*]. Ed. Arthur Crook. N.Y., 1961.
914.2   DA566.4 T5

74.39 Hoffman, Frederick J. *The Twenties. American Writing in the Postwar Decade.* Rev. ed. N.Y., 1962. (Orig. ed. 1955.)
810.90   PS221 H58

74.40 MacDonald, Dwight. *Against the American Grain.* N.Y., 1962.
917.3   E169.1 M136

74.41 Becker, George J., ed. *Documents of Modern Literary Realism.* Princeton, 1963.
809.91   PN56 R3 B4

74.42 Bradbury, John M. *Renaissance in the South. A Critical History of the Literature, 1920-1960.* Chapel Hill, N.C., 1963.
810.975   PS261 B624

74.43 Gold, Herbert, ed. *First Person Singular. Essays for the Sixties.* N.Y., 1963.
814.54   PS688 G58

74.44 Hope, Alec D. *Australian Literature, 1950-62.* Melbourne, 1963.
828.9999409   PR9453 H6

74.45 Hough, Graham G. *The Dream and the Task. Literature and Morals in the Culture of Today.* London, 1963.
801   PN49 H66

74.46 Howe, Irving. *A World More Attractive. A View of Modern Literature and Politics.* N.Y., 1963. Rpt. Freeport, N.Y., 1970.
809.04   PN771 H6

74.47 Langford, Richard E., ed. *Essays in Modern American Literature.* Deland, Fla., 1963.
  PS121 L27

74.48 Morgan, Howard W. *Writers in Transition. Seven Americans.*
N.Y., 1963.
928.1   PS221 M57

74.49 Rubin, Louis D. *The Faraway Country. Writers of the Modern
South.* Seattle, 1963.
810.975   PS261 R63

74.50 Spender, Stephen H. *The Struggle of the Modern.* London &
Berkeley, 1963.
809.04   PN771 S625

74.51 Cowley, Malcolm, ed. *After the Genteel Tradition. American
Writers, 1910-1930.* Rev. ed. Carbondale, Ill., 1964. (Orig. ed. N.Y.,
1937.)
810.904   PS221 C645

74.52 Fiedler, Leslie A. *Waiting for the End.* N.Y., 1964. Rpt. 1970.
810.9   PS221 F44

74.53 Fraser, George S. *The Modern Writer and His World. Continuity and Innovation in Twentieth-Century English Literature.* Rev.
ed. London & N.Y., 1964. (Orig. ed. London, 1953.)
820.904   PR471 F72

74.54 Holloway, John. *The Colours of Clarity. Essays on Contemporary Literature and Education.* London, 1964.
809.04   PN771 H58

74.55 Cruise O'Brien, Conor. *Writers and Politics.* London & N.Y.,
1965.
824.914   PR6053 R8 W7

74.56 Ellmann, Richard, and Charles Feidelson, eds. *The Modern Tradition. Backgrounds of Modern Literature.* N.Y., 1965.
808.8891   PN49 E5

74.57 Stewart, John L. *The Burden of Time. The Fugitives and Agrarians. The Nashville Groups of the 1920's and 1930's, and the Writing
of John Crowe Ransom, Allen Tate, and Robert P. Warren.* Princeton, 1965.
810.904   PS255 N3 S7

74.58 Strauman, Heinrich. *American Literature in the Twentieth Century.* 3rd ed. N.Y., 1965. (Orig. ed. 1951.)
810.904   PS221 S8

74.59 Browne, Ray B., Donald M. Winkelman, and Allen Hayman,
eds. *New Voices in American Studies. Mid-America Conference on
Literature, History, Popular Culture and Folklore, Purdue Univ.,
1965.* W. Lafayette, Ind., 1966.
917.03   E169.1 M6213

74.60 Cronin, Anthony. *A Question of Modernity.* London, 1966.
809.04   PN771 C7

74.61 Enright, Dennis J. *Conspirators and Poets.* London & Chester Springs, Pa., 1966.
809.04   PN710 E6

74.62 Kramer, Dale. *Chicago Renaissance. The Literary Life in the Midwest, 1900-1930.* N.Y., 1966.
810.9005   PS221 K67

74.63 Muste, John M. *Say That We Saw Spain Die. Literary Consequences of the Spanish Civil War.* Seattle, 1966.
946.081   DP269.8 L5 M8

74.64 Benson, Frederick R. *Writers in Arms. The Literary Impact of the Spanish Civil War.* N.Y., 1967, N.Y.U. Studies in Comp. Lit., 1.
908.933   DP269.8 L5 B4

74.65 Cowley, Malcolm. *Think Back on Us . . . A Contemporary Chronicle of the 1930's.* Ed. Henry Dan Piper. Carbondale, Ill., 1967.
810.9005   PS3505 O956 T45

74.66 French, Warren G., ed. *The Thirties. Fiction, Poetry, Drama.* Deland, Fla., 1967.
810.90052   PS221 F68

74.67 Kampf, Louis. *On Modernism. The Prospects for Literature and Freedom.*Cambridge, Mass., 1967.
001.2   AZ361 K3

74.68 Ruland, Richard. *The Rediscovery of American Literature. Premises of Critical Taste, 1900-1950.* Cambridge, Mass., 1967.
801.950973   PS221 R8

74.69 Tipple, John O., ed. *Crisis of the American Dream. A History of American Social Thought, 1920-1940.* N.Y., 1967.
917.30391   HN64 T56

74.70 Tucker, Martin. *Africa in Modern Literature. A Survey of Contemporary Writing in English.* N.Y., 1967.
820   PR9798 T8

74.71 Goodheart, Eugene. *The Cult of the Ego. The Self in Modern Literature.* Chicago, 1968.
809.933   PN710 G58

74.72 International Congress of the P.E.N. Clubs. *The Writer as Independent Spirit. Proceedings of 34th Congress, N.Y., 1966.* N.Y., 1968.
808.02   PN131 I6

74.73 Weintraub, Stanley. *The Last Great Cause. The Intellectuals and the Spanish Civil War.* N.Y., 1968.
820.93   PR478 S6 W4

74.74 Alter, Robert. *After the Tradition. Essays on Modern Jewish Writing.* N.Y., 1969.
809.89174924   PJ5017 A4

74.75 French, Warren G., ed. *The Forties. Fiction, Poetry, Drama.* Deland, Fla., 1969.
810.9005   PS221 F6

74.76 Hilfer, Anthony C. *The Revolt from the Village, 1915-1930.* Chapel Hill, N.C., 1969.
810.90052   PS228 C54 H5

74.77 Hoskins, Katherine B. *Today the Struggle. Literature and Politics in England During the Spanish Civil War.* Austin, Tex., 1969.
820.900912   PR478 S6 H6

74.78 Scott, Nathan A. *Negative Capability. Studies in the New Literature and the Religious Situation.* New Haven, 1969.

74.79 Durr, Robert A. *Poetic Vision and the Psychedelic Experience.* Syracuse, N.Y., 1970.
821.009   PR408 I5 D8

74.80 Eagleton, Terence. *Exiles and Émigrés. Studies in Modern Literature.* N.Y., 1970.
820.900912   PR474 E2

74.81 Fox, Hugh. *The Living Underground. A Critical Overview.* Troy, N.Y., 1970.
811.5409   PS325 F69

74.82 Gibson, Donald B., ed. *Five Black Writers. Essays on Wright, Ellison, Baldwin, Hughes, and Le Roi Jones.* N.Y. & London, 1970.
810.9896   PS153 N5 G5

74.83 *Sense and Sensibility in Twentieth-Century Writing. A Gathering in Memory of Wm. Van O'Connor.* Ed. Brom Weber. London & Carbondale, Ill., 1970.
820.9009   PR403 S4

74.84 Bradbury, Malcolm. *The Social Context of Modern English Literature.* N.Y., 1971.
820.90091   PR471 B67

74.85 Churchill, Allen. *The Literary Decade.* Englewood Cliffs, N.J., 1971.
810.90052   PS221 C5

74.86 Moore, Harry T. *Age of the Modern and Other Literary Essays.* Carbondale, Ill., 1971.
809.04   PN771 M64

74.87 Ray, Paul C. *The Surrealist Movement in England.* Ithaca, N.Y., 1971.
820.900912   PR478 S85 R3

74.88 *Twentieth-Century Literature in Retrospect.* Ed. Reuben A. Brower. Cambridge, Mass., 1971. Harvard English Studies, 2.
820.9   PR473 T85

§75. Poetry

75.1 Irish, Wynot R. *The Modern American Muse. A Complete Bibliography of American Verse, 1900-1925.* Syracuse, N.Y., 1950.
016.8115   Z1231 P7 I7

75.2 Anderson, Hugh. *Guide to Australian Poets.* Melbourne, 1953.
Z4024 P6 A65

75.3 Tate, Allen. *Sixty American Poets, 1896-1944. Selected with Preface and Critical Notes.* Rev. ed. Washington, D.C.: Library of Congress, 1954. (Orig. ed. 1945.) Rpt. Detroit, 1969.
016.81152   Z1231 P7 U55

75.4 Shapiro, Nat, ed. *Popular Music. An Annotated Index of American Popular Songs [1920-1964].* 5 vols. N.Y., 1964-69.
ML120 U5 S5

75.5 Woolmer, J. Howard. *A Catalogue of the Imagist Poets.* N.Y., 1966.
016.80881   Z2014 P7 W75

•

75.6 Lowell, Amy. *Tendencies in Modern American Poetry.* Boston, 1917. Rpt. 1928; N.Y., 1969, 1970.
811.5209   PS324 L8

75.7 Untermeyer, Louis. *American Poetry Since 1900.* N.Y., 1923.
PS324 U63

75.8 Williams, Charles. *Poetry at Present.* Oxford, 1930. Rpt. Freeport, N.Y., 1969.
821.009   PR601 W58

75.9 Hughes, Glenn. *Imagism and the Imagists. A Study in Modern Poetry.* Stanford, 1931. Rpt. N.Y., 1959.
821.9109   PR605 I6 H8

75.10 Blackmur, Richard P. *The Double Agent. Essays in Craft and Elucidation.* N.Y., 1935. Rpt. Gloucester, Mass., 1962.
811.09   PS324 B6

75.11 Winters, Yvor. *Primitivism and Decadence. A Study of American Experimental Poetry.* N.Y., 1937. Rpt. 1969.
811.5209   PS324 W5

75.12 Brooks, Cleanth. *Modern Poetry and the Tradition.* Chapel Hill, N.C., 1939. Rpt. N.Y., 1965.
808.1   PN1136 B75

75.13 Daiches, David. *Poetry and the Modern World. A Study of Poetry in England Between 1900 and 1939.* Chicago, 1940. Rpt. 1948; N.Y., 1969.
821.9109   PR601 D25

75.14 Gregory, Horace, and Marya Zaturenska. *A History of American Poetry, 1900-1940.* N.Y., 1942. Rpt. 1969.
811.509   PS324 G7

75.15 Spender, Stephen. *Poetry Since 1939.* London, 1946. Arts in Britain, 1.
821.9109   PR601 S55

75.16 Leavis, Frank R. *New Bearings in English Poetry. A Study of the Contemporary Situation.* 2nd ed. London & N.Y., 1950. (Orig. ed. London, 1932.) Rpt. Ann Arbor, 1960.
821.9109   PR601 L4

75.17 Southworth, James G. *Some Modern American Poets.* Oxford, 1950.
811.509   PS305 S6

75.18 Waggoner, Hyatt H. *The Heel of Elohim. Science and Values in Modern American Poetry.* Norman, Okla., 1950.
811.509   PS324 W3

75.19 Bogan, Louise. *Achievement in American Poetry, 1900-1950.* Chicago, 1951.
811.509   PS221 B56

75.20 Blackmur, Richard P. *Language as Gesture. Essays in Poetry.* N.Y., 1952.
808.1   PN1055 B55

75.21 Southworth, James G. *More Modern American Poets.* London & N.Y., 1954.
811.5   PS324 S6

75.22 Quinn, Mary B. *The Metaphoric Tradition in Modern Poetry. Essays on the Work of Ezra Pound, Wallace Stevens, William Carlos Williams, T. S. Eliot, Hart Crane, Randall Jarrell, and William Butler Yeats.* New Brunswick, N.J., 1955. Rpt. N.Y., 1966.
811.509   PS324 Q5

75.23 Krieger, Murray. *The New Apologists for Poetry.* Minneapolis, 1956. Rpt. Bloomington, Ind., 1963.
808.1   PN1031 K7

75.24 Schlauch, Margaret. *Modern English and American Poetry. Techniques and Ideologies.* London, 1956.
821.9109   PR601 S33

75.25 Blackmur, Richard P. *Form and Value in Modern Poetry.* Garden City, N.Y., 1957.
821.09   PR503 B55

75.26 Langbaum, Robert W. *The Poetry of Experience. The Dramatic Monologue in Modern Literary Tradition.* London & N.Y., 1957. Rpt. N.Y., 1963.
821.09   PR509 M6 L3

75.27 Alvarez, Alfred. *Stewards of Excellence. Studies in Modern English and American Poets.* N.Y., 1958. Rpt. 1971. British title, *The Shaping Spirit* (London, 1958).
821.91209   PR610 A4

75.28 Pacey, William C. Desmond. *Ten Canadian Poets. A Group of Biographical and Critical Essays.* Toronto, 1958. Rpt. 1966.
819.1   PR9165 P3

75.29 Beach, Joseph W. *Obsessive Images. Symbolism in the Poetry of the 1930's and 1940's.* Ed. William Van O'Connor. Minneapolis, 1960.
811.52091   PS310 S9 B4

75.30 Currey, Ralph N. *Poets of the 1939-1945 War.* London & N.Y., 1960. Writers and Their Work, 127.
821.9   PR604 C8

75.31 Rosenthal, Macha L. *The Modern Poets. A Critical Introduction.* N.Y., 1960. Rpt. 1965.
821.9109   PR601 R6

75.32 Jennings, Elizabeth J. *Poetry Today (1957-1960).* London, 1961. Suppl. to *British Book News.*
821.91   PR601 J4

75.33 Cambon, Glauco. *Recent American Poetry.* Minneapolis, 1962.
811.509   PS324 C27

75.34 Cambon, Glauco. *The Inclusive Flame. Studies in American Poetry.* Bloomington, Ind., 1963. (Orig. Italian ed. 1956.)
811.09   PS305 C313

75.35 Deutsch, Babette. *Poetry in Our Time. A Critical Survey of Poetry in the English-speaking World, 1900-1960.* 2nd ed. Garden City, N.Y., 1963. (Orig. ed. N.Y., 1952.)
821.9109   PR601 D43

75.36 Ossman, David, ed. *The Sullen Art. Interviews with Modern Poets.* N.Y., 1963.
811.5409   PS324 O8

75.37 Press, John. *Rule and Energy. Trends in British Poetry Since the Second World War.* N.Y., 1963.
821.9109   PR601 P69

75.38 Loftus, Richard J. *Nationalism in Modern Anglo-Irish Poetry.* Madison, Wis., 1964.

821.91093   PR8771 L6

75.39 National Poetry Festival Held in the Library of Congress October 22-24, 1962. *Proceedings.* Washington, D.C., 1964.

PS301 N3

75.40 Donoghue, Denis. *Connoisseurs of Chaos. Ideas of Order in Modern American Poetry.* N.Y., 1965.

811.009   PS316 D65

75.41 Stepanchev, Stephen. *American Poetry Since 1945. A Critical Survey.* N.Y., 1965.

811.5409   PS324 S68

75.42 Bowra, Cecil M. *Poetry and Politics, 1900-1960.* Cambridge, 1966.

809.193   PN1081 B6

75.43 Dembo, Lawrence S. *Conceptions of Reality in Modern American Poetry.* Berkeley, 1966.

811.509   PS324 D45

75.44 Dudek, Louis. *The Making of Modern Poetry in Canada. Essential Articles on Contemporary Canadian Poetry in English.* Toronto, 1967.

811.5209   PR9171 D8

75.45 Rosenthal, Macha L. *The New Poets. American and British Poetry Since World War II.* N.Y., 1967.

821.91409   PS326 R6

75.46 Hollander, John, ed. *Modern Poetry. Essays in Criticism.* N.Y., 1968.

821.9109   PR610 H6

75.47 Maxwell, Desmond E. S. *Poets of the Thirties.* London & N.Y., 1969.

821.91209   PR610 M3

75.48 Dodsworth, Martin, ed. *The Survival of Poetry. A Contemporary Survey by Donald Davie, Martin Dodsworth, Barbara Hardy, Derwent May, Gabriel Pearson and Anthony Thwaite.* London, 1970.

821.91409   PR611 D6

75.49 Mazzaro, Jerome, ed. *Modern American Poetry. Essays in Criticism.* N.Y., 1970.

811.409   PS323 M3

75.50 Spears, Monroe K. *Dionysus and the City. Modernism in Twentieth-Century Poetry.* N.Y., 1970.

821.909   PS323.5 S65

75.51 Rexroth, Kenneth. *American Poetry in the Twentieth Century.*
N.Y., 1971.
811.509   PS323.5 R4

75.52 Sisson, Charles H. *English Poetry, 1900-1950. An Assessment.*
London, 1971.
821.91209   PR610 S47

§76. Drama and Theater

76.1 Thomson, Ruth G. *Index to Full Length Plays, 1895-1944.*
2 vols. Boston, 1946-56.
016.8125   Z5781 T5

76.2 Ireland, Norma O. *Index to Full Length Plays, 1944-1964.* Boston,
1965.
016.80882   Z5781 T52

76.3 Salem, James M. *A Guide to Critical Reviews.* 5 vols. Metuchen,
N.J., 1966-71.
    Pt. 1. *American Drama from O'Neill to Albee.*
    Pt. 2. *The Musical from Rodgers-and-Hart to Lerner-and-Lowe.*
    Pt. 3. *British and Continental Drama from Ibsen to Pinter.*
    Pt. 4. *The Screenplay from The Jazz Singer to Dr. Strangelove.*
2 vols.
016.8092   Z5782 S34

76.4 Adelman, Irving, and Rita Dworkin, eds. *Modern Drama. A
Checklist of Critical Literature on Twentieth-Century Plays.* Metuchen, N.J., 1967.
016.809204   Z5781 A35

76.5 Palmer, Helen H., and Anne J. Dyson, eds. *European Drama
Criticism, 1900-1966.* Hamden, Conn., 1968. *Supplement to January
1970,* 1970.
016.8092   Z5781 P2

76.6 Breed, Paul F., and Florence M. Sniderman. *Dramatic Criticism
Index. A Bibliography of Commentaries on Playwrights from Ibsen
to Avant-Garde.* Detroit, 1970.

76.7 Patterson, Charlotte A., ed. *Plays in Periodicals. An Index to
English Language Scripts in Twentieth Century Journals.* Includes a
few plays from earlier periods. Boston, 1970.
016.8229108   Z5781 P3

76.8 Keller, Dean H. *Index to Plays in Periodicals.* Includes a few
plays from earlier periods. Metuchen, N.J., 1971.
016.80882   Z5781 K43

76.9 *Who's Who in the Theatre. A Biographical Record of the Contemporary Stage.* 14th ed. by Freda Gaye. London, 1967. (Orig. ed. 1912.)
927.92   PN2012 W5

•

76.10 *Modern Drama.* 1958- . 4/yr. Annual bibliography since 1965.
809.2   PN1861 M55

76.11 *Gambit. An International Theatre Review.* 1963- . 4/yr.
PN6111 G3

76.12 *Black Theatre. A Periodical of the Black Theatre Movement.* 1968- . 6/yr.

•

76.13 Seldes, Gilbert. *The Seven Lively Arts.* N. Y., 1924. Rpt. 1957; with revisions, 1962.
792.0973   PN2221 S43

76.14 Gard, Robert E. *Grassroots Theater. A Search for Regional Arts in America.* Madison, Wis., 1935.
792   PN2267 G3

76.15 Mantle, Burns. *Contemporary American Playwrights.* N.Y., 1938.
812.509   PS351 M32

76.16 Davis, Hallie Flanagan. *Arena. The History of the Federal Theatre.* N.Y., 1940. Rpt. 1965.
792.0973   PN2266 D37

76.17 Bentley, Eric R. *The Playwright as Thinker. A Study of Drama in Modern Times.* N.Y., 1946. Rpt., 1955, 1967. British title *The Modern Theatre. A Study of Dramatists and the Drama.*
808.2   PN1851 B4

76.18 Clark, Barrett H., and George Freedley. *A History of Modern Drama.* N.Y., 1947.
809.2   PN1861 C55

76.19 Gagey, Edmond M. *Revolution in American Drama.* N.Y., 1947. Rpt. Freeport, N.Y., 1971.
812.509   PS351 G3

76.20 Downer, Alan S. *Fifty Years of American Drama, 1900-1950.* Chicago, 1951.
812.509   PS351 D6

76.21 Bentley, Eric R. *In Search of Theater.* N.Y., 1953. Rpt. 1954.
792.0904   PN2189 B4

76.22 Krutch, Joseph W. *The American Drama since 1918. An Informal History.* Rev. ed. N.Y., 1957. (Orig. ed. 1939.)
812.509   PS351 K7

76.23 Donoghue, Denis. *The Third Voice. Modern British and American Verse Drama.* Princeton, 1959. Rpt. N.Y., 1966.
822.9109   PR736 D6

76.24 Downer, Alan S. *Recent American Drama.* Minneapolis, 1961.
812.5209   PS351 D63

76.25 *Contemporary Theatre.* Stratford-upon-Avon Studies, 4. London & N.Y., 1962.
822.9109   PR737 C6

76.26 Gascoigne, Bamber. *Twentieth-Century Drama.* London, 1962.
809.2   PN1861 G3

76.27 Price, Julia S. *The Off-Broadway Theatre.* N.Y., 1962.
792.097471   PN2277 N5 P7

76.28 Himelstein, Morgan Y. *Drama Was a Weapon. The Left-Wing Theatre in New York, 1929-1941.* New Brunswick, N.J., 1963.
792.097471   PN2277 N5 H5

76.29 Brustein, Robert S. *The Theatre of Revolt. An Approach to the Modern Drama.* Boston, 1964.
809.2   PN2189 B7

76.30 Rabkin, Gerald. *Drama and Commitment. Politics in the American Theatre of the Thirties.* Bloomington, Ind., 1964.
812.52093   PS338 P6 R3

76.31 Bogard, Travis, and William I. Oliver, eds. *Modern Drama. Essays in Criticism.* N.Y., 1965.
809.2   PN1851 B6

76.32 Meserve, Walter J., ed. *Discussions of [Modern] American Drama.* Boston, 1965.
812.509   PS351 M47

76.33 Williams, Raymond. *Modern Tragedy.* Stanford & London, 1966.
809.916   PN1897 W5

76.34 *American Theatre.* Stratford-upon-Avon Studies, 10. London & N.Y., 1967.
812.5209   PS351 A8

76.35 Bentley, Eric R. *The Theatre of Commitment, and Other Essays on Drama in Our Society.* N.Y., 1967.
792.015   PN2037 B43

76.36 Bigsby, Christopher W. *Confrontation and Commitment. A Study of Contemporary American Drama, 1959-66.* London, 1967.
812.5409   PS351 B48

76.37 Golden, Joseph. *The Death of Tinker Bell. The American Theatre in the Twentieth Century.* Syracuse, N.Y., 1967.
792.0973   PN2266 G63

76.38 Mathews, Jane D. *The Federal Theatre, 1935-1939. Plays, Relief, and Politics.* Princeton, 1967.
792.0973   PN2266 M33

76.39 Taylor, John R. *The Rise and Fall of the Well-Made Play.* N.Y., 1967.
822.809   PR731 T3

76.40 Brown, John Russell, ed. *Modern British Dramatists. A Collection of Essays.* Englewood Cliffs, N.J., 1968.
822.91409   PR737 B7

76.41 Styan, John L. *The Dark Comedy. The Development of Modern Comic Tragedy.* 2nd ed. London, 1968. (Orig. ed. 1962.)
809.2   PN1861 S75

76.42 Williams, Raymond. *Drama from Ibsen to Brecht.* London, 1968. Rev. ed. (Orig. ed. 1953 as *Drama from Ibsen to Eliot.*)
809.2   PN1851 W48

76.43 Abramson, Doris E. *Negro Playwrights in the American Theatre, 1925-1959.* N.Y., 1969.
812.509   PS351 A2

76.44 Esslin, Martin. *The Theatre of the Absurd.* Rev. ed. Garden City, N. Y., 1969. (Orig. ed. 1961.)
809.2   PN1861 E8

76.45 *Free Southern Theater. A Documentary of the South's Radical Black Theater, with Journals, Letters, Poetry, Essays, and a Play Written by Those Who Built It.* Ed. Thomas C. Dent et. al. Indianapolis, Ind., 1969.
792.0975   PN2297 F7

76.46 Porter, Thomas E. *Myth and Modern American Drama.* Detroit, 1969.
812.509   PS351 P6

76.47 Taylor, John R. *The Angry Theatre. New British Drama.* Rev. ed. N. Y., 1969. (Orig. ed. 1962.) English title *Anger and After. A Guide to the New British Drama.*
822.91409   PR736 T3

76.48 Esslin, Martin. *Brief Chronicles. Essays on Modern Theatre.* London, 1970.
809.204   PN1861 E78

76.49 Lewis, Allan. *American Plays and Playwrights of the Contemporary Theatre.* Rev. ed. N.Y., 1970. (Orig. ed. 1965.)
812.509   PS351 L4

76.50 Taylor, John R. *The Second Wave. British Drama for the Seventies.* London & N.Y., 1971.
822.91409   PR736 T34

76.51 Wellwarth, George E. *The Theater of Protest and Paradox. Developments in the Avant-Garde Drama.* Rev. ed. N.Y., 1971. (Orig. ed. 1964.)
809.204   PN1861 W4

§77. Fiction

77.1 Astrinsky, Aviva, ed. *A Bibliography of South African English Novels, 1930-1960.* Cape Town, 1965. Rpt. 1970.
016.823   Z3608 L5 A85

77.2 Bufkin, Ernest C. *The Twentieth-Century Novel in English. A Checklist.* Athens, Ga., 1967.
016.82391208   Z2014 F5 B93

77.3 Hubble, Gregory V., ed. *Modern Australian Fiction. A Bibliography, 1940-1965.* Perth, 1969.

77.4 Nevius, Blake. *The American Novel. Sinclair Lewis to the Present.* Goldentree Bibliographies. N.Y., 1970.
016.8135209   Z1231 F4 N4

•

77.5 *Modern Fiction Studies. A Critical Quarterly.* 1955-   .
808.3   PS379 M55

77.6 *Critique. Studies in Modern Fiction.* 1956-   . 3/yr. Succeeds *Faulkner Studies,* 1952-56.
PN3503 C7

•

77.7 Van Doren, Carl. *Contemporary American Novelists, 1900-1920.* N. Y., 1922. Rpt. 1931, 1971.
813.009   PS379 V3

77.8 Beach, Joseph W. *The Outlook for American Prose.* Chicago, 1926. Rpt. Freeport, N. Y., Westport, Conn.; Pt. Washington, N.Y., 1968.
818.520809/810.90052   PS379 B4

77.9 Michaud, Regis. *The American Novel To-day. A Social and Psychological Study.* Boston, 1928. (Orig. French ed. 1926.) Rpt. N.Y., 1967.
813.009   PS371 M53

77.10 Beach, Joseph W. *The Twentieth-Century Novel. Studies in Technique.* N.Y., 1932.
808.3   PN3503 B4

77.11 Hartwick, Harry. *The Foreground of American Fiction.* N.Y., 1934. Rpt. 1967.
813.009   PS379 H3

77.12 Hatcher, Harlan H. *Creating the Modern American Novel.* N.Y., 1935. Rpt. 1965.
813.509   PS379 H34

77.13 Ford, Nick A. *The Contemporary Negro Novel. A Study in Race Relations.* Boston, 1936. Rpt. College Park, Md., 1968.
813.5209   PS374 N4 F6

77.14 Muller, Herbert J. *Modern Fiction. A Study of Values.* N.Y., 1937.
808.3   PN3503 M8

77.15 Eldershaw, M. Barnard [pseud.]. *Essays in Australian Fiction.* Melbourne, 1938. Rpt. Freeport, N.Y., 1970.
823.009   PR9503 E5

77.16 Boynton, Percy H. *America in Contemporary Fiction.* Chicago, 1940. Rpt. N.Y., 1963.
813.509   PS379 B65

77.17 Beach, Joseph W. *American Fiction, 1920-1940.* N.Y., 1941. Rpt. 1960.
813.509   PS379 B38

77.18 Wilson, Edmund. *The Boys in the Back Room. Notes on California Novelists.* San Francisco, 1941. Rpt. Folcroft, Pa., 1969.
PS379 W5

77.19 Geismar, Maxwell. *Writers in Crisis. The American Novel Between Two Wars. Ring Lardner, Ernest Hemingway, John Dos Passos, William Faulkner, Thomas Wolfe, John Steinbeck.* Boston, 1942. Rpt. N.Y., 1971.
813.5209   PS379 G4

77.20 Kazin, Alfred. *On Native Grounds. An Interpretation of Modern American Prose Literature.* N. Y., 1942. (Abridged ed. with new postscript, Garden City, N.Y., 1956.) Rpt. 1963.
810.9   PS379 K3

77.21 Reed, Henry. *The Novel Since 1939.* London, 1946. The Arts in Britain, 4.
823.9109   PR884 R4

77.22 Burgum, Edwin B. *The Novel and the World's Dilemma.* N.Y., 1947. Rpt. 1963.
809.3   PN3503 B8

77.23 O'Connor, William Van, ed. *Forms of Modern Fiction. Essays Collected in Honor of Joseph Warren Beach.* Minneapolis, 1948. Rpt. Bloomington, Ind., 1959.
PN3355 M5

77.24 Geismar, Maxwell. *The Last of the Provincials. The American Novel, 1915-1925.* 2nd ed. Boston, 1949. (Orig. ed. 1947.)
813.509   PS379 G36

77.25 Kiely, Benedict. *Modern Irish Fiction. A Critique.* Dublin, 1950.
823.9109   PR8797 K5

77.26 Warfel, Harry R. *American Novelists' of Today.* N.Y., 1951.
813.509   PS379 W3

77.27 Aldridge, John W., ed. *Critiques and Essays on Modern Fiction, 1920-1951. Representing the Achievement of Modern American and British Critics.* N.Y., 1952.
808.3   PN3355 A8

77.28 Prescott, Orville. *In My Opinion. An Inquiry into the Contemporary Novel.* Indianapolis, Ind., 1952. Rpt. Freeport, N.Y., 1971.
813.5409   PR881 P7

77.29 Savage, Derek S. *The Withered Branch. Six Studies in the Modern Novel.* London, 1950; N.Y., 1952.
823.9109   PR884 S3

77.30 Geismar, Maxwell. *Rebels and Ancestors. The American Novel, 1890-1915. Frank Norris, Stephen Crane, Jack London, Ellen Glasgow, Theodore Dreiser.* Boston 1953.
813.409   PS379 G38

77.31 Hughes, Carl M. *The Negro Novelist. A Discussion of the Writings of American Negro Novelists, 1940-1950.* N.Y., 1953. Rpt. Freeport, N.Y., 1967.
813.509   PS374 N4 H8

77.32 Gelfant, Blanche H. *The American City Novel. Theodore Dreiser, Thomas Wolfe, Sherwood Anderson, Edith Wharton, John Dos Passos, James T. Bishop, Willard Motley. and Others.* Norman, Okla., 1954. Rpt. 1969.
813.509   PS374 C5 G4

77.33 Humphrey, Robert. *Stream of Consciousness in the Modern Novel.* Berkeley, 1954. Rpt. 1962.
808.3   PN3365 H8

77.34 Friedman, Melvin. *Stream of Consciousness. A Study in Literary Method.* New Haven, 1955.
809.3   PN3448 P8 F7

77.35 Lewis, Richard W. B. *The Picaresque Saint. Representative Figures in Contemporary Fiction.* Philadelphia, 1956. Rpt. 1961.
809.3   PN3503 L4

77.36 O'Connor, Frank [Michael O'Donovan]. *The Mirror in the Roadway. A Study of the Modern Novel.* N.Y., 1956. Rpt. Freeport, N.Y., 1970.
809.33   PN3491 O3

160 / *The Modern Period*

77.37 Rideout, Walter B. *The Radical Novel in the United States, 1900-1954. Some Interrelations of Literature and Society.* Cambridge, Mass., 1956. Rpt. N.Y., 1966.
813.509   PS379 R5

77.38 Hicks, Granville, ed. *The Living Novel. A Symposium.* N.Y., 1957.
813.504   PS379 H5

77.39 O'Faolain, Sean. *The Vanishing Hero. Studies in Novelists of the Twenties.* Boston, 1957. Rpt. Freeport, N.Y., 1971.
823.91409   PR888 H4 O3

77.40 Zabel, Morton D. *Craft and Character. Texts, Method, and Vocation in Modern Fiction.* N.Y., 1957.
823.804   PR823 Z3

77.41 Frohock, Wilbur M. *The Novel of Violence in America.* 2nd ed. Dallas, Tex., 1958. (Orig. ed. 1950.)
813.509   PS379 F7

77.42 Fuller, Edmund. *Man in Modern Fiction. Some Minority Opinions on Contemporary American Writing.* N.Y., 1958.
813.509   PS379 F8

77.43 Daiches, David. *The Novel and the Modern World.* Rev. ed. Chicago, 1960. (Orig. ed. 1939.)
823.912   PR881 D3

77.44 Hassan, Ihab H. *Radical Innocence. Studies in the Contemporary American Novel.* Princeton, 1961.
813.509   PS379 H32

77.45 Schorer, Mark, ed. *Modern British Fiction.* N.Y., 1961.
823.9109   PR883 S3

77.46 Gindin, James J. *Postwar British Fiction. New Accents and Attitudes.* Berkeley, 1962.
823.914   PR881 G5

77.47 Ludwig, Jack B. *Recent American Novelists.* Minneapolis, 1962.
813.5   PS379 L82

77.48 Malin, Irving. *New American Gothic.* Carbondale, Ill., 1962.
813.5409   PS379 M28

77.49 Balakian, Nona, and Charles Simmons, eds. *The Creative Spirit Present. Notes on Contemporary American Fiction.* Garden City, N.Y., 1963.
813.509   PS379 B29

77.50 Broes, Arthur T., et al. *Lectures on Modern Novelists.* Pittsburgh, Pa., 1963. Carnegie Series in English, 7.
PS379 C3

77.51 Burgess, Anthony [John A. B. Wilson]. *The Novel To-day.* London, 1963. Supplement to *British Book News.*
PR881 W52

77.52 Church, Margaret. *Time and Reality. Studies in Contemporary Fiction.* Chapel Hill, N. C., 1963.
809.3   PN3503 C5

77.53 Eisinger, Chester E. *Fiction of the Forties.* Chicago, 1963.
813.509   PS379 E4

77.54 Litz, A. Walton., ed. *Modern American Fiction. Essays in Criticism.* N. Y., 1963.
823.0904   PS379 L5

77.55 Hoffman, Frederick J. *The Modern Novel in America, 1900-1950.* Rev. ed. Chicago, 1963. (Orig. ed. 1951.)
813.509   PS379 H6

77.56 Allen, Walter E. *The Modern Novel in Britain and the United States.* N. Y., 1964. English title *Tradition and Dream.*
823.9109   PR881 A4

77.57 Edel, Leon. *The Modern Psychological Novel.* Rev. ed. N. Y., 1964. (Orig. ed. *The Psychological Novel: 1900-1950,* Philadelphia, 1955.)
809.3   PN3448 P8 E3

77.58 Feied, Frederick. *No Pie in the Sky. The Hobo as American Cultural Hero in the Works of Jack London, John Dos Passos, and Jack Kerouac.* N. Y., 1964.
813.093   PS3523 O46 Z6235

77.59 Hardy, John E. *Man in the Modern Novel.* Seattle, 1964. Rpt. 1966.
823.912093   PR881 H35

77.60 Klein, Marcus. *After Alienation. American Novels in Mid-Century.* Cleveland, 1964. Rpt. Freeport, N. Y., 1970.
813.509   PS379 K5

77.61 Millgate, Michael. *American Social Fiction. James to Cozzens.* Edinburgh & N. Y., 1964.
813.093   PS379 M48

77.62 Mizener, Arthur. *The Sense of Life in the Modern Novel.* Boston, 1964.
813.509   PS371 M59

77.63 Moore, Harry T., ed. *Contemporary American Novelists.* Carbondale, Ill., 1964.
813.5409   PS379 M64

77.64 Witham, W. Tasker. *The Adolescent in the American Novel, 1920-1960.* N. Y., 1964.
813.5093   PS374 Y6 W5

77.65 Baumbach, Jonathan. *The Landscape of Nightmare. Studies in the Comtemporary American Novel.* N.Y., 1965.
813.509   PS379 B35

77.66 Davie, Donald, ed. *Russian Literature and Modern English Fiction. A Collection of Critical Essays.* Chicago & Toronto, 1965.
891.709003   PG2981 G7 D3

77.67 Gleason, Judith I. *This Africa. Novels by West Africans in English and French.* Evanston, Ill., 1965.
809.3   PQ3984 G4

77.68 Gossett, Louise Y. *Violence in Recent Southern Fiction.* Durham, N.C., 1965.
813.5093   PS261 G6

77.69 Meyer, Roy W. *The Middle Western Farm Novel in the Twentieth Century.* Lincoln, Neb., 1965.
813.5093   PS374 F3 M4

77.70 Rippier, Joseph S. *Some Postwar English Novelists.* Frankfurt/Main, 1965.

77.71 West, Paul. *The Modern Novel.* 2nd ed. 2 vols. London, 1965. (Orig. ed. 1963.)
809.3   PN3448 P8 W4

77.72 Blotner, Joseph L. *The Modern American Political Novel, 1900-1960.* Austin, Tex., 1966.
813.5093   PS374 P6 B55

77.73 Derrett, M. E. *The Modern Indian Novel in English. A Comparative Approach.* Brussels, 1966.
823.009   PR9737 D4

77.74 French, Warren G. *The Social Novel at the End of an Era.* Carbondale, Ill., 1966.
813.52093   PS379 F68

77.75 Friedman, Alan. *The Turn of the Novel. The Transition to Modern Fiction.* N.Y., 1966. Rpt. 1970.
823.9109   PR881 F78

77.76 Holman, C. Hugh. *Three Modes of Modern Southern Fiction. Ellen Glasgow, William Faulkner, Thomas Wolfe.* Athens, Ga., 1966.

813.5209   PS379 H64

77.77 Lytle, Andrew N. *The Hero with the Private Parts. Essays.* Baton Rouge, La., 1966.
814.52.   PS3523 Y88 H4

77.78 Stevens, Joan. *The New Zealand Novel, 1860-1965.* 2nd ed. Wellington, 1966. (Orig. ed. 1962.)
823   PR9635 S7

77.79 Stuckey, William J. *The Pulitzer Prize Novels. A Critical Backward Look.* Norman, Okla., 1966.
813.509   PS379 S78

77.80 Cooperman, Stanley R. *World War I and the American Novel.* Baltimore, 1967.
810.9005   PS221 C63

77.81 Harper, Howard M. *Desperate Faith. A study of Bellow, Salinger, Mailer, Baldwin, and Updike.* Chapel Hill, N.C., 1967.
813.5209   PS379 H27

77.82 Hoffman, Frederick J. *The Art of Southern Fiction. A Study of Some Modern Novelists.* Carbondale, Ill., 1967.
813.009   PS261 H48

77.83 Rabinovitz, Rubin. *The Reaction Against Experiment in the English Novel, 1950-1960.* N.Y., 1967.
823.9109   PR881 R3

77.84 Scholes, Robert E. *The Fabulators,* N.Y., 1967.
813.509   PS379 S37

77.85 Hall, James W. *The Lunatic Giant in the Drawing Room. The British and American Novel Since 1930.* Bloomington, Ind., 1968.
823.9109   PR881 H28

77.86 Madden, David, ed. *Proletarian Writers of the Thirties.* Carbondale, Ill., 1968.
810.90052   PS379 M258

77.87 Madden, David, ed. *Tough Guy Writers of the Thirties.* Carbondale, Ill., 1968.
813.5209   PS379 M26

77.88 Ratcliffe, Michael. *The Novel Today.* London, 1968.
823.9109   PR884 R3

77.89 Rhodes, Harold W. *New Zealand Fiction Since 1945. A Critical Survey of Recent Novels and Short Stories.* Dunedin, 1968.
823.009   PR9637 R48

77.90 Klein, Marcus, ed. *The American Novel Since World War II.* Greenwich, Conn., 1969.
813.5409   PS379 K52

77.91 Schulz, Max F. *Radical Sophistication. Studies in Contemporary Jewish-American Novelists.* Athens, O., 1969.
813.509   PS379 S394

77.92 Sherman, Bernard. *The Invention of the Jew. Jewish-American Education Novels, 1916-1964.* N.Y., 1969.
813.5093   PS153 J4 S5

77.93 *Southern Fiction Today. Renascence and Beyond.* Ed. George Core. Athens, Ga., 1969.
813.5409   PS261 S52

77.94 Tischler, Nancy M. *Black Masks. Negro Characters in Modern Southern Fiction.* University Park, Pa., 1969.
813.509   PS374 N4 T5

77.95 Bergonzi, Bernard. *The Situation of the Novel.* London, 1970.
823.03   PR881 B4

77.96 Galloway, David D. *The Absurd Hero in American Fiction. Updike, Styron, Bellow, Salinger.* Rev. ed. Austin, Tex., 1970. (Orig. ed. 1966.)
813.54093   PS379 G24

77.97 Ramchand, Kenneth. *The West Indian Novel and Its Background.* London & N. Y., 1970.
823.009   PR9324 R3

77.98 Cooke, Michael, ed. *Modern Black Novelists. A Collection of Critical Essays.* Englewood Cliffs, N.J., 1971.
809.3304   PN3503 C6

77.99 Gindin, James J. *Harvest of a Quiet Eye. The Novel of Compassion.* Bloomington, Ind., 1971.
823.03   PR861 G5

77.100 Lebowitz, Naomi. *Humanism and the Absurd in the Modern Novel.* Evanston, Ill., 1971.
809.33   PN3499 L4

77.101 Panichas, George A., ed. *The Politics of Twentieth Century Novelists.* N.Y., 1971.
809.33   PN3503 P3

77.102 Pinsker, Sanford. *The Schlemiel as Metaphor. Studies in the Yiddish and American Jewish Novel.* Carbondale, Ill., 1971.
809.88924   PJ5124 P5

77.103 Tanner, Tony. *City of Words. American Fiction, 1950-1970.* London & N.Y., 1971.
813.03   PS379 T3

77.104 Watkins, Floyd C. *The Flesh and the Word. Eliot, Hemingway, Faulkner.* Nashville, Tenn., 1971.
810.90052   PS121 W35

§78. Language

78.1 Avis, Walter S. *A Bibliography of Writings on Canadian English (1857-1965).* Toronto, 1965.
Z1379 A85

78.2 *Current Slang. A Quarterly Glossary of Slang Expressions Presently in Use.* 1966- .

•

78.3 Kennedy, Arthur G. *Current English. A Study of Present-Day Usages and Tendencies, Including Pronunciation, Spelling, Grammatical Practice, Word Coining, and the Shifting of Meanings.* Boston, 1935. Rpt. Westport, Conn., 1970.
420   PE1075 K4

78.4 Partridge, Eric, and John W. Clark. *British and American English Since 1900. With Contributions on English in Canada, South Africa, Australia, New Zealand, and India.* London, 1951. Rpt. N.Y., 1968.
420.904   PE1087 P3

78.5 Lloyd, Donald J., and Harry R. Warfel. *American English in Its Cultural Setting.* N.Y., 1956.
425   PE1105 L58

78.6 Gold, Robert S. *A Jazz Lexicon.* N.Y., 1964.
781.5703   ML102 J3 G6

78.7 Rosten, Leo C. *The Joys of Yiddish. A Relaxed Lexicon of Yiddish, Hebrew, and Yinglish Words Often Encountered in English.* N.Y., 1968.
492.4932   PN6231 J5 R67

78.8 Major, Clarence. *Dictionary of Afro-American Slang.* N.Y., 1970.

427.09   PE3727 N4 M3

78.9 Landy, Eugene E. *The Underground Dictionary.* N.Y., 1971.
427.09   PE3721 L3

12. Criticism

§79. Bibliographies, Guides

79.1 Elton, William. *A Guide to the New Criticism.* Chicago, 1951. (Orig. title *A Glossary of the New Criticism,* 1949.)
PN1031 E6

79.2 Hall, Vernon, ed. *Literary Criticism, Plato Through Johnson.* Goldentree Bibliographies. N.Y., 1970.
016.809   Z6514 C97 H3

●

79.3 *Contemporary Literature.* 1960- . 4/yr. Until 1967 *Wisconsin Studies in Contemporary Literature.* Annual review on Criticism.
809.04   PN2 W55

79.4 *Yearbook of Comparative Criticism.* 1968- . Catalogued separately.

●

79.5 Hyman, Stanley E. *The Armed Vision. A Study in the Methods of Modern Literary Criticism.* Abr. ed. N.Y., 1955. (Orig. ed. 1948.)
801   PN94 H9

79.6 Daiches, David. *Critical Approaches to Literature.* Englewood Cliffs, N. J., 1956. Rpt. N.Y., 1965.
801   PN81 D3

79.7 Goldberg, Gerald J., and Nancy Marmer, eds. *The Modern Critical Spectrum. The Major Schools of Modern Literary Criticism Explained and Illustrated for Today's Reader.* N.Y., 1962.
801.9   PN94 G6

79.8 Scott, Wilbur S., ed. *Five Approaches of Literary Criticism. An Arrangement of Contemporary Critical Essays.* N.Y., 1962.
809   PN94 S28

79.9 Crews, Frederick C. *The Pooh Perplex. A Freshman Casebook.*
N.Y., 1963.
823.912   PR6025 I65 W65

79.10 Kaplan, Charles, ed. *The Overwrought Urn. A Potpourri of Parodies of Critics Who Triumphantly Present the Real Meanings of Authors from Jane Austen to J. D. Salinger.* N.Y., 1969.
809   PN6231 C75 K3

§80. Surveys

80.1 Spingarn, Joel E. *A History of Literary Criticism in the Renaissance.* 2nd ed. N.Y., 1908. (Orig. ed. 1899.) Rpt. 1938, 1963. Columbia Studies in Comp. Lit.
801.9   PN88 S6

80.2 Saintsbury, George. *A History of English Criticism. Being the English Chapters of "A History of Criticism and Literary Taste in Europe," Revised, Adapted, and Supplemented.* Edinburgh, 1911. Rpt. 1955, 1962.
820.1   PR63 S3

80.3 Foerster, Norman. *American Criticism. A Study in Literary Theory from Poe to the Present.* Boston, 1928. Rpt. N.Y., 1962.
810.9   PS62 F6

80.4 Ransom, John C. *The New Criticism.* Norfolk, Conn., 1941.
801   PN1031 R3

● Atkins, John W. H. *English Literary Criticism.*
80.5 *The Medieval Phase.* N.Y., 1943. Rpt. 1961.
801.9   PN99 G7 A8

80.6 *The Renascence.* 2nd ed. London, 1951. Rpt. N.Y., 1968. (Orig. ed. 1947.)
801.950942   PN99 G7 A83

80.7 *Seventeenth and Eighteenth Centuries.* London, 1951. Rpt. London & N.Y., 1959, 1966.
801   PN99 G7 A78

80.8 Tillotson, Geoffrey. *Criticism and the Nineteenth Century.* London, 1951. Rpt. Hamden, Conn., 1967.
820.9008   PR463 T5

80.9 O'Connor, William Van. *An Age of Criticism: 1900-1950.* Chicago, 1952. Rpt. 1966.
801   PN99 U52 O3

80.10 Temple, Ruth Z. *The Critic's Alchemy. A Study of the Introduction of French Symbolism into England.* N.Y., 1953. Rpt. New Haven, Conn., 1962.
820.903   PR468 S9 T4

80.11 Stovall, Floyd, ed. *The Development of American Literary Criticism.* Chapel Hill, N. C., 1955. Rpt. New Haven, Conn., 1965.
801   PN99 U5 S75

80.12 Wellek, René. *A History of Modern Criticism, 1750-1950.* 4 vols. Vol. 5: The Twentieth Century, in progress. New Haven, 1955-
801   PN86 W4

80.13 Pritchard, John P. *Criticism in America. An Account of the Development of Critical Techniques from the Early Period of the Republic to the Middle Years of the Twentieth Century.* Norman, Okla., 1956. Rpt. 1967.
801   PN99 U5 P69

80.14 Wimsatt, William K., and Cleanth Brooks. *Literary Criticism. A Short History.* N.Y., 1957.
801   PN86 W5

80.15 Hyman, Stanley E. *Poetry and Criticism. Four Revolutions in Literary Taste.* N.Y., 1961.
801.9   PN86 H9

80.16 Parks, Edd W. *Ante-Bellum Southern Literary Criticism.* Athens, Ga., 1962.
810.9   PN99 U52 P3

80.17 Watson, George G. *The Literary Critics. A Study of English Descriptive Criticism.* Harmondsworth, Eng., 1962.
809   PR63 W3

80.18 Hall, Vernon. *A Short History of Literary Criticism.* N.Y.,

801.9   PN86 H3

80.19 Pritchard, John P. *Literary Wise Men of Gotham. Criticism in New York, 1815-1860.* Baton Rouge, La., 1963.
PN99 U52 P7

80.20 Lemon, Lee T. *The Partial Critics.* N.Y., 1965.
801.951   PN94 L4

80.21 Karanikas, Alexander. *Tillers of a Myth. Southern Agrarians as Social and Literary Critics.* Madison, Wis., 1966.
810.9005   PS221 K27

80.22 Demetz, Peter. *Marx, Engels, and the Poets. Origins of Marxist Literary Criticism.* Rev. ed. Trans. Jeffrey L. Sammons. Chicago, 1967. (Orig. German ed. Stuttgart, 1959.)
335.4388   PN98 C6 D413

80.23 Marks, Emerson R. *The Poetics of Reason. English Neoclassical Criticism.* N.Y., 1968.
801.950942   PR445 M28

80.24 *The Critical Temper. A Survey of Modern Criticism on English and American Literature from the Beginnings to the Twentieth Century.* Ed. Martin Tucker. 3 vols. N.Y., 1969.
820.9   PR83 C764

80.25 Gross, John. *The Rise and Fall of the Man of Letters. A Study of the Idiosyncratic and the Humane in Modern Literature.* N.Y., 1969.
820.9   PR63 G7

80.26 Bradbury, Malcolm, and David Palmer, eds. *Contemporary Criticism.* Stratford-upon-Avon Studies, 12. London, 1971.

§81. Collections of Critical Essays

81.1 Stallman, Robert W., ed. *Critiques and Essays in Criticism, 1920-1948. Representing the Achievement of Modern British and American Critics.* N.Y., 1949.
801   PN81 S67

81.2 Crane, Ronald S., ed. *Critics and Criticism Ancient and Modern. By R. S. Crane, W. R. Keast, Richard McKeon, Norman MacLean, Elder Olson, Bernard Weinberg.* Chicago, 1952. Abr. ed. 1957.
801   PN81 C8

81.3 West, Ray B., ed. *Essays in Modern Literary Criticism.* N.Y., 1952.
801   PN85 W4

81.4 Johnston, Kevin W. Grahame, ed. *Australian Literary Criticism.* Melbourne, 1962.
828.99994   PR9414 J6

81.5 Zabel, Morton D., ed. *Literary Opinions in America. Essays Illustrating the Status, Methods, and Problems of Criticism in the United States in the Twentieth Century.* 3rd ed. 2 vols. N.Y., 1962. (Orig. ed. in 1 vol., 1937.)
820.82   PN771 Z2

81.6 Sutton, Walter E., ed. *Modern American Criticism.* Englewood Cliffs, N.J., 1963. Princeton Studies: Humanistic Scholarship in America.
810.904   PN99 U5 S8

81.7 Nyren, Dorothy, ed. *A Library of Literary Criticism: Modern American Literature.* 3rd ed. N.Y., 1964. (Orig. ed. 1960.)
810.904   PS221 N9

81.8 Times Literary Supplement. *The Critical Moment. Literary Criticism in the 1960's. Essays from the London Times Literary Supplement* [*July 26 and Sept. 27, 1963*]. N.Y., 1964.
801.9   PN85 T5

81.9 Temple, Ruth Z., and Martin Tucker, eds. *A Library of Literary Criticism: Modern British Literature.* 3 vols. N.Y., 1966.
820.90091   PR473 T4

81.10 Semmler, Clement, ed. *Twentieth Century Australian Literary Criticism.* Melbourne, 1967.
820.9994   PR9453 S4

81.11 *The Disciplines of Criticism. Essays in Literary Theory, Interpretation, and History.* Ed. Peter Demetz et al. New Haven, 1968.
809   PN36 W4

81.12 Grebstein, Sheldon N., ed. *Perspectives in Contemporary Criticism. A Collection of Recent Essays by American, English, and European Literary Critics.* N.Y., 1968.
809   PN511 G69

81.13 Pacey, William C. Desmond. *Essays in Canadian Criticism, 1938-1968.* Toronto, 1969.
810.9   PR9114 P3

81.14 Albrecht, Milton C., ed. *The Sociology of Art and Literature. A Reader.* N.Y., 1970.
700   NK650 S6 A4

81.15 *Determinations. Critical Essays* [from *Scrutiny*]. ed. Frank R. Leavis. N.Y., 1970.
820.9   PR67 D4

81.16 Mandel, Eli, ed. *Contexts of Canadian Criticism.* Chicago, 1971.

§82. Statements by Individual Critics

82.1 More, Paul E. *Shelburne Essays.* 11 vols. London, N.Y. & Boston, 1904-21. Rpt. N.Y., 1967.
820.4   PR99 M7

82.2 Babbitt, Irving. *Rousseau and Romanticism.* Boston, 1919. Rpt. 1924; N.Y., 1955, 1957.
809.03   PN603 B3

82.3 Richards, Ivor A. *Principles of Literary Criticism.* London & N.Y., 1924. Rpt. 1959; N.Y., 1961.
801.9   PN81 R5

82.4 Read, Herbert E. *Reason and Romanticism. Essays in Literary Criticism.* London, 1926. Rpt. N.Y., 1963.
809   PN511 R35

82.5 Eliot, T[homas] S. *For Lancelot Andrewes. Essays on Style and Order.* London, 1928.
082   PN511 E43

82.6 Richards, Ivor A. *Practical Criticism. A Study of Literary Judgment.* London, 1929. Rpt. 1935, 1948, 1956; N.Y., 1956, 1964.
PN1031 R48

82.7 Hulme, Thomas E. *Speculations. Essays on Humanism and the Philosophy of Art.* 2nd ed. London & N.Y., 1936. (Orig. ed. 1924.) Rpt. London, 1954; N.Y. 1961, 1963.
192   B1646 H83 S7

82.8 James, David G. *Scepticism and Poetry. An Essay on the Poetic Imagination.* London, 1937. Rpt. N.Y., 1960.
808.1   PN1031 J3

82.9 Lewis, Clive S. *Rehabilitations and Other Essays.* London, 1939.
820.4   PR99 L4

82.10 Blackmur, Richard P. *The Expense of Greatness.* N.Y., 1940. Rpt. Gloucester, Mass., 1958.
820.4   PR473 B56

82.11 Orwell, George. *Inside the Whale, and Other Essays.* London, 1940. (Rpt. Harmondsworth, Eng., 1957, 1960, as *Selected Essays.*) Rpt. Harmondsworth, 1962, 1964, 1966, 1967.
824.91   PR6029 R8 I6

82.12 Wilson, Edmund. *The Wound and the Bow. Seven Studies in Literature.* Boston, 1941. Rpt. 1947; N.Y., 1965.
809   PN511 W633

82.13 Burke, Kenneth. *A Grammar of Motives.* N.Y., 1945. Rpt. Berkeley, 1969.
191.9   B945 B773 G7

82.14 Orwell, George. *Dickens, Dali, and Others. Studies in Popular Culture.* N.Y. & London, 1946. British title *Critical Essays.*
824.91   PR6029 R8 D5

82.15 Sprigg, Christopher St. John [pseud. Christopher Caudwell]. *Illusion and Reality. A Study of the Sources of Poetry.* New ed. London, 1946. (Orig. ed. 1937.) Rpt. 1947, 1949, 1955, 1970.
808.1   PN1031 S75

82.16 Winters, Yvor. *In Defense of Reason.* N.Y., 1947.
801   PS121 W53

82.17 Wilson, Edmund. *The Triple Thinkers. Twelve Essays on Literary Subjects.* N.Y., 1948. (Orig. ed. . . . *Ten Essays* . . . , 1938.) Rpt. 1963.
809.03   PN511 W63

82.18 Auden, W[ystan] H. *The Enchafèd Flood. Or the Romantic Iconography of the Sea.* N.Y., 1950.
809.03   PN56 S4 A8

82.19 Burke, Kenneth. *A Rhetoric of Motives.* N.Y., 1950. Rpt. N.Y., 1955; Berkeley, 1969.
149.94   B840 B8

82.20 Eliot, T[homas] S. *The Sacred Wood. Essays on Poetry and Criticism.* 7th ed. London, 1950. (Orig. ed. 1920.)
801.95   PN511 E44

82.21 Eliot, T[homas] S. *Selected Essays.* Rev. ed. N.Y., 1950. (Orig. ed. London & N.Y., 1932.)
814.5   PN511 E443

82.22 Stallman, Robert W., ed. *The Critic's Notebook.* Minneapolis, 1950.
801   PN81 S66

82.23 Trilling, Lionel. *The Liberal Imagination. Essays on Literature and Society.* N.Y., 1951. Rpt. 1953.
804   PS3539 R56 L5

82.24 Leavis, Frank R. *The Common Pursuit.* London & N.Y., 1952. Rpt. N.Y., 1964.
820.9   PR99 L35

82.25 Burke, Kenneth. *Counter-Statement.* 2nd ed. Los Altos, Calif., 1953. (Orig. ed. N.Y., 1931.) Rpt. with new Addendum, Berkeley, 1968.
809   PN511 B79

82.26 Crane, Ronald S. *Languages of Criticism and the Structure of Poetry.* The Alexander Lectures, 1950-51. Toronto, 1953. Rpt. 1964.
PN1042 C7

82.27 Langer, Susanne K. *Feeling and Form. A Theory of Art Developed from "Philosophy in a New Key."* London & N.Y., 1953.
153   BF458 L29

82.28 Tate, Allen. *The Forlorn Demon. Didactic and Critical Essays.* Chicago, 1953. Rpt. Freeport, N.Y., 1971.
804   PN37 T28

82.29 Hulme, Thomas E. *Further Speculations.* Ed. Sam Hynes. Minneapolis, 1955. Rpt. Lincoln, Neb., 1962.
192.9   B1646 H83 F8

82.30 Frye, Northrop. *Anatomy of Criticism. Four Essays.* Princeton, 1957. Rpt. N.Y., 1966.
801   PN81 F75

82.31 Langer, Susanne K. *Philosophy in a New Key. A Study in the Symbolism of Reason, Rite, and Art.* 3rd ed. London & Cambridge, Mass., 1957. (Orig. ed. 1942.)
153   BF458 L3

82.32 Levin, Harry T. *Contexts of Criticism.* Cambridge, Mass., 1957. Rpt. N.Y., 1963. Harvard Studies in Comp. Lit., 22.
804   PN511 L36

82.33 Rahv, Philip. *Image and Idea. Twenty Essays on Literary Themes.* Rev. ed. N.Y., 1957. (Orig. ed. 1949.)
809   PN511 R27

82.34 Winters, Yvor. *The Function of Criticism. Problems and Exercises.* Denver, 1957.
801   PN85 W5

82.35 Cunningham, James V. *Tradition and Poetic Structure. Essays in Literary History and Criticism.* Denver, 1960.
821.09   PR503 C8

82.36 Holloway, John. *The Charted Mirror. Literary and Critical Essays.* London, 1960.
820.4   PR6015 O416 C5

82.37 Lerner, Laurence D. *The Truest Poetry. An Essay on the Question: What is Literature?* London, 1960.
801   PN49 L45

82.38 Lane, Robert E. *The Liberties of Wit. Humanism, Criticism and the Civic Mind.* New Haven, 1961. Rpt. Hamden, Conn., 1970.
801.9   PN81 L3

82.39 Auden, W[ystan] H. *The Dyer's Hand and Other Essays.* N.Y., 1962.
828.912   PR6001 U4 D9

82.40 Kermode, John Frank. *Puzzles and Epiphanies. Essays and Reviews, 1958-1961.* London, 1962.
809.04   PR473 K4

82.41 Ong, Walter J. *The Barbarian Within and Other Fugitive Essays and Studies.* N.Y., 1962.
814.54   PN511 O55

82.42 Swallow, Alan. *An Editor's Essays of Two Decades.* Seattle & Denver, 1962.
814.54   PN511 S75

82.43 Hyman, Stanley E. *The Promised End. Essays and Reviews, 1942-1962.* Cleveland, 1963.
809   PN511 H9

82.44 Wain, John. *Essays on Literature and Ideas.* N.Y., 1963.
820.9   PR99 W24

82.45 Wimsatt, William K. *Hateful Contraries. Studies in Literature and Criticism.* Lexington, Ky., 1965.
809   PN85 W49

82.46 Brophy, Brigid. *Don't Never Forget. Collected Views and Reviews.* London, 1966.
828.91408   PR6052 R583 D6

82.47 Burke, Kenneth. *Language as Symbolic Action. Essays on Life, Literature, and Method.* Berkeley, 1966.
801.95   PN511 B793

82.48 Robson, William W. *Critical Essays.* London, 1966.
820.9   PR99 R63

82.49 Sontag, Susan. *Against Interpretation. And Other Essays.* N.Y., 1966.
809.04   PN771 S62

82.50 Burke, Kenneth. *The Philosophy of Literary Form. Studies in Symbolic Action.* 2nd ed. Baton Rouge, La., 1967. (Orig. ed. 1941.)
801   PN511 B795

82.51 Crane, Ronald S. *The Idea of the Humanities and Other Essays.* 2 vols. Chicago, 1967.
001.308   PN50 C7

82.52 Levin, Harry T. *Why Literary Criticism Is Not an Exact Science.* Cambridge, Mass., 1967.
801.95   PN85 L473

82.53 Daiches, David. *More Literary Essays.* Edinburgh & Chicago, 1968.
820.9   PR99 D26

82.54 Tate, Allen. *Essays of Four Decades.* Chicago, 1968.
818.5208   PS3539 A74 A16

82.55 Barker, George. *Essays.* London, 1969.
808.108   PR6003 A68 A16

82.56 Housman, A[lfred] E. *The Confines of Criticism. The Cambridge Inaugural, 1911.* London, 1969.
801.95   PR4809 H15 A66

82.57 Kronenberger, Louis. *The Polished Surface. Essays in the Literature of Worldliness.* N.Y., 1969.
809.933   PN56 W67 K7

82.58 McLuhan, Herbert Marshall. *The Interior Landscape. The Literary Criticism of Marshall McLuhan, 1943-1962.* Ed. Eugene McNamara. N.Y., 1969.
820.9   PR99 M28

82.59 Rahv, Philip. *Literature and the Sixth Sense.* Boston, 1969.
809   PN761 R26

82.60 Hobsbaum, Philip. *Theory of Criticism.* Bloomington, Ind., 1970.
801.95   PN81 H52

82.61 Frye, Northrop. *The Stubborn Structure. Essays on Criticism and Society.* Ithaca, N.Y., 1970.
801.95   PN81 F76

82.62 Hoggart, Richard. *Speaking to Each Other. Essays.* Vol. I: *About Society,* Vol. II: *About Literature.* N.Y., 1970.
301.08   AC8 H7532

82.63 McCarthy, Mary T. *The Writing on the Wall and Other Literary Essays.* London & N.Y., 1970.
809   PS3525 A1435 A16

82.64 Rexroth, Kenneth. *The Alternative Society. Essays from the Other World.* N.Y., 1970.
081   PS3535 E923 A16

82.65 Rexroth, Kenneth. *With Eye and Ear.* N.Y., 1970.
814.52   PS3535 E923 A16

82.66 Rodway, Allan E. *The Truths of Fiction.* London, 1970.
820.1   PN81 R6

82.67 Richards, Ivor A. *Sciences and Poetries. A Reissue of "Science and Poetry" (1926, 1935) with Commentary.* N.Y., 1970.
821.009   PN1031 R5

82.68 Wellek, René. *Discriminations. Further Concepts of Criticism.* New Haven, 1970.
801.9508   PN81 W36

82.69 Fiedler, Leslie A. *The Collected Essays of Leslie Fiedler.* 2 vols. N.Y., 1971.
814.54   PS3556 I34 A16

82.70 Frye, Northrop. *The Critical Path. An Essay on the Social Context of Literary Criticism.* Bloomington, Ind., 1971.
801.95   PN81 F754

§83. The Critical Idiom

These works either examine or exemplify various critical schools (formalist, mythic, etc.) or critical concepts (irony, symbol, etc.).

83.1 Kuntz, Joseph M. *Poetry Explication. A Checklist of Interpretations Since 1925 of British and American Poems Past and Present.* Rev. ed. Denver, 1962. (Orig. ed. by J. M. Kuntz and George Arms. N.Y., 1950.)
016.82109   Z2014 P7 K8

83.2 Walcutt, Charles C., and J. Edwin Whitesell, eds. *The Explicator Cyclopedia.* Vol. I: *Modern Poetry,* Vol. II: *Traditional Poetry,* Vol. III: *Prose.* Chicago, 1966-69.
820.9   PR401 E9

83.3 Kiell, Norman. *Psychoanalysis, Psychology and Literature. A Bibliography.* Madison, Wis., 1963.
016.80993   Z6511 K5

83.4 Shibles, Warren A. *Metaphor. An Annotated Bibliography and History.* Whitewater, Wis., 1971.
011   Z7004 M4 S5

●

83.5 *American Imago. A Psychoanalytical Journal for Culture, Science, and the Arts.* 1939- . 4/yr.
BF173 A2 A55

83.6 *Explicator.* 1942- . 10/yr.
PR1 E9

83.7 *Satire Newsletter.* 1963- . 2/yr. Annual bibliography.
PN169 S35

83.8 *Genre.* 1968- . 4/yr.
801.95   PN80 G4

●

83.9 Turner, Francis McD. *The Element of Irony in English Literature. An Essay.* Cambridge, 1926.
PR931 T8

83.10 Bodkin, Maud. *Archetypal Patterns in Poetry. Psychological Studies of Imagination.* Oxford, 1934. Rpt. 1948, 1951, 1963.
808.1   PN1031 B63

83.11 Lovejoy, Arthur O. *The Great Chain of Being. A Study of the History of an Idea.* Cambridge, Mass., 1936. Rpt. 1957; N.Y., 1960.
119   B105 C5 L6

83.12 Worcester, David. *The Art of Satire.* Cambridge, Mass., 1940. Rpt. N.Y., 1960, 1969.
808.7   PN6149 S2 W6

83.13 Lovejoy, Arthur O. *Essays in the History of Ideas.* Baltimore, 1948. Rpt. N.Y., 1955, 1960.
104   B945 L583 E7

83.14 Sedgewick, Garnett G. *Of Irony, Especially in Drama.* 2nd ed. Toronto, 1948. (Orig. ed. 1935.) Rpt. Cambridge, 1967.
808.2   PN1680 S4

83.15 Chase, Richard V. *Quest for Myth.* Baton Rouge, La., 1949. Rpt. N.Y., 1969.
398   BL313 C47

83.16 Bodkin, Maud. *Studies of Type-Images in Poetry, Religion, and Philosophy.* London, 1951.
201   BL51 B62

83.17 Brower, Reuben A. *The Fields of Light. An Experiment in Critical Reading.* N.Y., 1951. Rpt. 1962.
809   PN83 B78

83.18 Graves, Robert. *The White Goddess. A Historical Grammar of Poetic Myth.* 3rd ed. London, 1952. (Orig. ed. 1948.) Rpt. N.Y., 1966.
809.1   PN1077 G7

83.19 Shumaker, Wayne. *Elements of Critical Theory.* Berkeley, 1952.
801   PN81 S46

83.20 Feidelson, Charles. *Symbolism and American Literature.* Chicago, 1953. Rpt. 1959.
810.903   PS201 F4

83.21 Goodman, Paul. *The Structure of Literature.* Chicago, 1954.
801   PN45 G6

83.22 Richards, Ivor A. *Speculative Instruments.* Chicago, 1955. Rpt. N.Y., 1967.
412   P325 R5

83.23 Tindall, William Y. *The Literary Symbol.* N.Y., 1955. Rpt. Bloomington, Ind., 1955.
809   PN56 S9 T5

83.24 Leyburn, Ellen D. *Satiric Allegory: Mirror of Man.* New Haven, 1956. Rpt. Hamden, Conn., 1969. Yale Studies in English, 130.
827.00915   PR931 L46

83.25 Hoffman, Frederick J. *Freudianism and the Literary Mind.* 2nd ed. Baton Rouge, La., 1957. (Orig. ed. 1945.) Rpt. 1967.
809.04   PN49 H6

83.26 Beardsley, Monroe C. *Aesthetics. Problems in the Philosophy of Criticism.* N.Y., 1958.
701.17   BH201 B4

83.27 Cary, Joyce. *Art and Reality. Ways of the Creative Process.* N.Y., 1958. Rpt. Freeport, N.Y., 1970.
701.15   NX165 C36

83.28 Hopkins, Kenneth. *Portraits in Satire.* London, 1958. Rpt. St. Clair Shores, Mich., 1971.
821.609   PR935 H6

83.29 Sutherland, James R. *English Satire.* Cambridge, 1958. Rpt. 1962.
827.09   PR931 S8

83.30 Campbell, Joseph. *The Masks of God.* 4 vols. N.Y., 1959-68.
291.143   BL311 C27

83.31 Honig, Edwin. *Dark Conceit. The Making of Allegory.* Evanston, Ill., 1959. Rpt. N.Y., 1966.
809.93   PN56 A5 H6

83.32 Beebe, Maurice, ed. *Literary Symbolism. An Introduction to the Interpretation of Literature.* San Francisco, 1960.
809.91   PN56 S9 B4

83.33 Elliott, Robert C. *The Power of Satire. Magic, Ritual, Art.* Princeton, 1960.
808.7   PN6149 S2 E37

83.34 Fiedler, Leslie A. *No! in Thunder. Essays on Myth and Literature.* Boston, 1960.
809   PN511 F5

83.35 Fraiberg, Louis B. *Psychoanalysis and American Literary Criticism.* Detroit, 1960.
810.93   PS78 F7

83.36 Seward, Barbara. *The Symbolic Rose.* N.Y., 1960.
809.93   PN56 R75 S4

83.37 Tave, Stuart M. *The Amiable Humorist. A Study in the Comic Theory and Criticism of the Eighteenth and Early Nineteenth Centuries.* Chicago, 1960.
827.0903   PR935 T3

83.38 Knox, Norman D. *The Word "Irony" and Its Context, 1500-1755.* Durham, N.C., 1961.
422   PE1599 I7 K55

83.39 Brower, Reuben A., and Richard Poirier, eds. *In Defense of Reading. A Reader's Approach to Literary Criticism.* N.Y., 1962.
801.9   PR67 B7

83.40 Bruner, Jerome S. *On Knowing. Essays for the Left Hand.* Cambridge, Mass., 1962.
121   LB885 B778

83.41 Highet, Gilbert. *The Anatomy of Satire.* Princeton, 1962.
809.7   PN6149 S2 H5

83.42 Mazzeo, Joseph A., ed. *Reason and Imagination. Studies in the History of Ideas, 1600-1800.* N.Y., 1962.
901.93   CB411 M3

83.43 Wheelwright, Philip E. *Metaphor and Reality.* Bloomington, Ind., 1962.
412   P325 W43

83.44 Frye, Northrop. *Fables of Identity. Studies in Poetic Mythology.* N.Y., 1963.
821.09   PR503 F7

83.45 Righter, William. *Logic and Criticism.* London & N.Y., 1963.
801.9   BH39 R5

83.46 Slote, Bernice, ed. *Myth and Symbol. Critical Approaches and Applications by Northrop Frye, L. C. Knights and Others.* Lincoln, Neb., 1963.
809.91   PN501 S55

83.47 Wimsatt, William K., ed. *Explication as Criticism. Selected Papers from the English Institute, 1941-1952.* N.Y., 1963.
801.9   PN81 W482

83.48 Fletcher, Angus J. *Allegory. The Theory of a Symbolic Mode.* Ithaca, N.Y., 1964.
809   PN56 A5 F5

83.49 Hirst, Désirée. *Hidden Riches. Traditional Symbolism from the Renaissance to Blake.* London & N.Y., 1964.
820.91   PN56 S9 H5

83.50 Weisinger, Herbert. *The Agony and the Triumph. Papers on the Use and Abuse of Myth.* E. Lansing, Mich., 1964.
809   PN710 W45

83.51 Black, Edwin. *Rhetorical Criticism. A Study in Method.* N.Y., 1965.
801.9   PN4121 B518

83.52 Dyson, Anthony E. *The Crazy Fabric. Essays in Irony.* London & N.Y., 1965.
820.9   PR149 I7 D9

83.53 Handy, William J. *A Symposium on Formalist Criticism.* Austin, Tex., 1965.

83.54 International Federation for Modern Languages and Literature. *Literary History and Literary Criticism. Acta of the Ninth Congress, 1963.* Ed. Leon Edel. N.Y., 1965.
PN31 I52

83.55 Kernan, Alvin B. *The Plot of Satire.* New Haven, 1965.
827.009   PN6147 K4

83.56 Bremner, Robert H., ed. *Essays on History and Literature.* Columbus, O., 1966.
907.2   D13 B69

83.57 Casey, John. *The Language of Criticism.* London & N.Y., 1966.
801.95   PR77 C3

83.58 Vickery, John B., ed. *Myth and Literature. Contemporary Theory and Practice.* Lincoln, Neb., 1966.
809.933   PN56 M94 V5

83.59 Damon, Philip, ed. *Literary Criticism and Historical Understanding. Selected Papers from the English Institute.* N.Y., 1967.
801.95   PN81 D35

83.60 McDowell, Frederick P., ed. *The Poet as Critic.* Evanston, Ill., 1967.
809.1   PN1136 M25

83.61 Paulson, Ronald. *The Fictions of Satire.* Baltimore, 1967.
809.7   PN6149 S2 P33

83.62 Campbell, Joseph. *The Hero with a Thousand Faces.* 2nd ed. Princeton, 1968. (Orig. ed. 1949.)
291.13   BL313 C28

83.63 Hinchliffe, Arnold P. *The Absurd.* The Critical Idiom, 5. London, 1968.
809.04   PN771 H5

83.64 Morrison, Claudia C. *Freud and the Critic. The Early Use of Depth Psychology in Literary Criticism.* Chapel Hill, N.C., 1968.
810.9005   PS78 M6

83.65 *The Uses of Myth. Papers Relating to the Anglo-American Seminar on the Teaching of English at Dartmouth College, New Hampshire, 1966.* Ed. Paul A. Olson. NCTE. Champaign, Ill., 1968.
809.915   LB1631 U8

83.66 Wheelwright, Philip E. *The Burning Fountain.* Rev. ed. Bloomington, Ind., 1968. (Orig. ed. 1954.)
401.9   P106 W57

83.67 Adams, Hazard. *The Interests of Criticism. An Introduction to Literary Theory.* N.Y., 1969.
801.95   PN81 A36

83.68 Campbell, Joseph. *The Flight of the Wild Gander. Explorations in the Mythological Dimension.* N.Y., 1969.
291.13   BL304 C35

83.69 Corbett, Edward P., ed. *Rhetorical Analyses of Literary Works.* N.Y., 1969.
820.9   PR14 C6

83.70 Furst, Lilian R. *Romanticism.* The Critical Idiom, 2. London, 1969.
809.914   PN603 F78

83.71 Hodgart, Matthew J. *Satire.* N.Y., 1969.
809.7   PN6149 S2 H6

83.72 Johnson, Robert V. *Aestheticism.* The Critical Idiom, 3. London, 1969.
701.1709034   BH221 G73 J6

83.73 Kitagawa, Joseph M., and Charles H. Long, eds. *Myths and Symbols. Studies in Honor of Mircea Eliade.* Chicago, 1969.
200.4   BL25 M85

83.74 Lincoln, Eleanor T., ed. *Pastoral and Romance. Modern Essays in Criticism.* Englewood Cliffs, N.J., 1969.
809.933   PN56 P3 L5

83.75 Merivale, Patricia. *Pan the Goat-God. His Myth in Modern Times.* Cambridge, Mass., 1969. Harvard Studies in Comp. Lit., 30.
809.933   PN57 P25 M4

83.76 Muecke, Douglas C. *The Compass of Irony.* London & N.Y., 1969.
809.91   PN56 I65 M8

83.77 Ruthven, Kenneth K. *The Conceit.* London, 1969. The Critical Idiom, 4.
821.0093   PR535 M37 R8

83.78 Beer, Gillian. *The Romance.* The Critical Idiom, 10. London, 1970.
809.385   PN56 R6 B4

83.79 Burnshaw, Stanley. *The Seamless Web. Language-Thinking; Creature-Knowledge; Art-Experience.* London & N.Y., 1970.
153.35   BF408 B86

83.80 Dipple, Elizabeth. *Plot.* The Critical Idiom, 12. London, 1970.
808   PN218 D5

83.81 Elliott,Robert C. *The Shape of Utopia. Studies in a Literary Genre.* Chicago, 1970.
809.933   PN56 U8 E5

83.82 Gass, William H. *Fiction and the Figures of Life.* N.Y., 1970.
809.3   PN3353 G36

83.83 Grant, Damian. *Realism.* The Critical Idiom, 9, London, 1970.
809.912   PN56 R3 G7

83.84 Kallich, Martin. *The Association of Ideas and Critical Theory in Eighteenth Century England. A History of a Psychological Method in English Criticism.* The Hague, 1970.
121   PN99 G72 K3

83.85 MacQueen, John. *Allegory.* The Critical Idiom, 14. London, 1970.
809.915   PN56 A5 M33

83.86 Muecke, Douglas C. *Irony,* The Critical Idiom, 13. London, 1970.
809.91   BH301 I7 M8

83.87 Pollard, Arthur. *Satire.* The Critical Idiom, 7. London, 1970.
809.7   PN6149 S2 P6

83.88 *Psychoanalysis and Literary Process.* Ed. Frederick C. Crews. Cambridge, Mass., 1970.
820.9   PR14 P76

83.89 Slatoff, Walter J. *With Respect to Readers. Dimensions of Literary Response.* Ithaca, N.Y., 1970.
807.1173   PN61 S58

83.90 Slochower, Harry. *Mythopoesis. Mythic Patterns in the Literary Classics.* Detroit, 1970.
809.933   PN56 M95 S5

83.91 Spivey, Ted R. *The Coming of the New Man. A Study of Literature, Myth, and Vision Since 1750.* N.Y., 1970.
809.04   PN701 S6

83.92 Chadwick, Charles. *Symbolism.* The Critical Idiom, 16. London, 1971.
841.00915   PQ439 C47

83.93 Furst, Lilian R., and Peter N. Skrine, eds. *Naturalism.* The Critical Idiom, 18. London, 1971.
809.912   B828.2 F87

83.94 Marinelli, Peter V. *Pastoral.* The Critical Idiom, 15. London, 1971.
809.912   PN56 P3 M3

83.95 Paulson, Ronald, ed. *Satire. Modern Essays in Criticism.* Englewood Cliffs, N.J., 1971.
809.7   PN6149 S2 P35

83.96 Toliver, Harold E. *Pastoral Forms and Attitudes.* Berkeley, 1971.
820.914   PR408 P3 T6

§84. Book Reviews

84.1 Gray, Richard A., ed. *A Guide to Book Review Citations. A Bibliography.* Columbus, O., 1969.
016.0281   Z1035 A1 G7

84.2 *Book Review Digest.* 1905-   . 10/yr with annual cumulations. Five-year index cumulations.
Z1219 C95

84.3 *An Index to Book Reviews in the Humanities.* 1960-   . Annual. 4/yr until 1963.
028.1016   Z1035 A1 I63

84.4 *Book Review Index.* 1965-   . Annual. 4/yr until 1968.
028   Z1035 A1 B6

84.5 *New York Times Book Review.* 1896-   . 52/yr.

•

84.6 *Times Literary Supplement.* 1902-   . 52/yr.
AP4 T45

84.7 *Critic.* 1943- . 6/yr. Until 1957 *Books on Trial.*
015.73   Z1219 Z9 B6

84.8 *New York Review of Books.* 1963- . 24/yr.
028.105   AP2 N655

84.9 *Book World.* 1967- . 52/yr. Formerly *N.Y. Herald Tribune Book Review,* 1924-62, and *Book Week,* 1963-66.

§85. Journals of Criticism

85.1 *Books Abroad. An International Literary Quarterly.* 1927- .
Z1007 B717

85.2 *Scrutiny. A Quarterly Review.* 1932-53. Rpt. Cambridge, 1963, 20 vols. plus index.
AP4 S45

85.3 *Babel. A Multi-Lingual Critical Review.* 1940- . 4/yr.
805   PN1 B3

85.4 *Essays in Criticism. A Quarterly Journal of Literary Criticism.* 1951- .
PR1 E75

85.5 *Critical Review, Melbourne-Sydney.* 1958- . Annual.

85.6 *Criticism. A Quarterly for Literature and the Arts.* 1959- .
AS30 W3 A2

85.7 *Review of English Literature.* London. 1960-67. 8 vols. 4/yr.
PR1 R35

85.8 *Thoth. Syracuse University Graduate Studies in English.* 1961- . 3/yr.
PR1 T45

85.9 *Critical Survey. The Journal of the Critical Quarterly Society.* 1962- . 2/yr.
805   PN2 C7

85.10 *Paunch.* 1963- . 3/yr.

85.11 *Hollins Critic.* 1964- . 5/yr.

85.12 *Cambridge Quarterly.* 1965- .

85.13 *Style.* 1967- . 3/yr.

85.14 *Notes on Mississippi Writers.* 1968- . 3/yr.

85.15 *Ariel. A Review of International English Literature.* 1970- . 4/yr.

85.16 *Studies in Black Literature.* 1970- . 3/yr.

85.17 *Notes on Contemporary Literature.* 1971- . 5/yr.

Part Two. The Book

13. Bibliography

§86. Bibliographies, Guides, Periodicals

86.1 Hart, Horace. *Bibliotheca Typographica. In usum eorum qui libros amant. A List of Books About Books.* Rochester, N.Y., 1933. Rpt. Ann Arbor, 1971.
016.070573   Z1002 H255

86.2 McKerrow, Ronald B. *An Introduction to Bibliography for Literary Students.* 2nd imprint with corrections. Oxford, 1928. (Orig. imprint 1927.) Rpt. 1949.
Z1001 M16

86.3 Van Hoesen, Henry B., and Frank K. Walter. *Bibliography, Practical, Enumerative, Historical. An Introductory Manual.* N.Y., 1928. Rpt. 1971.
001.552   Z1002 V25

86.4 Besterman, Theodore. *The Beginnings of Systematic Bibliography.* 2nd ed. Oxford, 1936. (Orig. ed. 1935.) Rpt. N.Y., 1968.
010   Z1001.3 B4

86.5 Malclès, Louise-Noëlle. *Les sources du travail bibliographique.* 3 vols. Geneva, 1950-58.
016.01   Z1002 M4

86.6 Binns, Norman E. *An Introduction to Historical Bibliography.* 2nd ed. London, 1962. (Orig. ed. 1953.)
655.09   Z4 B55

86.7 Lowy, George. *A Searcher's Manual.* Hamden, Conn., 1965.
025.2   Z689 L6

86.8 Astbury, Raymond G. *Bibliography and Book Production.* Oxford & N.Y., 1967.
655.442   Z1002 A85

86.9 Downs, Robert B., and Frances B. Jenkins, eds. *Bibliography. Current State and Future Trends.* Urbana, Ill., 1967.
016.016   Z1002 D62

86.10 Esdaile, Arundell. *Manual of Bibliography*. 4th ed. by Roy Stokes. N.Y., 1967. (Orig. ed. *The Student's Manual of Bibliography*, London, 1931.)
010   Z1001 E75

86.11 Williamson, Derek. *Historical Bibliography*. Hamden, Conn., 1967.
655.57309   Z4 W76

86.12 Collison, Robert L. *Bibliographies. Subject and National. A Guide to Their Contents, Arrangement, and Use*. 3rd ed. London, 1968. (Orig. ed. N.Y., 1951.)
016.016   Z1002 C7

86.13 Stokes, Roy B. *The Function of Bibliography*. London, 1969.
010   Z1001 S84

86.14 Hackman, Martha L. *The Practical Bibliographer*. Englewood Cliffs, N.J., 1970.
010   Z1000 H2

86.15 Robinson, Anthony M. L. *Systematic Bibliography. A Practical Guide to the Work of Compilation*. 3rd ed. Cape Town, London, & Hamden, Conn., 1971. (Orig. ed. 1963.)
010.28   Z1001 R66

•

86.16 *Library. A Quarterly Review of Bibliography*. 1889-   . Since 1920, *Transactions of the Bibliographical Society* as subtitle.
010.5   Z671 L69

86.17 Bibliographical Society. London. *Transactions*. 1892-1919. 15 vols. Rpt. Nendeln, Liechtenstein, 1967.
                   Z1008 B587

    86.18 Cole, George W. *An Index to Bibliographical Papers Published by the Bibliographical Society and the Library Association, London, 1877-1932*. Chicago, 1933.
016.01   Z1008 B585

86.19 *Bulletin of Bibliography and Magazine Notes*. 1897-   . 4/yr.
                   Z1007 B94

86.20 *Papers of the Bibliographical Society of America*. 1906-   . 4/yr.
                   Z1008 B51 P

86.21 *Edinburgh Bibliographical Society. Transactions*. 1938-   . Supersedes *Publications*, 1896-1935. 15 vols.
                   Z1008 E24

86.22 *Studies in Bibliography. Papers of the Bibliographical Society of Virginia*. 1948-   . Annual.
010.6275549   Z1008 V55

86.23 *Selective Checklist of Bibliographical Scholarship.* Ed. Howell J. Heaney and Rudolf Hirsch. Cumulated annual lists from *Studies in Bibliography.* Charlottesville, Va.
  Series A. 1949-1955. 1957.
  Series B. 1956-1964. 1966.
    Z1002 V59

86.24 *Cambridge Bibliographical Society. Transactions.* 1949- . Annual.
  010.6242   Z1008 C2

86.25 *Inter-American Review of Bibliography. Revista Interamericana de Bibliografía.* 1951- . 4/yr.
  010.5   Z1007 R4317

86.26 *Bibliography, Documentation, Terminology.* 1961- . UNESCO. 6/yr.
    Z1007 B5775

86.27 *Proof. Yearbook of American Bibliographic and Textual Studies.* 1971-

§87. Editing and Textual Criticism

87.1 Glaister, Geoffrey A. *An Encyclopedia of the Book. Terms Used in Paper-Making, Printing, Bookbinding and Publishing. With Notes on Illuminated Manuscripts, Bibliophiles, Private Presses, and Printing Societies.* Cleveland & London, 1960. British title *Glossary of the Book.*
  655.03   Z118 G55

87.2 *CEAA Newsletter.* Center for Editions of American Authors. 1968- . Annual.

•

87.3 Briquet, Charles M. *Les filigranes. Dictionnaire historique des marques du papier dès leur apparition vers 1282 jusqu'en 1600.* 2nd ed. 4 vols. Leipzig, 1923. (Orig. ed. 1907.) Rpt. N.Y., 1966.
  676.2802703   Z237 B845

87.4 Greg, Walter W. *The Calculus of Variants. An Essay on Textual Criticism.* Oxford, 1927.
    PA47 G7

87.5 Chapman, Robert W. *Cancels. With Eleven Facsimiles in Collotype.* London & N.Y., 1930.
  655.25   Z242 C2 C4

87.6 Carter, John, and Graham Pollard. *An Enquiry into the Nature of Certain Nineteenth Century Pamphlets.* London, 1934. Rpt. N.Y., 1971.
098.3   Z1024 C32

87.7 McKerrow, Ronald B. *Prolegomena for the Oxford Shakespeare. A Study in Editorial Method.* Oxford, 1939. Rpt. 1969.
822.33   PR3071 M26

87.8 Bowers, Fredson T. *Principles of Bibliographical Description.* Princeton, 1949. Rpt. N.Y., 1962.
010.1   Z1001 B78

87.9 Bühler, Curt F., James G. McManaway, and Lawrence C. Wroth. *Standards of Bibliographical Description.* Philadelphia, 1949.
010.1   Z1001 B9

87.10 *Nineteenth-Century English Books. Some Problems in Bibliography.* Third Annual Windsor Lectures by Gordon N. Ray, Carl J. Weber, and John Carter. Urbana, Ill., 1952.
094.4   Z2014 F5 N5

87.11 Bowers, Fredson T. *Textual and Literary Criticism.* Cambridge, 1959.
801.9   P47 B6

87.12 Foxon, David F. *Thomas J. Wise and the Pre-Restoration Drama. A Study in Theft and Sophistication.* London, 1959. Supp. to Biblio. Soc. Pubs., 19.
024.8   Z989 W8 F6

87.13 Dearing, Vinton A. *Methods of Textual Editing. A Paper Delivered at a Seminar . . . Clark Library, 12 May 1962 . . .* Los Angeles, 1962.
PN162 D4

87.14 Bowers, Fredson T. *Bibliography and Textual Criticism.* Oxford & N.Y., 1964.
010   Z1001 B775

● Editorial Conference. *Papers Given at the Editorial Conference, University of Toronto.*

    87.15 1965 *Editing Sixteenth Century Texts.* Ed. Richard J. Schoeck. Toronto, 1966.
808.02   PN162 E3

    87.16 1966. *Editing Nineteenth Century Texts.* Ed. John M. Robson. Toronto, 1967.
808.02   PN162 E3

    87.17 1967. *Editing Eighteenth Century Texts.* Ed. Donal I. B. Smith. Toronto, 1968.
808.02   PN162 E2

87.18 1968. *Editor, Author, and Publisher.* Ed. William J. Howard. Toronto, 1969.
808.02   PN155 E3

87.19 Schoenbaum, Samuel. *Internal Evidence and Elizabethan Dramatic Authorship. An Essay in Literary History and Method.* London & Evanston, Ill., 1966.
822.309   PR658 A9 S3

87.20 Modern Language Association. *Statement of Editorial Principles. A Working Manual for Editing Nineteenth Century American Texts.* N.Y., 1967.
808.02   PN162 M6

87.21 Wilson, Edmund. *The Fruits of the MLA.* N.Y., 1968. (Rpt. from *New York Review of Books,* Sept. 26, Oct. 10, 1968.)

87.22 Brack, O. M., and Warner Barnes, eds. *Bibliography and Textual Criticism. English and American Literature, 1700 to the Present.* Chicago, 1969.
801.959   PR77 B7

87.23 Hinman, Charlton, and Fredson Bowers. *Two Lectures on Editing. Shakespeare and Hawthorne.* Columbus, O., 1969.
808.02   PN162 H5

87.24 Modern Language Association. *Professional Standards and American Editions. A Response to Edmund Wilson.* N.Y., 1969.

87.25 Todd, William B. *Suppressed Commentaries on the Wiseian Forgeries. Addendum to an Enquiry.* Austin, Tex., 1969.
098.3   Z1024 C32 T6

87.26 Gottesman, Ronald, and Scott Bennett, eds. *Art and Error. Modern Textual Editing. Essays.* Bloomington, Ind., 1970.
808.02   PN162 G63

87.27 Thorpe, James E. *Principles of Textual Criticism.* San Marino, Calif., 1972.

14. Manuscripts

§88. Guides and Periodicals

88.1 Martin, Charles T. *The Record Interpreter. A Collection of Abbreviations, Latin Words and Names Used in English Historical Manuscripts and Records.* 2nd ed. London, 1910. (Orig. ed. 1892.) Rpt. 1935, 1949.
Z111 M23

88.2 Madan, Falconer. *Books in Manuscript. A Short Introduction to Their Study and Use. With a Chapter on Records.* 2nd ed. London, 1920. (Orig. ed. 1893.) Rpt. 1927; N.Y., 1969.
091   Z105 M17

88.3 Galbraith, Vivian H. *An Introduction to the Use of the Public Records.* London, 1934. Corrected rpt. 1952, 1963.
025.171   CD1043 G3

88.4 *Guide to the Records in the National Archives.* Washington, D.C., 1948.
353   CD3023 A46

88.5 Crick, Bernard R., and Miriam Alman, eds. *A Guide to Manuscripts Relating to America in Great Britain and Ireland.* London, 1961.
016.973   CD1048 U5 C7

88.6 Hamer, Philip M. *A Guide to Archives and Manuscripts in the United States. Compiled for the National Historical Publications Commission.* New Haven, 1961.
025.171   CD3022 A45

88.7 *Guide to the Contents of the Public Record Office.* 3 vols. London, 1963-68.
025.171   CD1043 A553

88.8 *Elsevier's Lexicon of Archive Terminology. French, English, German, Spanish, Italian, Dutch.* Amsterdam & N.Y., 1964.
025.171014   CD945 E4

88.9 Hepworth, Philip. *Archives and Manuscripts in Libraries.* 2nd ed. London, 1964. (Orig. ed. 1958.) Library Assoc. Pamphlet, 8.
025.171   Z5140 H4

88.10 Cappelli, Adriano. *Lexicon abbreviaturarum. Dizionario di abbreviature latine ed italiane.* 7th ed. Milan, 1967. (Orig. ed. 1899.)
471.8   Z111 C24

•

88.11 *Scriptorium. International Review of Manuscript Studies.* 1946- . 2/yr.
417.05   Z108 S35

88.12 *Manuscripts.* 1948- . 4/yr.
091.505   Z41 A2 A925

88.13 *Manuscripta.* 1954- . 3/yr.

88.14 *Quarendo. A Quarterly Journal from the Low Countries Devoted to Manuscripts and Printed Books.* 1971- .

§89. Handwriting

89.1 Wright, Andrew. *Court-Hand Restored. Or, the Student's Assistant in Reading Old Deeds, Charters, Records, etc.* 10th ed. by Charles J. Martin. London, 1912. (Orig. ed. 1776.) Rpt. N.Y., 1971.
Z113 W95

89.2 Johnson, Charles, and Hilary Jenkinson. *English Court Hand, A.D. 1066-1500. Illustrated Chiefly from the Public Records.* 2 vols. London, 1915. Rpt. N.Y., 1967.
421.7   Z115 E5 J6

89.3 Jenkinson, Hilary. *The Later Court Hands in England from the Fifteenth to the Seventeenth Century. Illustrated from the Common Paper of the Scriveners' Company of London, the English Writing Masters, and the Public Records.* Cambridge, 1927. Rpt. N.Y., 1968.
745.61   Z115 E5 J57

89.4 Tannenbaum, Samuel A. *The Handwriting of the Renaissance. Being the Development and Characteristics of the Script of Shakespeare's Time.* N.Y., 1930. Rpt. 1967.
421.7   Z113 T17

89.5 Judge, Cyril B. *Specimens of Sixteenth-Century English Handwriting Taken from Contemporary Public and Private Records.* Cambridge, Mass., 1935.
421.7   Z113 J91

89.6 Fairbank, Alfred, and Berthold Wolpe. *Renaissance Handwriting. An Anthology of Italic Scripts.* London, 1960.
417   Z115 I8 F3

89.7 Wright, Cyril E. *English Vernacular Hands from the Twelfth to the Fifteenth Centuries.* Oxford, 1960.
421.7   Z115 E5 W7

89.8 Denholm-Young, Noël. *Handwriting in England and Wales.* 2nd ed. Cardiff, 1964. (Orig. ed. 1954.)
417.7   Z115 E5 D45

89.9 Dawson, Giles E., and Laetitia Kennedy-Skipton. *Elizabethan Handwriting, 1500-1650. A Manual.* N.Y., 1966.
652.10942   Z43 D264

89.10 Hector, Leonard C. *The Handwriting of English Documents.* 2nd ed. London, 1966. (Orig. ed. 1958.)
421.7   Z115 E5 H4

89.11 Whalley, Joyce I. *English Handwriting, 1540-1853. An Illustrated Survey Based on Material in the National Art Library, Victoria and Albert Museum.* London, 1969.
745.61   Z43 W5

§90. Catalogues

90.1 Ricci, Seymour de. *Census of Medieval and Renaissance Manuscripts in the United States and Canada.* 3 vols. N.Y., 1935-40. Rpt. 1961. *Supplement.* Ed. Christopher U. Faye and William H. Bond. N.Y., 1962.
016.091   Z6620 U5 R5

90.2 Richardson, Ernest C. *A List of Printed Catalogues of Manuscript Books.* N.Y., 1935. Rpt. as *Union World Catalog of Manuscript Books, Vol. 3.* N.Y., 1968.
016.016091   Z6601 A1 R4   ·

90.3 *British Manuscripts Project. A Checklist of the Microfilms Prepared in England and Wales for the American Council of Learned Societies, 1941-1945.* Ed. Lester K. Born. Washington, D.C.: Library of Congress, 1955.
016.025179   Z6620 G7 U5

90.4 Ker, Neil R. *Catalogue of Manuscripts Containing Anglo-Saxon.* London, 1957.
016.829   Z6605 A56 K4

90.5 *American Literary Manuscripts. A Checklist of Holdings in Academic, Historical, and Public Libraries in the United States. Compiled and Published Under the Auspices of the American Literature*

Group, Modern Language Association of America. . . Austin, Tex. 1960. Rpt., 1971. New edition in progress.
016.81   Z6620 U5 M6

90.6 Ker, Neil R. *English Manuscripts in the Century After the Norman Conquest.* Oxford, 1960.
421.7   Z115 E5 K4

90.7 *The National Union Catalog of Manuscript Collections. Based on Reports from American Repositories of Manuscripts.* 1962- . Vol. for 1959-61, Ann Arbor; 1962, Hamden, Conn.; 1963-64, Washington, D.C. Now an annual issued by the Library of Congress.
Z6620 U5 N3

90.8 Ker, Neil R. *Medieval Manuscripts in British Libraries.* Vol. I, *London.* Oxford, 1969- .
011   Z6620 G7 K4

90.9 Sinclair, Keith V. *Descriptive Catalogue of Medieval and Renaissance Western Manuscripts in Australia.* Sydney, 1969.
016.091   Z6620 A8 S55

●

90.10 Aberdeen University Library. *A Catalogue of the Medieval Manuscripts* . . . Ed. Montague R. James. Cambridge, 1932.
016.091   Z6621 A13

90.11 Bodleian Library. Oxford. *A Summary Catalogue of Western Manuscripts* . . . Ed. Falconer Madan. 7 vols. Oxford, 1895-1953.
Z6621 O96 W4

90.12 British Museum. *The Catalogues of the Manuscript Collection.* Rev. ed. by Theodore C. Skeat. London, 1962. (Orig. ed. 1951.)
016.091   Z6621 B844

● British Museum. *Catalogue of Manuscripts.* London.
    90.13 *Arundel* and *Burney.* Ed. Josiah Forshall. 3 vols. 1834-41.
    90.14 *Cottonian Library.* Ed. Joseph Planta. 1802.
    90.15 *Harleian.* 4 vols. 1808-12.
    90.16 *Landsdowne.* Ed. Francis Douce and Henry Ellis. 1819.
    90.17 *Stowe.* 2 vols. 1895-96.
    Z6621 B85

90.18 British Museum. *Catalogue of Additions to the Manuscripts in the British Museum in the Years* [*1783-1935*]. 20 vols. London, 1850- . (Orig. ed. for 1841-45 by Frederic Madden, 5 vols., 1850, rpt. 1964.)
016.091   Z6621 B842

90.19 British Museum. *Catalogue of Romances in the Department of Manuscripts* . . . 3 vols. London, 1883-1910. Rpt. 1961-63.
Z6621 B87 R7

● Cambridge University. *A Descriptive Catalogue of the Manuscripts-* . . . Ed. Montague R. James. Cambridge.

90.20 *Christ's College.* 1905.

90.21 *Clare College.* 1905.

90.22 *Corpus Christi College.* 2 vols. 1909-12.

90.23 *Emanuel College.* 1904.

90.24 *Fitzwilliam Museum.* 1895.

90.25 *Gonville and Gaius College.* 3 vols. 1907-14.

90.26 *Jesus College.* 1895.

90.27 *King's College.* 1895.

90.28 *McClean Collection.* 1912.

90.29 *Magdalene College.* 1909.

90.30 *Pembroke College.* 1905.

90.31 *Peterhouse.* 1899.

90.32 *Queen's College.* 1905.

90.33 *St. Catharine's College.* 1925.

90.34 *St. John's College.* 1913.

90.35 *Sidney Sussex College.* 1895.

90.36 *Trinity Hall.* 1907.
016.091   Z6621 C174 C-T

90.37 Columbia University. *Manuscript Collections in the Columbia University Libraries. A Descriptive List.* N.Y., 1959.
016.091   Z6621 N48

90.38 Edinburgh University Library. *Index to Manuscripts.* Ed. L. W. Sharp and C. P. Finlayson. 2 vols. Boston, 1964.

90.39 Edinburgh University Library. *A Descriptive Catalogue of the Western Mediaeval Manuscripts in Edinburgh University Library.* Ed. Catherine R. Borland. Edinburgh, 1916.
Z6621 E23

90.40 Eton College. *Descriptive Catalogue of the Manuscripts* . . . Ed. Montague R. James. Cambridge, 1895.
Z6621 E85 J2

90.41 Folger Shakespeare Library. Washington, D.C. *Catalog of Manuscripts.* 3 vols. Boston, 1971.

90.42 John Rylands Library. Manchester. *Catalogue of Printed Books and Manuscripts* . . . Ed. Edward G. Duff. 3 vols. Manchester, 1899.
Z921 M18

90.43 Lambeth Palace. *A Descriptive Catalogue of the Manuscripts in the Library of Lambeth Palace.* Ed. Montague R. James. Cambridge, 1932.
016.091   Z6621 L82 J

90.44 National Library of Scotland. *Catalogue of Manuscripts Acquired Since 1925.* 3 vols. Edinburgh, 1938-68.
016.091   Z6621 E192

90.45 New York Public Library. *Dictionary Catalogue of the Manuscript Division, the New York Public Library, Research Libraries.* 2 vols. Boston, 1967.
091.1   Z6621 N5518

90.46 Oxford University. *Catalogue of the Manuscripts of Balliol College, Oxford.* Ed. Roger A. B. Mynors. Oxford, 1963.
016.091   Z6621 O92

90.47 University of Pennsylvania Library. *Catalogue of Manuscripts- . . . to 1800.* Philadelphia, 1965.
018.1   Z6621 P44

15. Publishing and the Book Trade

§91. Historical and General Studies

91.1 *Penrose Annual. Review of the Graphic Arts.* 1895- .
TR925 P4

91.2 *American Book Trade Directory. Lists of Publishers and Book-sellers.* N.Y., 1915- . Biennial.
658.809001552   Z475 A5

91.3 *Books and Bookmen.* 1955- . 12/yr.
Z2005 B62

91.4 *Private Press Books.* 1960- . Annual.
015   Z1028 P7

91.5 *Small Press Review.* 1967- . 4/yr.

●

91.6 McMurtrie, Douglas C. *The Invention of Printing. A Bibliography.* Chicago, 1942. Rpt. N.Y., 1962.
016.65511   Z117 M18

●

91.7 Duff, Edward G. *The Printers, Stationers, and Bookbinders of Westminster and London from 1476 to 1535.* Cambridge, 1906. Rpt. N.Y., 1971.
338.4707050942   Z151.2 D85

91.8 Plomer, Henry R. *A Dictionary of the Booksellers and Printers Who Were at Work in England, Scotland and Ireland from 1641 to 1667.* London, 1907. Rpt. 1968.
655.00942   Z151 D52
. . . *Printers and Booksellers . . . 1668 to 1725.* London, 1922. Rpt. 1968.
655.00942   Z151 D53
. . . *Printers and Booksellers . . . 1726 to 1775.* London, 1932. Rpt. 1968.
655.00942   Z151 D54

91.9 McKerrow, Ronald B., et al. *A Dictionary of Printers and Booksellers in England, Scotland, and Ireland, and of Foreign Printers of English Books, 1557-1640.* London, 1910. Rpt. 1968. Bibliographical Society Monograph, 13.
655.0942   Z151 D51

91.10 Sadleir, Michael. *Excursions in Victorian Bibliography.* London, 1922.
Z2013 S12

91.11 Peddie, Robert A., ed. *Printing. A Short History of the Art.* London, 1927.
Z124 P375

91.12 Simpson, Percy. *Proof-Reading in the Sixteenth, Seventeenth, and Eighteenth Centuries.* London, 1935. Rpt. with New Fwd., 1970.
686.2255   Z254 S625

91.13 Blakey, Dorothy. *The Minerva Press, 1790-1820.* Oxford, 1939.
655.4421   Z232 M66 B6

91.14 Aldis, Harry G. *The Printed Book. Revised and Brought Up to Date by John Carter and Brooke Crutchley.* 3rd ed. Cambridge, 1951. (Orig. ed. 1916.)
655.1   Z4 A63

91.15 Lehmann-Haupt, Hellmut. *The Book in America. A History of the Making and Selling of Books in the United States.* 2nd ed. N.Y., 1951. (Orig. ed. 1939.)
655.473   Z473 L522

91.16 Mumby, Frank A. *Publishing and Bookselling. A History from the Earliest Times to the Present Day.* 4th ed. London, 1956. (Orig. ed. 1910 as *The Romance of Book Selling.* Rpt. Metuchen, N.J., 1967.)
655.442   Z323 M95

91.17 Blagden, Cyprian. *The Stationers' Company. A History, 1403-1959.* London & Cambridge, Mass., 1960.
655.44212   Z329 S79 B5

91.18 Gettmann, Royal A. *A Victorian Publisher. A Study of the Bentley Papers.* Cambridge, 1960.
655.4421   Z325 B45 G4

91.19 Harman, Eleanor, ed. *The University as Publisher.* Toronto, 1961.
655.409713541   Z483 T6 H3

91.20 Sutton, Walter E. *The Western Book Trade. Cincinnati as a Nineteenth-Century Publishing and Book-Trade Center. Containing a Directory of Cincinnati Publishers, Booksellers, and Members of Allied Trades, 1796-1880, and a Bibliography.* Columbus, O., 1961.
655.477178   Z473 S93

91.21 Barnes, James J. *Free Trade in Books. A Study of the London Book Trade Since 1800.* Oxford, 1964.
655.442   Z323 B35

91.22 Plant, Marjorie. *The English Book Trade. An Economic History of the Making and Sale of Books.* 2nd ed. London, 1965. (Orig. ed. 1939.)
655.00942   Z151 P67

91.23 Bingley, Clive. *Book Publishing Practice.* London & Hamden, Conn., 1966.
655.442   Z278 B5

91.24 McKenzie, Donald F. *The Cambridge University Press, 1696-1712. A Bibliographical Study.* 2 vols. Cambridge, 1966.
655.44259   Z325 C26 M3

91.25 Grannis, Chandler B. *What Happens in Book Publishing.* 2nd ed. N.Y., 1967. (Orig. ed. 1957.)
655.473   Z471 G7

91.26 Hawes, Gene R. *To Advance Knowledge. A Handbook on American University Press Publishing.* N.Y., 1967.
655.594   Z231.5 U6 H3

91.27 Franklin, Colin. *The Private Presses.* London & Chester Springs, Pa., 1969.
094.1 / 655   Z231.5 P7 F7

91.28 Bennett, Henry S. *English Books and Readers, 1475 to 1557. Being a Study in the History of the Book Trade from Caxton to the Incorporation of the Stationers' Company.* 2nd ed. Cambridge, 1969. (Orig. ed. 1952.)
658.809655573   Z151 B4

91.29 ——. *. . . 1558-1603. . . . in the Reign of Elizabeth I.* Cambridge, 1965.
655.442   Z151.3 B4

91.30 ——. *. . . 1603-1640. . . . in the Reigns of James I and Charles I.* Cambridge, 1970.
338.476555730942   Z151.4 B45

91.31 Humanities Research Council of Canada. *Guide to Scholarly Publishing in Canada.* Ottawa, 1971.

§92. Incunabula

92.1 Duff, Edward G. *Early English Printing. A Series of Facsimiles of All the Types Used in England During the XVth Century, with Some of Those Used in the Printing of English Books Abroad.* London, 1896. Rpt. N.Y., 1970.
686.20942   Z151.2 D84

92.2 Peddie, Robert A. *Fifteenth-Century Books. A Guide to Their Identification. With a List of the Latin Names of Towns and an Extensive Bibliography of the Subject.* London, 1913. Rpt. N.Y., 1969.
016.016093   Z240 A1 P4

92.3 Stillwell, Margaret B. *Incunabula and Americana, 1450-1800. A Key to Bibliographical Study.* N.Y., 1930. Rpt. 1961.
093   Z240 A1 S8

92.4 Peddie, Robert A. *Place Names in Imprints. An Index to the Latin and Other Forms Used on Title Pages.* London, 1932. Rpt. Detroit, 1968; N.Y., 1970.
929.4   Z125 P37

92.5 Bühler, Curt F. *The Fifteenth-Century Book. The Scribes, the Printers, the Decorators.* Philadelphia, 1960.
093   Z240 B924

92.6 Besterman, Theodore. *Early Printed Books to the End of the Sixteenth Century. A Bibliography of Bibliographies.* 2nd ed. N.Y., 1961. (Orig. ed. London, 1940.) Rpt. 1969.
016.016093   Z1002 B562

92.7 Goff, Frederick R. *Incunabula in American Libraries. A Third Census of Fifteenth-Century Books Recorded in North American Collections.* N.Y., 1964. (1st Census, 1919, ed. George P. Winship.)
016.093   Z240 G58

92.8 Scholderer, Victor. *Fifty Essays in Fifteenth- and Sixteenth-Century Bibliography.* Ed. Dennis E. Rhodes. Amsterdam, 1966.
093   Z1005 S374

92.9 Heilbronner, Walter L. *Printing and the Book in Fifteenth-Century England. A Bibliographical Survey.* Charlottesville, Va., 1967.
016.655142   Z151.2 H4

§93. National and Book Trade Bibliography: Great Britain, Australia, New Zealand, and India

93.1 Growoll, Adolf. *Three Centuries of English Booktrade Bibliography. An Essay on the Beginnings of Booktrade Bibliography Since the Introduction of Printing and in England since 1595. Also a List of the Catalogues, etc., Published for the English Booktrade from 1595-1902, by Wilberforce Eames.* N.Y., 1903. Rpt. London, 1964.
Z2001 A1 G8

93.2 Conover, Helen F. *Current National Bibliographies.* Washington, D.C.; Library of Congress, 1955. Rpt. N.Y., 1968.
016.015   Z1002 A2 U583

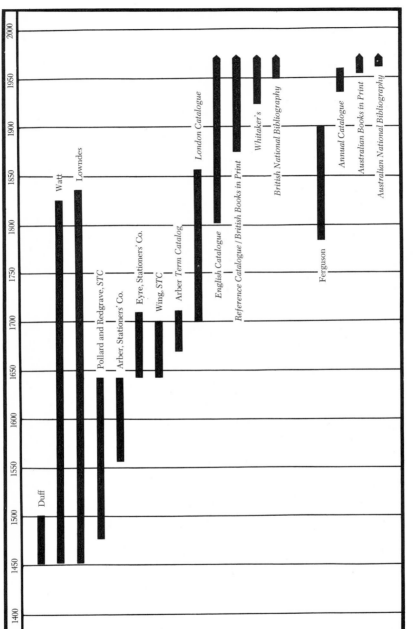

National and book trade bibliography, retrospective and current:
Great Britain and Australia.

93.3 Linder, LeRoy H. *The Rise of Current Complete National Bibliography*. N.Y., 1959.
015   Z1001.3 L5

•

93.4 Duff, Edward G. *Fifteenth Century English Books. A Bibliography of Books and Documents Printed in England and of Books for the English Market Printed Abroad.* London, 1917.
Z240 D852

93.5 Watt, Robert. *Bibliotheca Britannica. Or, a General Index to British and Foreign Literature.* 4 vols. Edinburgh, 1824. Rpt. N.Y., 1965.
011   Z2001 W34

93.6 Lowndes, William T. *The Bibliographer's Manual of English Literature. Containing an Account of Rare, Curious, and Useful Books, Published in or Relating to Great Britain and Ireland, from the Invention of Printing, with Bibliographical and Critical Notices . . .* New ed. 6 vols. London, 1865. (Orig. ed. 1834 in 4 vols.) Rpt. Detroit, 1967, in 8 vols.
015.42   Z2001 L92

93.7 British Museum. *Catalogue of Books Printed in the Fifteenth Century Now in the British Museum.* Ed. Alfred W. Pollard, Victor Scholderer, and George D. Painter. London, 1908-
016.093   Z240 B85

93.8 Faye, Christopher U. *Fifteenth Century Printed Books at the University of Illinois.* Urbana, Ill., 1949.
016.093   Z240 F32

93.9 British Museum. *The Short-Title Catalogue of Books Printed in the German-Speaking Countries and German Books Printed in Other Countries from 1455 to 1600 Now in the British Museum.* London, 1962.
015.43   Z2222 B73

93.10 British Museum. *Short-Title Catalogue of Books Printed in the Netherlands and Belgium and of Dutch and Flemish Books Printed in Other Countries from 1470 to 1600 Now in the British Museum.* Ed. Alfred F. Johnson and Victor Scholderer. London, 1965.
015.492   Z2402 B7

93.11 London. Guildhall Library. *A List of Books Printed in the British Isles and of English Books Printed Abroad Before 1701 in Guildhall Library.* 2 vols. London, 1966-67.
015.42   Z2002 L62

204 / *Publishing and the Book Trade*

93.12 Bibliographical Society. London. *Hand-Lists of Books Printed by London Printers, 1501-1556.* Ed. Edward G. Duff et al. London, 1913.
Z152 L8 B5

93.13 Maunsell, Andrew. *The First Part of the Catalogue of English Printed Books. Which concerneth such matters of Divinitie, as have bin either written in our owne Tongue, or translated out of anie other language: And have bin published . . .* London, 1595. Rpt. Farnborough, Eng., 1965.
Z2002 M3

93.14 Adams, Herbert M., ed. *Catalogue of Books Printed on the Continent of Europe, 1501-1600, in Cambridge Libraries.* 2 vols. London, 1967.
018.5   Z1014 A38

93.15 British Museum. *Catalogue of Books in the Library of the British Museum Printed in England, Scotland, and Ireland, and of Books in English Printed Abroad to the Year 1640.* Ed. George Bullen. 3 vols. London, 1884.
Z2002 B86

93.16 Cambridge University Library. *Early English Printed Books in the University Library, Cambridge (1475-1640).* Ed. Charles E. Sayle. 4 vols. Cambridge, 1900-1907. Rpt. N.Y., 1971.
015.42   Z2002 C172

93.17 Arber, Edward, ed. *A Transcript of the Registers of the Company of Stationers of London, 1554-1640.* 5 vols. London, 1875-77. Rpt. Birmingham, Eng., 1894; N.Y., 1950; Gloucester, Mass., 1967.
655.442   Z2002 L64

93.18 Greg, Walter W., ed. *A Companion to Arber. Being a Calendar of Documents . . . with Text and Calendar of Supplementary Documents.* Oxford, 1967.
655.42   Z151.3 G68

93.19 Greg, Walter W., and Eleanore Boswell. *Records of the Court of the Stationers' Company, 1576 to 1602, from Register B.* London, 1930.
655.142   Z329 S79

93.20 Jackson, William A. *Records of the Court of the Stationers' Company, 1602 to 1640.* London, 1957.
655.142   Z329 S79

93.21 John Rylands Library. Manchester. *Catalogue of Books in the John Rylands Library, Printed in England, Scotland, and Ireland,*

and of Books in English Printed Abroad to the End of the Year
1640. Ed. Edward G. Duff. Manchester, 1895.
Z2002 J65

93.22 Pollard, Alfred W., and Gilbert R. Redgrave. *A Short-Title Catalogue of Books Printed in England, Scotland, and Ireland, and of English Books Printed Abroad, 1475-1640.* London, 1926. Rpt. 1946, 1948, 1963, 1969. A new edition is in preparation. *a finding list*
015.42   Z2002 P77

93.23 Woodward, Gertrude L. *English Books and Books Printed in England Before 1641, in the Newberry Library. A Supplement to the Record in the Short Title Catalogue.* Chicago, 1939.
015.42   Z2012 N531

93.24 Morrison, Paul G. *Index of Printers, Publishers, and Booksellers in A. W. Pollard and G. R. Redgrave STC . . .* Charlottesville, Va., 1950.
015.42   Z2002 P77

93.25 Ramage, David, et al. *A Finding-List of English Books to 1640 in Libraries in the British Isles (Excluding the National Libraries and the Libraries of Oxford and Cambridge). Based on the Numbers in . . . STC 1475-1640.* Durham, Eng., 1958.
015.42   Z2002 P772 R3

93.26 Bishop, William W. *A Checklist of American Copies of "Short-Title Catalogue" Books.* 2nd ed. Ann Arbor, 1950. (Orig. ed. 1944.) Rpt. N. Y., 1968.
015.42   Z2002 P772 B5

93.27 Hazlitt, William C. *Hand-Book to the Popular, Poetical, and Dramatic Literature of Great Britain, from the Invention of Printing to the Restoration.* London, 1867. Rpt. N.Y., 1961.
Z2012 H3

93.28 Gray, George J., ed. *A General Index to Hazlitt's Handbook and His Bibliographical Collections, 1867-1889.* London, 1893. Rpt. N.Y., 1961.
Z2012 H35

93.29 [London, William]. *Catalogue of the Most Vendible Books in England Orderly and Alphabetically Digested.* London, 1657. *Supplement . . . till June the First 1658,* and *Catalogue . . . till Easter-Term 1660.* 1658-60. Rpt. in 1 vol., 1965.
015.42   Z2002 L67

93.30 British Museum. *Catalogue of the Pamphlets, Books, Newspapers, and Manuscripts Relating to the Civil War, the Commonwealth, and Restoration, Collected by George Thomason, 1640-1661.* 2 vols. London, 1908. Rpt. Nendeln, Liechtenstein, 1969.
Z2018 B85

93.31 Aldis, Harry G. *A List of Books Printed in Scotland Before 1700. Including Those Printed Furth of the Realm for Scottish Booksellers, with Brief Notes on Printers and Stationers.* Edinburgh, 1904. Rpt. N.Y., 1970. Pubs. Edin. Biblio. Soc., 7.
015.41   Z2051 A55

93.32 Hazlitt, William C. *Bibliographical Collections and Notes on Early English Literature, 1474-1700.* 4 series and 2 supp. London, 1876-1903. Rpt. N.Y., 1961.
Z2012 H33-37

93.33 Dix, Ernest R. *Catalogue of Early Dublin-Printed Books, 1601-1700. With an Historical Introduction and Bibliographical Notes by C. Winston Dugan.* 3 vols. Dublin, 1898-1912. Rpt. N.Y., 1971.
Z2032 D61

93.34 Clough, Eric A. *A Short-Title Catalogue Arranged Geographically of Books Printed and Distributed by Printers, Publishers and Booksellers in the English Provincial Towns and in Scotland and Ireland Up to and Including the Year 1700.* London, 1969.
015.42   Z2002 C62

93.35 Eyre, George E. B., ed. *A Transcript of the Registers of the Worshipful Company of Stationers from 1640 to 1708 A. D.* 3 vols. London, 1913-14. Rpt. N.Y., 1950, 1967.
655.442   Z2002 L653

93.36 Wing, Donald G. *Short-Title Catalogue of Books Printed in England, Scotland, Ireland, and Wales, and British America and of English Books Printed in Other Countries, 1641-1700.* 3 vols. N.Y., 1945-51.
015.42   Z2002 W5

93.37 Morrison, Paul G. *Index of Printers, Publishers, and Booksellers in Donald Wing's STC . . .* Charlottesville, Va., 1955.
015.42   Z2002 W5

93.38 Alden, John E. *Bibliographica Hibernica. Additions and Corrections to Wing.* Charlottesville, Va., 1955.
Z2032 A4

93.39 Hiscock, Walter G. *The Christ Church Supplement to Wing's Short-Title Catalogue, 1641-1700.* Oxford, 1956.
015.42   Z2002 W5 O9

93.40 Alden, John E. *Wing Addenda and Corrigenda. Some Notes on Materials in the British Museum.* Charlottesville, Va., 1958.
Z2002 P78 A43

93.41 Wolf, Edwin. *A Check-List of the Books in the Library Company of Philadelphia in and Supplementary to Wing's Short-Title Catalogue, 1641-1700.* Philadelphia, 1959.
Z2002 P78 W6

93.42 Wing, Donald G. *A Gallery of Ghosts. Books Published Between 1641-1700 Not Found in the Short-Title Catalogue.* N.Y., 1967.
015.42   Z2002 W5

93.43 Cameron, William J. *A Short-Title Catalogue of Books Printed in Britain and British Books Printed Abroad, 1641-1700, Held in Australian Libraries.* Sydney, 1962.
Z2002 C22

93.44 Cameron, William J., and Diana J. Carroll, eds. *Short-Title Catalogue of Books Printed in the British Isles, the British Colonies and the United States of America and of English Books Printed Elsewhere, 1701-1800, Held in the Libraries of the Australian Capital Territory.* 3 vols. Canberra, 1966-70.
018.109947   Z2002 C23

93.45 Arber, Edward. *The Term Catalogues, 1668-1709. A Contemporary Bibliography of English Literature in the Reigns of Charles II, James II, William and Mary, and Anne.* 3 vols. London, 1903-6. Rpt. N. Y., 1965.
Z2002 A31

93.46 [Clavell, Robert]. *A Catalogue of Books Printed in England Since the Dreadful Fire of London in 1666. To the end of Michaelmas term 1695* . . . 4th ed. London, 1696. Prev. eds. 1673, 1675, 1680-81. All eds. Rpt. Farnborough, Eng., 1965.
015.42   Z2001 C55

93.47 *Bibliotheca annua* [1699-1703]. *Or, the Annual Catalogues for the Year* . . . . *Being an Exact Catalogue of All English and Latin Books Printed in England* . . . 4 vols. London, 1700-1704. Rpt. in 2 vols., 1964.
015.42   Z2002 B52

93.48 [*Monthly Catalogue*, 1714-17. Ed. Bernard Lintott]. *A Catalogue of All Books, Sermons, and Pamphlets* . . . London, 1714-17. Rpt. 1964.
Z2005 M64

93.49 *Monthly Catalogue* [*1723-30*] *Containing an Exact Register of All Books, Sermons, Plays, Poetry, and Miscellaneous Pamphlets, Printed and Published in London, or the Universities* . . . *With a Compleat Index to the Whole.* London, 1725-29. Rpt. in 2 vols., 1964.
015.42   Z2002 M62

93.50 [*Monthly Chronicle*]. *A Register of Books, 1728-1732, Extracted from the Monthly Chronicle.* London, 1964.
016.82   Z2002 R4

93.51 *Gentleman's Magazine, 1731-51. The Lists of Books, Collected with Annual Indexes and the Index to the First Twenty Years Compiled by Edward Kimber (1752).* London, 1966.
015.42   Z2002 K5

93.52 [*London Magazine,* 1732-66]. *The Monthly Catalogues from The London Magazine, 1732-66, with the Index for 1732-58, Compiled by Edward Kimber.* London, 1966.
015.42   Z2002 M64

93.53 *The Annual Catalogue. Or, a New and Compleat List of All the New Books, New Editions of Books, Pamphlets, etc., Published . . .* 2 vols. London, 1737-38. Rpt. in 1 vol. 1965.
015.42   Z2002 A55

93.54 [*British Magazine*]. *The Lists of Books from the British Magazine, 1746-50, Collected with Annual Indexes.* London, 1965.
015.42   Z2001 B73

93.55 Wiles, Roy McK. *Serial Publication in England Before 1750.* Cambridge, 1957. Includes "Short-Title Catalogue of Books Published in Fascicules Before 1750."
655.5   Z323 W5

93.56 *The London Catalogue of Books in All Languages . . . Since 1700.* London, 1800. Prev. eds. 1773, 1786, 1791, 1799.
Z2001 E5

93.57 *The London Catalogue of Books . . .* [1800-1844]. 8 issues plus supplement. London, 1811-44.
Z2001 E5

93.58 *The London Catalogue of Books Published in Great Britain. With Their Sizes, Prices, and Publishers' Names. From 1814 to 1855.* London, 1855. Prev. eds. 1846, 1849, 1851, 1855.
Z2001 E5

93.59 Peddie, Robert A., and Quintin Waddington. *The English Catalogue of Books (Including the Original 'London' Catalogue). Giving in One Alphabet, Under Author, Title and Subject, the Size, Price, Month and Year of Publication, and Publisher of Books Issued in the United Kingdom of Great Britain and Ireland, 1801-1836.* London, 1914. Rpt. N.Y., 1963.
Z2001 E517

93.60 *The English Catalogue of Books Published, 1801-1951.* 16 vols. London, 1864-1952. Rpt. N.Y., 1963.
Z2001 E52

93.61 *English Catalogue of Books. Being a Continuation of the "London" and "British" Catalogues, with the Publications of Learned and Other Societies . . .* 1835- . Annual. Rpt. covering 1835-1965 in 20 vols., N.Y., 1963.
015.42   Z2001 E52

93.62 [Low, Sampson]. *The British Catalogue of Books Published from October 1837 to December 1852. Containing the Date of Publication, Size, Price, Publisher's Name, and Edition.* London, 1853.
Z2001 E51

93.63 *Publisher. The Journal of the Publishing Industry.* 1837- . 52/yr. Until 1958 *Publishers' Circular and Booksellers' Record;* 1959-66 *British Books.*
655.5   Z2005 P97

93.64 *The Bookseller. The Organ of the Book Trade.* 1858- . 52/yr.
Z2005 W57

93.65 *Reference Catalogue of Current Literature. A National Inclusive Book-Reference Index of Books in Print and On Sale in the United Kingdom* . . . 1874-1961. Succeeded by *British Books in Print.*
015.42   Z2001 R33

93.66 Dobell, Bertram. *Catalogue of Books Printed for Private Circulation . . . Described and Annotated.* London, 1906. Rpt. Detroit, 1966.
011   Z1028 D63

93.67 *Whitaker's Cumulative Book List. The Complete List of All Books Published in the United Kingdom* . . . 1924- . 4/yr with annual and 5-yr cumulations.
015.42   Z2005 W59

93.68 *Books.* London. 1929-68. 12/yr.
010.5   Z1009 N28 B6

93.69 *British Book News. A Guide to Books Published in the Commonwealth and Empire.* 1940- . 12/yr.
016   Z1035 B838

93.70 *British National Bibliography.* 1950- . 52/yr with quarterly and annual cumulations. *Index 1950-54,* 1955; *1955-59,* 1961; *1960-64,* 1967. *Cumulated Subject Catalogue, 1951-54,* 2 vols., 1958; . . . *1955-59,* 3 vols., 1963; . . . *1960-64,* 3 vols., 1968. London.
015.42   Z2001 B75

93.71 *British Books in Print.* 1962- . Annual.
Z2001 R33

●

93.72 Ferguson, John A. *Bibliography of Australia [1784-1900].* 7 vols. Sydney, 1941-69.
016.994   Z4011 F47

93.73 Foxcroft, Albert B., ed. *The Australian Catalogue. A Reference Index to the Books and Periodicals Published and Still Current in the Commonwealth of Australia.* Melbourne, 1911. Rpt. London, 1961.
015.94   Z4011 F69

93.74 *Annual Catalogue of Australian Publications.* Canberra, 1936-
60. 25 vols.
Z4011 C22

93.75 *Books Published in Australia. List of Books Supplied to the
National Library, Canberra, Under the Provisions of the Copyright
Act.* 1946-60. 12/yr.
Z4011 C26

93.76 *Australian Books in Print.* 1956- . Annual. Formerly *Book-
buyers Reference Book.*
015.94   Z4011 B62/ A85

93.77 *Australian National Bibliography.* 1961- . 52/yr with monthly
and annual cumulations.
015   Z4015 A96

●

93.78 *New Zealand National Bibliography.* 1967- . 12/yr with annual
cumulations.
015

93.79 *New Zealand Books in Print.* Ed. Barbara Collie. 4th ed. Wellington & London, 1969. (Orig. ed. 1957.)
Z4101 N56

●

93.80 *Indian Books in Print, 1955-67. A Select Bibliography of English
Books Published in India.* Delhi, 1969.
015.54   Z3201 S52

§94. National and Book Trade Bibliography:
The United States and Canada

94.1 *A Catalogue of All the Books, Printed in the United States, with
the Prices, and Places Where Published, Annexed. Published by the
Booksellers in Boston.* Boston, 1804. (Z1215 C35). Rpt. in *Book-
Trade Bibliography in the United States in the Nineteenth Century,*
by Adolf Growoll. N.Y., 1898. Rpt. 1939, 1969.
015.73   Z473 G76

94.2 Evans, Charles. *American Bibliography. A Chronological Dictio-
nary of All Books, Pamphlets, and Periodical Publications Printed in
the United States of America from the Genesis of Printing in 1639
Down to and Including the Year 1800. With Bibliographical and
Biographical Notes.* Vol. 13 ed. Clifford K. Shipton; Vol. 14 ed.
Roger P. Bristol. 14 vols. Chicago & Worcester, Mass., 1903-59. Rpt.
N.Y., 1941-42, vols. 1-12.
015.73   Z1215 E923

94.3 *Checklist of Additions to Evans' American Bibliography in the Rare Book Division of the New York Public Library.* Comp. Lewis M. Stark and Maud D. Cole. N.Y., 1960.
015.73   Z1215 E95

94.4 Bristol, Roger P. *Index of Printers, Publishers, and Booksellers Indicated by Charles Evans in His "American Bibliography."* Charlottesville, Va., 1961.
015.73   Z1215 E9233

94.5 Bristol, Roger P. *Supplement to Evans' "American Bibliography."* Charlottesville, Va., 1970.
94.6 *Index* . . . Charlottesville, Va., 1971.
015.73   Z1215 E92334

94.7 Shipton, Clifford K., and James E. Mooney. *National Index of American Imprints Through 1800. The Short-Title Evans.* 2 vols. Barre, Mass., 1970.
015.73   Z1215 S495

94.8 Shaw, Ralph R., and Richard H. Shoemaker. *American Bibliography. A Preliminary Checklist, 1801 to 1819.* 22 vols. N.Y., 1958-66.
015.73   Z1215 S48

94.9 Shoemaker, Richard H. *A Checklist of American Imprints for 1820-1830.* 10 vols. (An 11th vol. is planned.) N.Y., 1964-71.
015.73   Z1215 S5

94.10 Sampson Low Co., London. *The American Catalogue of Books. Or, English Guide to American Literature, Giving the Full Title of Original Works Published in the United States Since the Year 1800. With Especial Reference to Works of Interest to Great Britain. With Prices at Which They May Be Obtained in London.* London, 1856.
Z1215 L91

94.11 Stevens, Henry. *Catalogue of the American Books in the Library of the British Museum at Christmas, MDCCCLVI.* London, 1866. Rpt. Nendeln, Liechtenstein, 1969.
Z1207 B862

94.12 Sabin, Joseph, et al. *Bibliotheca Americana. A Dictionary of Books Relating to America, from Its Discovery to the Present Time.* Completed by Robert W. Vail. 29 vols. N.Y., 1868-1936. Rpt. in 15 vols., 1936; in 2 vols., 1966.
015.73   Z1201 S22

94.13 Roorbach, Orville A. *Bibliotheca Americana. Catalogue of American Publications, Including Reprints and Original Works, from 1820 to 1852, Inclusive. Together with a List of Periodicals Published in the United States.* N. Y., 1852. *Supplements,* 1852-61. 3 vols., 1855-61. Rpt. in 4 vols. N. Y., 1939; Metuchen, N.J., 1967.
015.73   Z1215 A3

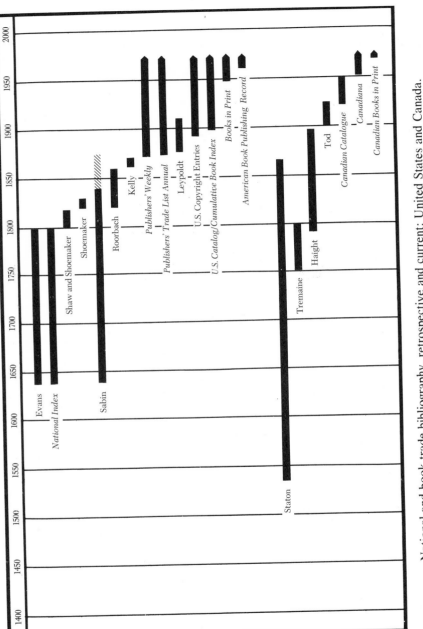

National and book trade bibliography, retrospective and current: United States and Canada.
(The dotted section of the Sabin bar indicates the reduced comprehensiveness for this period.)

94.14 Kelly, James. *The American Catalogue of Books (Original and Reprints) Published in the United States from Jan. 1861. to Jan. 1871.* 2 vols. N. Y., 1866-71. Rpt. in 1 vol. Metuchen, N.J., 1967.
015.73   Z1215 A3

94.15 *Publishers' Weekly. The Book Industry Journal.* 1872-   .
        Z1219 P98

✓**94.16** *Publishers' Trade List Annual.* 1873-   . 1971 ed. in 6 vols. A gathering of trade catalogues. Indexed since 1948 in *Books in Print* and since 1957 in *Subject Guide to Books in Print.*
015.73   Z1215 P97

94.17 Leypoldt, Frederick, et al. *The American Catalogue . . . Author and Title Entries of Books in Print and for Sale (Including Reprints and Importations), 1876-1910.* N.Y., 15 vols. Rpt. in 13 vols., 1941.
015.73   Z1215 A52

94.18 *Annual American Catalogue, 1886-1909.* 22 vols. N.Y., 1887-1911.
        Z1215 A7

94.19 U.S. Copyright Office. *Catalog of Copyright Entries.* New Series 1891-1946. Series 3. 1947-   . Pt. 1. *Books and Pamphlets, Including Serials and Contributions to Periodicals.* 2/yr.
        Z1219 U58 C

94.20 *United States Catalog. Books in Print January 1, 1928.* 4th ed. N.Y., 1928. Prev. eds. 1900, 1903, 1912.
        Z1215 U6

✓**94.21** *Cumulative Book Index. International Bibliography of Books Published in the English Language.* 1898-   . 11/yr with quarterly and annual cumulations. From 1928 to 1956 appeared also in 4-, 5-, or 6-yr cumulations as *Cumulative Book Index. A World List of Books in the English Language . . . Supplementing the United States Catalog Fourth Edition.*
        Z1219 M78/Z1215 U61

✓**94.22** *Books in Print. An Author-Title-Series Index to the Publishers' Trade List Annual.* 1948-   . Annual.
015.73   Z1215 P97

94.23 *Booklist. A Guide to Current Books.* 1905-   . 23/yr. In 1956 combined with *Subscription Books Bulletin* and had added title until 1969.
028.105   Z1035 A1 B65

94.24 *Paperbound Books in Print.* 1955-   . 12/yr with 2/yr cumulations.
016   Z1033 P3 P32

94.25 *American Book Publishing Record.* 1960-   . 12/yr with annual cumulation.
015   Z1219 A515

94.26 *BPR. Cumulative, 1960-1964. A Record of Book Production.*
4 vols. N.Y., 1968. . . . *1965-1969.* 5 vols. N.Y., 1970.
015.73   Z1201 A52

94.27 *Choice.* Amer. Library Assoc. 1964- . 11/yr.
Z1035 C5

●

94.28 *Books and Pamphlets Published in Canada Up to 1837, Copies of Which Are in the Public Reference Library, Toronto.* Ed. Frances M. Staton. Toronto, 1916. *Supplements,* 1919, 1926.
Z1365 T65

94.29 Staton, Frances M., and Marie Tremaine, eds. *A Bibliography of Canadiana. Being Items in the Public Library of Toronto, Canada, Relating to the Early History and Development of Canada.* Toronto, 1934. *Supplement.* Ed. Gertrude M. Boyle and Marjorie Colbeck, 1959.
016.971   Z1365 T64

94.30 Tremaine, Marie. *A Bibliography of Canadian Imprints, 1751-1800.* Toronto, 1952.
015.71   Z1365 T7

94.31 Haight, Willet R. *Canadian Catalogue of Books, 1791-1897.* 3 vols. Toronto, 1896-1904. Rpt. London, 1958.
015.71   Z1365 H16

94.32 Tod, Dorothea D., and Audrey Cordingley. *A Check-List of Canadian Imprints, 1900-1925.* Ottawa, 1950.
015.71   Z1365 T6

94.33 *The Canadian Catalogue of Books Published in Canada, About Canada, as Well as Those Written by Canadians, with Imprint, 1921-1949.* 1923-50. Annual. Rpt. in 2 vols., 1959.
015.71   Z1365 C222

94.34 *Canadiana. Publications of Canadian Interest Received by the National Library.* 1951- . 12/yr with annual cumulations.
015.71   Z1365 C23

94.35 *Quill and Quire. The Magazine of the Canadian Book Trade.* 1935- . 12/yr. Since 1960 "Canadian Booklist" in each issue, cumulated as *Books in Canada,* 2/yr.
655.505   Z487 Q8

94.36 *Canadian Books in Print.* 1967- . Annual.
015.71   Z1365 C2197

94.37 *Books in Canada.* 1971- . 18/yr.

16. Libraries

§95. Guides and Historical Studies

95.1 Downs, Robert B. *American Library Resources. A Bibliographical Guide.* Chicago, 1951. *Supplement, 1950-1961,* 1962.
016.016   Z1002 D6

95.2 *Bowker Annual of Library and Book Trade Information.* 1955- .
Until 1960 *American Library Annual.*
020.58   Z731 A47

95.3 Brummel, Leendert, and E. Egger. *Guide to Union Catalogues and International Loan Centers.* The Hague, 1961.
Z695.83 B68

95.4 Ash, Lee, and Denis Lorenz. *Subject Collections. A Guide to Special Book Collections and Subject Emphases as Reported by University, College, Public and Special Libraries in the United States and Canada.* 3rd ed. N.Y., 1967. (Orig. ed. 1958.)
026   Z688 A2 A8

95.5 *Aslib Directory.* [Association of Special Libraries and Information Bureaux.] 3rd ed. by Brian J. Wilson. 2 vols. London & N.Y., 1968-70. (Orig. ed. 1928.)
026.006242   Z791 A788

95.6 *Encyclopedia of Library and Information Service.* Ed. Allen Kent et al. N.Y., 1968- . 15 vols. planned.
020.3   Z1006 E57

95.7 Kruzas, Anthony T., ed. *Directory of Special Libraries and Information Centers.* 2nd ed. Detroit, 1968. (Orig. ed. 1963.)
026.000257   Z731 K7

95.8 Canadian Library Association. *Special Libraries and Information Centres in Canada. A Directory.* Rev. ed. by Beryl L. Anderson. Ottawa, 1970. (Preliminary ed. 1968.)
026.002571   Z673 C18515

95.9 Harrod, Leonard M. *The Librarians' Glossary. Terms Used in Librarianship and the Book Crafts.* 3rd ed. London, 1971. (Orig. ed. 1938.)
010.3   Z1006 H32

•

95.10 Streeter, Burnett H. *The Chained Library. A Survey of Four Centuries in the Evolution of the English Library.* London, 1931. Rpt. N.Y., 1970.
027   Z791 A1 S86

95.11 Burton, Margaret. *Famous Libraries of the World. Their History, Collections, and Administrations.* London, 1937.
027   Z721 B97

95.12 Esdaile, Arundell. *The British Museum Library. A Short History and Survey.* London, 1946.
027.542   Z792 B863 E8

95.13 Esdaile, Arundell. *National Libraries of the World. Their History, Administration, and Public Services.* 2nd ed. rev. by Francis J. Hill. London, 1957. (Orig. ed. 1934.)
027.5   Z721 E74

95.14 Oldman, Cecil B., et al. *English Libraries, 1800-1850.* London, 1958.
027.042   Z791 L8515

95.15 Wormald, Francis, and Cyril E. Wright, eds. *The English Library Before 1700. Studies in Its History.* London, 1958.
027.042   Z791 W7

95.16 Irwin, Raymond, and Ronald Staveley, eds. *The Libraries of London.* 2nd ed. London, 1961. (Orig. ed. by R. Irwin, 1949.) Corrected rpt., 1964.
027.0421   Z791 L852

95.17 Munby, Alan N. L. *Cambridge College Libraries.* 2nd ed. Cambridge, 1962. (Orig. ed. 1960.)
027.74259   Z792 M86

95.18 Ker, Neil R., ed. *Medieval Libraries of Great Britain. A List of Surviving Books.* 2nd ed. London, 1964. (Orig. ed. 1941.)
015.42   Z723 K47

95.19 English, Thomas H. *Roads to Research. Distinguished Library Collections of the Southeast.* Athens, Ga., 1968.
027.775   Z732 S92 E5

95.20 Wright, Louis B. *The Folger Library. Two Decades of Growth. An Informal Account.* Charlottesville, Va., 1968.
026.009753   Z733 W3 F555

95.21 Hobson, Anthony. *Great Libraries.* N.Y., 1970.
021.009   Z721 H66

§96. Periodicals

96.1 *Library Journal.* 1876- . 22/yr.
Z671 L7

96.2 *Bulletin of the New York Public Library, Astor, Lenox, and Tilden Foundations.* 1897- . 10/yr.
Z881 N6 B

96.3 *John Rylands Library Bulletin.* 1903- . 2/yr.
Z921 M18 B

96.4 *American Libraries. Bulletin of the American Library Association.* 1907- . 11/yr.
020.622   Z673 A5 B8

96.5 *Wilson Library Bulletin.* 1914- . 10/yr.
Z1217 W75

96.6 *Yale University Library Gazette.* 1926- . 4/yr.
Z733 Y17 G

96.7 *Library Quarterly. A Journal of Investigation and Discussion in the Field of Library Science.* 1931- .
020.5   Z671 L713

96.8 *Library Chronicle.* 1933- . 2/yr.
027.7748   Z733 P418

96.9 *Bodleian Library Record.* 1938- . 1 or 2/yr. Supersedes *Bodleian Quarterly Record,* 1914-38. 8 vols.
027.742   Z792 O94 B6

96.10 *Books at Brown.* 1938- . Irreg.
027.7745   Z733 P958 B6

96.11 *College and Research Libraries.* 1939- . 6/yr.
020.5   Z671 C6

96.12 *Princeton University Library Chronicle.* 1939- . 3/yr.
027.774967   Z733 P9 C5

96.13 *Colby Library Quarterly.* 1943- .
027.7741   Z881 W336

96.14 *Quarterly Journal of the Library of Congress.* 1943- .
027.5753   Z881 U5 Q3

96.15 *Newberry Library Bulletin.* 1944- . Irreg.
Z881 C524

96.16 *Journal of Documentation. Devoted to the Recording, Organization and Dissemination of Specialized Knowledge.* 1945- . 4/yr.
010.5   Z1007 J9

96.17 *University of Rochester Library Bulletin.* 1945- . 3/yr.
Z881 R676

96.18 *Harvard Library Bulletin.* 1947- . Suspended 1961-66. 4/yr.
027.7744   Z881 H3403

96.19 *American Society for Information Science Journal.* 1950- .
6/yr. Until 1969 *American Documentation.*

96.20 *Library Resources and Technical Services.* 1957- . 4/yr.
025.06273   Z671 L7154

96.21 *Private Library. Quarterly Journal of the Private Libraries Association.* 1957- .
                  Z990 P7

96.22 *RQ.* Reference Services Division. ALA. 1960- . 4/yr.

96.23 *Serif. Quarterly of the Kent State University Library.* 1964- .
                  Z671 S4

§97. Major Catalogues

97.1 British Museum. *General Catalogue of Printed Books.* 263 vols.
London, 1959-66. *Ten-Year Supplement, 1956-1965.* 50 vols. 1968.
Five-Year Supplement 1966-1970. Announced for 1971. *(Catalogue of
the Printed Books.* 95 vols. 1881-1900. *Supplement.* 15 vols. 1900-
1905. *General Catalogue . . .* 51 vols. Left incomplete, 1931-54.)
018.1   Z921 B87

97.2 London Library. *Catalogue of the London Library, St. James
Square, London.* 2nd ed. by Charles T. H. Wright and Christopher J.
Purnell. London, 1913-14. *Supplements, 1913-1950.* 3 vols. 1920-53.
          Z921 L6

●

The following two works in progress are superseding items 97.5
through 97.12.

97.3 *The National Union Catalog, Pre-1956 Imprints. A Cumulative
Author List Representing Library of Congress Printed Cards and
Titles Reported by Other American Libraries.* London, 1968- .
610 vols.
021.64   Z881 A1 U518

97.4 *The National Union Catalog: 1956-1967.* 120 vols. Totowa, N.J.,
1970-72.
018.10973   Z881 A1 U3742

97.5 *A Catalog of Books Represented by LC Printed Cards . . . to July
1942.* 167 vols. Ann Arbor, 1942-46. Rpt. 1949-50; N.Y., 1958, 1963,
1967.
          Z881 A1 C3

97.6 *Supplement: Aug. 1, 1942–Dec. 31, 1947.* 42 vols. Ann Arbor, 1948. Rpt. 1960, 1963, 1967.
Z881 A1 C312

97.7 [Second Supplement.] *LC Author Catalog. A Cumulative List . . . 1948-1952.* 24 vols. Ann Arbor, 1953. Rpt. N. Y., 1960, 1963, 1967.
018.1   Z881 U49 A2

97.8 *The National Union Catalog, 1952-1955 Imprints . . .* 30 vols. Ann Arbor, 1961.
018.1   Z881 A1 U374

97.9 *The National Union Catalog. A Cumulative Author List Representing LC Printed Cards and Titles Reported by Other American Libraries. Cumulation for 1953-57.* Union coverage 1956-57 only. 28 vols. Ann Arbor, 1958. Rpt. N. Y., 1961, 1966.
Z881 A1 U372

97.10 *The National Union Catalog . . . 1958-1962.* 54 vols. N.Y., 1963.
Z881 A1 U3722

The following work largely supersedes items 97.6 through 97.10.

97.11 *Library of Congress* [1942-1955] *and National Union Catalog* [1956-1962] *Author Lists, 1942-1962. A Master Cumulation.* 152 vols. Detroit, 1969-71.
Z881 A1 L63

97.12 *The National Union Catalog: Cumulation for 1963-67.* 72 vols. Ann Arbor, 1969.

97.13 *The National Union Catalog: Cumulation for 1968.* 12 vols. Washington, D.C., 1969.

97.14 *The National Union Catalog: Cumulation for 1969.* 13 vols. Washington D.C., 1970.

•

97.15 Crawford, James L., ed. *Bibliotheca Lindesiana. Catalogue of the Printed Books Preserved at Haigh Hall.* 4 vols. Aberdeen, 1910-13. Rpt. N.Y., 1970.
Z997 L739

97.16 Rothschild, Nathaniel M. V. *The Rothschild Library. A Catalogue of the Collection of Eighteenth-Century Printed Books and Manuscripts . . .* 2 vols. Cambridge, 1954. Rpt. London, 1969.
016.090942   Z997 R85

97.17 London University Library. *The Sterling Library. A Catalogue of the Printed Books and Literary Manuscripts Collected by Sir Louis Sterling and Presented by Him to the University of London.* Cambridge, 1954.
Z997 S83

97.18 British Museum. *The Lumley Library, the Catalogue of 1609.* Ed. Jayne Sears and Francis R. Johnson. London, 1956.
018.1   Z921 B898

97.19 New York Public Library. *Dictionary Catalog of the Henry W. and Albert A. Berg Collection of English and American Literature.* 5 vols. Boston, 1969.
016.82   Z2011 N55

97.20 Fales Library. New York University. *Fales Library Checklist.* Ed. Theodore Grieder. 2 vols. N.Y., 1970.
016.82303   Z2014 F5 F34

· **97.21** Folger Shakespeare Library. Washington, D. C. *Catalog of Printed Books.* 28 vols. Boston, 1970.

17. Special Topics

§98. Antiquarian Books

98.1 McKay, George L. *American Book Auction Catalogues, 1713-1934. A Union List.* N. Y., 1937. Rpt. Detroit, 1967, with Additions from *Bull. N.Y. Public Libr.*, 50 (1946), 177-84; 52 (1948), 401-12.
018.3 Z999 M15

• Munby, Alan N. L. *Phillipps Studies.* 5 vols. Cambridge, 1951-60.
98.2 I. *The Catalogues of Manuscripts and Printed Books of Sir Thomas Phillipps. Their Composition and Distribution.* 1951.
018.2 Z997 P553 M8

98.3 II. *The Family Affairs of Sir Thomas Phillipps.* 1952.
920.1 Z997 P553 M83

98.4 III & IV. *The Formation of the Phillipps Library.* 1954-56.
010 Z989 M77

98.5 V. *The Dispersal of the Phillipps Library.* 1960.
027.142 Z997 P553 M82

98.6 *The Bookman's Concise Dictionary.* Preface by F. C. Avis. London & N.Y., 1956.
010.3 Z1006 B59

98.7 Hertzberger, Menno. *Dictionary for the Antiquarian Booktrade in French, English, German, Swedish, Danish, Italian, Spanish, and Dutch.* Paris, 1956.
655.403 Z282 D5

98.8 Taylor, Archer. *Catalogues of Rare Books. A Chapter in Bibliographical History.* Lawrence, Kan., 1958.
016.09 Z721 T3

98.9 *Bookman's Glossary.* 4th ed. by Mary C. Turner. N.Y., 1961. (Orig. ed. 1925.)
010.3 Z1006 B6

98.10 Thompson, Anthony. *Vocabularium bibliothecarii. English, French, German, Spanish, Russian.* 2nd ed. Paris 1962. (Orig. ed. 1953.)
020.3   Z1006 T47

98.11 Carter, John. *ABC for Book-Collectors.* 4th ed. N.Y., 1966. (Orig. ed. 1951.) Rpt. 1970.
010.3   Z1006 C37

●

98.12 *Book-Auction Records. A Priced and Annotated Annual Record of London, New York, Montreal. Melbourne, Edinburgh and Glasgow Book-Auctions.* 1902-   . Subtitle and coverage varies.
017.3   Z1000 B65

98.13 *American Book Collector. A Monthly Magazine for Book Collectors.* Metuchen, N.J. 1931-35. 6 vols.
010.5   Z1007 A47

98.14 *AB Bookman's Weekly. For the Specialist Book World.* 1948-   .
Z999 A01 A5

98.15 *American Book Collector.* Chicago. 1950-   . 10/yr. Until 1955 *Amateur Book Collector.*
010.5   Z990 A5

98.16 *Directory of Dealers in Secondhand and Antiquarian Books in the British Isles.* 1951-   . Biennial.
655.5   Z327 D57

98.17 *Book Collector.* 1952-   . 4/yr.
010.5   Z990 B6

98.18 *Book Dealers in North America. A Directory of Dealers in Secondhand and Antiquarian Books in Canada and the United States of America.* London, 1954-   . Biennial.
655.47   Z475 B63

98.19 *Bookman's Price Index. An Annual Guide to the Values of Rare and Other Out-of-Print Books.* 1965-   .
018   Z1000 B74

§99. Microforms and Reprints

99.1 *Union List of Microfilms. Philadelphia Bibliographical Center and Union Library Catalogue.* Rev. ed. Ann Arbor, 1951. (Orig. ed. 1942.) *Cumulation, 1949-1959.* 2 vols. Ann Arbor, 1961.
016.099   Z1033 M5 P5

99.2 *Guide to Microforms in Print.* 1961-   . Annual.
016.099   Z1033 M5 G8

99.3 *Subject Guide to Microforms in Print.* 1961- . Biennial.
016.099   Z1033 M5 S8

99.4 Tilton, Eva M., ed. *A Union List of Publications in Opaque Microforms.* 2nd ed. N.Y., 1964. (Orig. ed. 1959.)
016.099   Z1033 M5 T5

99.5 U. S. Library of Congress. *National Register of Microform Masters.* 1965- . Annual.
Z1003 M5 N3

99.6 Hawken, William R. *Copying Methods Manual.* Chicago, 1966. Libr. Technology Pubs., 11.
655.3   Z48 H32

99.7 *Guide to Reprints.* 1967- . Annual.
011   Z1000.5 G8

99.8 *Newspapers on Microfilm.* 6th ed. Washington, D.C., 1967.
Z6945 U5 N43

99.9 *Announced Reprints.* 1969- . 4/yr.
016.655573   Z265 A55

99.10 Williams, Sam, ed. *Reprints in Print. Serials.* New ed. Dobbs Ferry, N.Y., 1970. (Orig. ed. 1967.)
011   Z1033 S5 W55

§100. Computers

100.1 *Computers and the Humanities.* 1966- . 5/yr. Annual bibliography.

100.2 *Computer Studies in the Humanities and Verbal Behavior.* 1968- . 4/yr.

100.3 *Hephaistos. A Quarterly Devoted to Computer Research in the Humanities.* 1970- .

•

100.4 Literary Data Processing Conference. *Proceedings, Sept. 9, 10, 11–1964. Yorktown Heights, N.Y.* Ed. Jess B. Bessinger. White Plains, N.Y., 1965.
P98 L57

100.5 Glickman, Robert J., and Gerrit J. Staalman. *Manual for the Printing of Literary Texts and Concordances by Computers.* Toronto, 1966.
655.28   Z253.3 G55

100.6 Bowles, Edmund A., ed. *Computers in Humanistic Research. Readings and Perspectives.* Englewood Cliffs, N.J., 1967.
001.3   AZ105 B6

100.7 Pritchard, Alan. *A Guide to Computer Literature. An Introductory Survey of the Sources of Information.* Hamden, Conn., 1969.
016.6518   Z6654 C17 P7

§101. Film and Records

101.1 *Variety. Films, Radio, Video, Music, Stage.* 1905- . 52/yr.
PN2000 V3

101.2 *Schwann Record and Tape Guide.* 1949- . 12/yr. Since 1969 spoken records and tapes are listed in semi-annual Supplementary Guide.
ML156.2 S385

●

101.3 National Council of Teachers of English. *The Motion Picture and the Teaching of English.* Ed. Marion C. Sheridan et al. N.Y., 1965.
791.43   PN1994 N32

101.4 *Literary Recordings. A Checklist of the Archive of Recorded Poetry and Literature in the Library of Congress.* Washington, D.C., 1966.
Z663.293 L5

101.5 Roach, Helen P. *Spoken Records.* 3rd ed. Metuchen, N.J., 1970. (Orig. ed. 1963.)
016.82   Z2011 R6

101.6 Enser, A. G. S. *Filmed Books and Plays. A List of Books and Plays from Which Films Have Been Made, 1928-1967. With a Supplementary List for 1968 and 1969.* Rev. ed. London, 1971. (Orig. ed. 1951.)
791.438   Z5784 M9 E55

101.7 Jinks, William. *The Celluloid Literature. Film in the Humanities.* Beverly Hills, Calif., 1971.
791.43   PN1994 J5

§102. Author-Audience Relationship

102.1 Collins, Arthur S. *Authorship in the Days of Johnson. Being a Study of the Relation between Author, Patron, Publisher and Public, 1726-1780.* London, 1928. Rpt. N.Y., 1970.
PN151 C6

102.2 Collins, Arthur S. *The Profession of Letters. A Study of the Relation of Author to Patron, Publisher, and Public, 1780-1832.* London, 1928. Rpt. N.Y., 1970.
PN151 C62

102.3 Cruse, Amy. *The Englishman and His Books in the Early Nineteenth Century.* N.Y., 1930. Rpt. 1968.
914.2033   PR457 C7

102.4 Leavis, Queenie D. *Fiction and the Reading Public.* London, 1932. Rpt. N.Y., 1965.
028.90942   PR821 L4

102.5 Cruse, Amy. *The Victorians and Their Reading.* Boston & London, 1935. Rpt. Boston, 1963. British title *The Victorians and Their Books.*
820.903   PR461 C7

102.6 Cruse, Amy, *After the Victorians.* London, 1938. Rpt. St. Clair Shores, Mich., 1971.
820.9008   PR461 C67

102.7 Mott, Frank L. *Golden Multitudes. The Story of Best Sellers in the United States.* N.Y., 1947. Rpt. 1960.
016   Z1033 B3 M6

102.8 Beljame, Alexandre. *Men of Letters and the English Public in the Eighteenth Century, 1660-1744.* Ed. Bonamy Dobrée. Trans. E. O. Lorimer from 1881 Fr. ed. London, 1948. Rpt. St. Clair Shores, Mich., 1971.
820.9004   PR441 B37

102.9 Hart, James D. *The Popular Book. A History of America's Literary Taste.* N.Y., 1950. Rpt. Berkeley, 1961.
028   Z1003 H328

102.10 Webb, Robert K. *The British Working Class Reader, 1790-1848. Literacy and Social Tension.* London, 1955.
331.8   HD8389 W42

102.11 Altick, Richard D. *The English Common Reader. A Social History of the Mass Reading Public, 1800-1900.* Chicago, 1957.
028.9   Z1003 A57

102.12 Hackett, Alice P. *Seventy Years of Best Sellers, 1895-1965.* N.Y., 1967.
655.473   Z1033 B3 H34

§103. Censorship

103.1 McCoy, Ralph E. *Freedom of the Press. An Annotated Bibliography.* Fwd. Robert B. Downs. Carbondale, Ill., 1968.
016.32344   KF4774 A1 M33

103.2 Meek, Oscar, ed. *Pornography, Obscenity and Censorship. A Selected Bibliography.* Santa Fe, N.M., 1969.
016.343740973   KF9444 A1 M4

•

103.3 *Newsletter on Intellectual Freedom.* 1952- . 6/yr.
Z671 N47

103.4 *Censorship. A Quarterly Report on Censorship of Ideas and the Arts.* London. 1964-67. 3 vols.
K3 E49

103.5 *Censorship Today.* 1968-70. 6/yr.
340   K3 E5

•

103.6 Fowell, Frank, and Frank Palmer. *Censorship in England.* London, 1913. Rpt. N.Y., 1969, 1970.
792.0942   PN2044 G6 F6

103.7 Ernst, Morris L., and William Seagle. *To the Pure. A Study of Obscenity and the Censor.* N.Y., 1928.
Z659 E72

103.8 Gillett, Charles R. *Burned Books. Neglected Chapters in British History and Literature.* 2 vols. N.Y., 1932. Rpt. Pt. Washington, N.Y., 1964.
098.1   Z1019 G47

103.9 Ould, Hermon, ed. *Writers in Freedom. A Symposium Based on the XVII International Congress of the P. E. N. Club, 1941.* London, 1941. Rpt. Pt. Washington, N.Y., 1970.
808.0668   PN131 I6

103.10 Craig, Alec. *Above All Liberties.* London, 1942. Rpt. N.Y., 1971.
098.120942   Z659 C87

103.11 Ould, Hermon, ed. *Freedom of Expression. A Symposium Based on the Conference Called by the London Centre of the International P. E. N. to Commemorate the Tercentenary of the Publications of Milton's Areopagitica: 22-26th August 1944.* London, 1944. Rpt. Pt. Washington, N.Y., 1970.
323.44   JC585 P2

103.12 McKeon, Richard P., et al. *The Freedom to Read. Perspective and Program.* N.Y., 1957.
323.445   Z657 M2

103.13 Paul, James C. N., and Murray L. Schwartz. *Federal Censorship. Obscenity in the Mail.* N.Y., 1961.
364.17   Z659 P3

103.14 Craig, Alec. *The Banned Books of England and Other Countries. A Study of the Conception of Literary Obscenity.* London, 1962. American title, *Suppressed Books*, Cleveland, 1963.
343.7

103.15 Hyde, Harford M. *History of Pornography.* London, 1964.
176.8   HQ458 H9

103.16 Bain, Kenneth B. [Richard Findlater, pseud.] *Banned! A Review of the Theatrical Censorship in Britain.* London, 1967.
301.152   KE B162b

103.17 Boyer, Paul S. *Purity in Print. The Vice-Society Movement and Book Censorship in America.* N.Y., 1968.
323.4450973   KF4775 B6

103.18 Hutchinson, Earl R. *"Tropic of Cancer" on Trial.* N.Y., 1968.
340   KF4775 H8

103.19 Rembar, Charles. *The End of Obscenity. The Trials of "Lady Chatterley," "Tropic of Cancer" and "Fanny Hill."* N.Y., 1968.
343.740973   KF9444 R4

103.20 Clor, Harry M. *Obscenity and Public Morality. Censorship in a Liberal Society.* Chicago, 1969.
343.740973   KF9444 C53

103.21 De Grazia, Edward. *Censorship Landmarks.* N.Y., 1969.
340   KF9444 A7 D4

103.22 Hewitt, Cecil R. *Books in the Dock.* London, 1969.
343.740942

103.23 Perrin, Noel. *Dr. Bowdler's Legacy. A History of Expurgated Books in England and America.* N.Y., 1969.
098   Z1019 P4

103.24 Thomas, Donald. *A Long Time Burning. A History of Literary Censorship in England.* London & N.Y., 1969.
340

103.25 Haight, Anne L. *Banned Books. Informal Notes on Some Books Banned for Various Reasons at Various Times and in Various Places.* 3rd ed. N.Y., 1970.
098.1   Z1019 H15

103.26 Hoyt, Olga G., and Edwin P. Hoyt. *Censorship in America.* N.Y., 1970.
301.154   KF4770 Z9 H6

103.27 Widmer, Eleanor J., ed. *Freedom and Culture. Literary Censorship in the 70's.* Belmont, Calif., 1970.
323.44   KF9444 A75 W5

18. Periodicals

§104. Bibliographies and Union Lists

104.1 *Tercentenary Handlist of English and Welsh Newspapers, Magazines and Reviews* [1620-1920]. London, 1920. Rpt. 1966.
016.052   Z6956 E5 T5

104.2 Crane, Ronald S., and Frederick B. Kaye. *A Census of British Newspapers and Periodicals, 1620-1800.* Chapel Hill, N.C., 1927. Rpt. N.Y., 1963; London, 1966.
016.072   Z6956 E5 C8

104.3 Tod, Dorothea D., and Audrey Cordingley. "A Bibliography of Canadian Literary Periodicals, 1789-1900." *Proc. & Trans. of the Royal Society of Canada,* 3rd Ser., 26, No. 2 (1932), 87-96.

104.4 Milford, Robert T., and Donald M. Sutherland. *A Catalogue of English Newspapers and Periodicals in the Bodleian Library, 1622-1800.* Oxford, 1936. Rpt. Nendeln, Liechtenstein, 1969.
Z1008 098

104.5 Gregory, Winifred. *American Newspapers, 1821-1936. A Union List of Files Available in the United States and Canada.* N.Y., 1937. Rpt. 1967.
016.071   Z6945 A53

104.6 Weed, Katherine K., and Richmond P. Bond. *Studies of British Newspapers and Periodicals from Their Beginning to 1800. A Bibliography.* Chapel Hill, N.C., 1946. Studies in Philology; Extra Series, 2.
016.072   Z6956 E5 W4

104.7 Stewart, Powell. *British Newspapers and Periodicals, 1632-1800. A Descriptive Catalogue of a Collection at the University of Texas.* Austin, 1950.
016.052   Z6956 E5 S85

104.8 Ward, William S. *Index and Finding List of Serials Published in the British Isles, 1789-1832.* Lexington, Ky., 1953.
016.052   Z6956 E5 W27

104.9 *British Union-Catalogue of Periodicals. A Record of the Periodicals of the World, from the Seventeenth Century to the Present Day, in British Libraries.* Ed. James D. Stewart et al. London, 1955-58, 4 vols. *Supplement to 1960,* 1962. Rpt. Hamden, Conn., 1968.
016.05   Z6945 B7

   104.10 British Union Catalogue of Periodicals. *New Periodical Titles.* 1964-   . 4/yr. with annual cumulation.
016.05   Z6945 B874

   Cumulation, 1960-1968, 1970.
016.05   Z7043 W9

104.11 Goggio, Emilio, et al. *A Bibliography of Canadian Cultural Periodicals (English and French from Colonial Times to 1950) in Canadian Libraries.* Toronto, 1955.
016.051   Z1369 G6

104.12 British Museum. *Periodical Publications.* Vols. 184-86 of *General Catalogue.* London, 1963.
018.1   Z921 B87

104.13 Goldwater, Walter. *Radical Periodicals in America, 1890-1950. A Bibliography with Brief Notes.* New Haven, 1964.
         Z7164 S67 G57

104.14 U. S. Library of Congress. *Union Lists of Serials. A Bibliography.* Ed. Ruth S. Freitag. Washington, D.C., 1964.
         Z6945 U5 U53

✔**104.15** *Union List of Serials in Libraries of the United States and Canada.* 3rd ed. by Edna B. Titus. 5 vols. N.Y., 1965. (Orig. ed. by Winifred Gregory, 1927.)
016.05   Z6945 U45

   ✔ **104.16** *New Serial Titles. A Union List of Serials Commencing Publication After December 31, 1949. [Supplement to the Union List of Serials Third Edition.]* 1953-   . 12/yr with quarterly, annual, and the following cumulations: *1950-1960,* 2 vols. Washington, D.C., 1961: *1961-1965,* 2 vols. N. Y., 1966; *1966-1969,* 2 vols., Washington, D.C., 1971.
016.05   Z6945 U5 S42

   104.17 *Subject Index to New Serial Titles, 1950-1965.* Ann Arbor, 1968.
016.5   Z6945 U5 S422

104.18 Paris. Bibliothèque Nationale. *Catalogue collectif des périodiques du début du XVIIe siècle à 1939, conservés dans les Biblio-*

230 / *Periodicals*

thèques des Paris et dans les Bibliothèques universitaires des Départements. Paris, 1967- . Vols. I & II in prep.; Vol. III, *J-Q,* 1967; Vol. IV, *R-Z,* 1969.
016.05   Z6945 P236

§105. Guides

105.1 Mullins, Edward L. C. *Texts and Calendars. An Analytical Guide to Serial Publications.* London, 1958. Royal Society Guides and Handbooks, 7.
016.942   Z2016 M8

105.2 *Index Bibliographicus. Directory of Current Periodical Abstracts and Bibliographies.* 4th ed. 4 vols. Paris, 1959- . Vol. I, *Science and Technology;* Vol. II, *Social Sciences;* Vol. III, *Humanities,* in prep.; Vol. IV, *General Bibliographies,* in prep. (Orig. ed. 1925.)
016.01   Z1002 I38

105.3 *International Guide to Literary and Art Periodicals.* 1960-61. Annual. Continued in *Trace.*
016.805   Z6941 I5

105.4 Toase, Mary, ed. *Guide to Current British Periodicals.* London, 1962.
016.052   Z6956 E5 T6

105.5 *Standard Periodicals Directory.* 1964- . Biennial.
016.051   Z6951 S78

105.6 *Directory of Published Proceedings.* Series SSH: Social Sciences/Humanities. 1968- . 4/yr with annual cumulated indexes.
        Z7409 D562

105.7 *International Directory of Back Issue Vendors. Periodicals, Newspapers/Newspaper Indexes, and Documents.* Ed. F. John Neverman. 2nd ed. N.Y., 1968. (Orig. ed. 1964.)
658.809655572025   Z286 P4 N4

105.8 Katz, William A., and Berry Gargal. *Magazines for Libraries. For the General Reader and Public, School, Junior College, and College Libraries.* N.Y., 1969.
016.05   Z6941 K2

105.9 Wall, C. Edward, ed. *Periodical Title Abbreviations.* Detroit, 1969.
050   Z6945 A2 W34

105.10 Gerstenberger, Donna, and George Hendrick. *Third Directory of Periodicals Publishing Articles on English and American Literature and Language.* Chicago, 1970. Prev. eds. 1959, 1965.
016.4205   Z2015 P4 G4

105.11 Levi, Doris J., and Nerissa L. Milton, eds. *Directory of Black Literary Magazines.* Washington, D.C., 1970.
016.051

105.12 Modern Language Association. *Directory of Journals and Series in the Humanities. A Data List of the Periodical Sources on the Master List of the MLA International Bibliography.* Ed. Harrison T. Meserole and Carolyn J. Bishop. N.Y., 1970.

✓ **105.13** *Irregular Serials and Annuals. An International Directory. A Classified Guide to Current Foreign and Domestic Serials, Excepting Periodicals Issued More Frequently Than Once a Year.* 2nd ed. Ed. Emery Koltay. N. Y., 1972. (Orig. ed. 1967.)
016.05   Z6941 I78

✓ **105.14** *Ulrich's International Periodicals Directory. A Classified Guide to a Selected List of Current Periodicals, Foreign and Domestic.* 2 vols. 14th ed. N. Y., 1971. (Orig. ed. 1932.) *1975- 76*
016.05   Z6941 U5

105.15 Woodworth, David. *Guide to Current British Journals.* London, 1971.
016.052   Z6956 G6 W66

§106. Historical Studies

106.1 Graham, Walter J. *The Beginnings of English Literary Periodicals. A Study of Periodical Literature, 1665-1715.* N.Y., 1926. Rpt. N.Y., 1971.
PN5124 P4 G7

106.2 Graham, Walter J. *English Literary Periodicals.* N.Y., 1930. Rpt. 1967.
820.5   PN5124 P4 G73

106.3 Mott, Frank L. *A History of American Magazines.* [1741-1930.] 4 vols. Cambridge, Mass., 1930-68.
051   PN4877 M63

106.4 Nesbitt, George L. *Benthamite Reviewing. The First Twelve Years of the Westminster Review, 1824-1836.* N.Y., 1934. Rpt. 1966.
052   PN5130 W45 N4

106.5 Thrall, Miriam M. *Rebellious Fraser's. Nol Yorke's Magazine in the Days of Maginn, Thackeray, and Charlyle.* N.Y., 1934. Rpt. 1966.
052   PN5130 F7 T5

106.6 Everett, Edwin M. *The Party of Humanity. The "Fortnightly Review" and Its Contributors, 1865-1874.* Chapel Hill, N.C., 1939. Rpt. N. Y., 1971.
052   PN5130 F6 E8

106.7 Marchand, Leslie A. *The Athenaeum. A Mirror of Victorian Culture.* Chapel Hill, N. C., 1941. Rpt. N.Y., 1971.
052   PN5130 A7 M3

106.8 Brigham, Clarence S. *History and Bibliography of American Newspapers, 1690-1820.* 2 vols. Worcester, Mass., 1947. *Supplement,* 1961.
016.071   Z6951 B86

106.9 Bauer, Josephine. *The London Magazine, 1820-29.* Copenhagen, 1953.
PN5130 L63 B3

106.10 Bond, Richmond P., ed. *Studies in the Early English Periodical.* Chapel Hill, N.C., 1957.
052   PN5116 B6

106.11 Clive, John L. *Scotch Reviewers. The Edinburgh Review, 1802-1815.* Cambridge, Mass. & London, 1957.
PN5140

106.12 Mott, Frank L. *American Journalism. A History, 1690-1960.* 3rd ed. N.Y., 1962. (Orig. ed. 1941.)
071.3   PN4855 M63

106.13 Peterson, Theodore B. *Magazines in the Twentieth Century.* 2nd ed. Urbana, Ill., 1964. (Orig. ed. 1956.)
051.09   PN4877 P4

106.14 Wiles, Roy McK. *Freshest Advices. Early Provincial Newspapers in England.* Columbus, O., 1965.
072.09   PN5115 W5

106.15 Bond, Richmond P. *The "Tatler." The Making of a Literary Journal.* Cambridge, Mass., 1971.
824.508   PR1365 T23 B6

§107. Indexes

107.1 Poole, William F., and William I. Fletcher. *Index to Periodical Literature, 1802-1881.* 2 vols. Rev. ed. Boston, 1882. *Supplements, 1882-1907.* 5 vols. 1888-1908. Rpt. N.Y., 1938, 1958.
AI3 P7

107.2 Bell, Marion V., and Jean C. Bacon. *Poole's Index, Date and Volume Key.* Chicago, 1957.
016.05   Z674 A75

107.3 Dearing, Vinton. *Transfer Vectors for Poole's Index to Periodical Literature.* I, Titles, Volumes, and Dates. Los Angeles, 1967-
AI3 P7

107.4 Wall, C. Edward, ed. *Cumulative Author Index to Poole's Index . . .* Ann Arbor, 1971.
050   AI3 W3

107.5 *Nineteenth Century Readers' Guide to Periodical Literature, 1890-1899. With Supplement Indexing, 1900-1922.* Ed. Helen G. Cushing and Adah V. Morris. 2 vols. N.Y., 1944.
050   AI3 R496

107.6 *Readers' Guide to Periodical Literature. An Author Subject Index to* [157] *Selected General Interest Periodicals of Reference Value in Libraries.* 1900-   . 22/yr.
          AI3 R48

107.7 *Annual Magazine Subject Index.* 1908-49. Rpt. as *Cumulated Magazine Subject Index, 1907-1949.* 43 vols. in 2. Boston, 1964.
          AI3 M26/ C76

107.8 *Internationale Bibliographie der Zeitschriftenliteratur . . . / International Bibliography of Periodical Literature Covering All Fields of Knowledge.* 1911-   . 2/yr.
          AI9 B7

107.9 *British Humanities Index.* 1962-   . 4/yr with annual cumulation. Continues *Subject Index to Periodicals,* 1916-61.
016.052   AI3 B7

107.10 *Canadian Periodical Index.* 1928-   . 12/yr with annual and 5-yr cumulations. Title 1948-63 *Canadian Index to Periodicals and Documentary Films.*
          AI3 C242

107.11 *America: History and Life. A Guide to Periodical Literature.* 1964-   . 4/yr.
016.917   Z1236 A48

107.12 Baer, Eleanora A. *Titles in Series. A Handbook for Librarians and Students.* 2nd ed. 2 vols. Washington, D. C., 1964. *Supplement,* Metuchen, N. J., 1967. *Second Supplement,* Metuchen, N.J., 1971.
011   AI3 B3

107.13 *Social Sciences and Humanities Index.* 1965-   . 4/yr with annual cumulation. Continues *International Index to Periodicals,* 1907-65.
          AI3 R49

107.14 *Wellesley Index to Victorian Periodicals, 1824-1900.* Ed. Walter E. Houghton. Toronto, 1966-   .
052   AI3 W45

107.15 *Catholic Periodical and Literature Index.* 1968-   . 6/yr with biennial cumulations. Combines *Catholic Periodical Index,* 1930-68, and *Guide to Catholic Literature,* 1888-1968.
051   AI3 C32

107.16 *Alternative Press Index. An Index to the Publications Which Amplify the Cry for Social Change and Social Justice.* 1969-   . 4/yr.
051.016   AI3 A27

107.17 Kujoth, Jean S. *Subject Guide to Periodical Indexes and Review Indexes.* Metuchen, N.J., 1969.
016.05   Z6293 K84

§108. General Periodicals

These are magazines aimed at the literate public. They often carry articles and book reviews of professional value to the student.

108.1 *Harper's Magazine.* 1850- . 12/yr.
AP2 H3

108.2 *Atlantic.* 1857- . 12/yr.
AP2 A8

108.3 *Catholic World.* 1865- . 12/yr.
AP2 C3

108.4 *Nation.* 1865- . 52/yr.
051   AP2 N2

108.5 *Contemporary Review. Incorporating the Fortnightly.* 1866- . 12/yr.
AP4 C7

108.6 *Christian Century. An Ecumenical Weekly.* 1884- .
BR1 C45

108.7 *New Statesman and Nation.* 1913- . 52/yr.
052   AP4 N64

108.8 *New Republic. A Journal of Politics and the Arts.* 1914- . 48/yr.
810.822   PS536 N4

108.9 *Manchester Guardian Weekly.* 1920- .
AP4 M25

108.10 *Commonweal. A Weekly Review of Public Affairs, Literature, and the Arts.* 1924- .
AP2 C6897

108.11 *Saturday Review.* 1924- . 52/yr. Until 1951 *Saturday Review of Literature.*
Z1219 S25

108.12 *New Yorker.* 1925- . 52/yr.
AP2 N6763

108.13 *Commentary.* 1945- . 12/yr.
296.05   DS101 C63

108.14 *National Review.* 1955- . 51/yr.
051   AP2 N3545

108.15 *Horizon.* New York. 1958- . 4/yr.
051   AP2 H788

§ 109. The Little Magazine

109.1 *Union List of Little Magazines. Showing Holdings of 1,037 Little Magazines in the Libraries of Indiana University, Northwestern University, Ohio State University, State University of Iowa, University of Chicago, and the University of Illinois.* Chicago, 1956.

109.2 *Index to American Little Magazines, 1920-1939.* Ed. Stephen H. Goode. Troy, N.Y., 1969.

109.3 *Index to Little Magazines, 1940-1942.* Ed. Stephen H. Goode. N.Y., 1967.

109.4 *Index . . . 1943-1947.* Ed. Stephen H. Goode. Denver, 1965.

109.5 *Index to Little Magazines.* 1948- . Annual to 1955; 3-yr cumulations 1949-52, 1953-55; 2-yr cumulations 1956- . *Earliest edition.*
051 / 805   AI3 I54

109.6 *Trace. A Chronicle of Living Literature, Comprising Annual Directories of (English Language) Poetry and Small Literary Magazines Appearing Throughout the World.* 1952-70. 3/yr.
PN2 T7

109.7 *Directory of Little Magazines and Small Presses.* 1965- . Annual.
Z6944 L5 D5

109.8 *Index to Commonwealth Little Magazines.* 1966- . Biennial.
016.052   AI3 I48

•

109.9 Hoffman, Frederick J., et al. *The Little Magazine. A History and a Bibliography.* Princeton, 1946. Rpt. N.Y., 1967.
052   PN4836 H6

109.10 Whittemore, Reed. *Little Magazines.* Minneapolis, 1963. Univ. of Minn. Pamphlets on Amer. Writers, 32.
051.09   PN4877 W45

109.11 *The Little Magazine and Contemporary Literature. A Symposium Held at the Library of Congress, 2-3 April 1965.* N.Y., 1966.
PN4888 L55 L5

•

109.12 *New Mexico Quarterly.* 1931-68. 38 vols.
AP2 N6168

109.13 *Western Review. A Literary Quarterly.* 1937-59. 23 vols.
051   AP2 W524

109.14 *Quarterly Review of Literature.* 1943- . 2 double nos./yr.
051   AP2 Q29

109.15 *Perspective. A Quarterly of Modern Literature.* 1947- .
810.5   AP2 P463

109.16 *Botteghe Oscure.* Rome. 1948-60. 25 vols. 2/yr.
PN6010 B6

109.17 *Epoch.* 1948- . Annual.
051   AP2 E68

109.18 *Beloit Poetry Journal.* 1950- . 4/yr.
PS301 B43

109.19 *Literary Review. An International Journal of Contemporary Writing.* 1957- . 4/yr.
051   AP2 L6377

109.20 *Prism International. A Journal of Contemporary Writing.* 1959- . 3/yr.
AP5 P67

109.21 *Transatlantic Review.* London & N.Y. 1959- . 4/yr.
051   AP1 T7

109.22 *Little Magazine.* 1965- . 4/yr. Until 1969 *Quest.*
AP2 Q43

109.23 *The Miscellany. A Davidson Review.* 1965- . 2/yr.

109.24 *Iowa Review.* 1970- . 4/yr.

§110. Reviews
A list of journals that combine creative, critical, and sometimes scholarly efforts.

110.1 *North American Review.* Old Series 1815-1940. New Series 1964- . 4/yr.
AP2 N83

110.2 *Cornhill Magazine.* 1860- . 4/yr.
AP4 C8

110.3 *Poet Lore. A National Quarterly of World Literature and the Drama.* 1889- .
PN2 P7

110.4 *Sewanee Review. America's Oldest Literary Quarterly.* 1892- .
AP2 S5

110.5 *Queen's Quarterly. A Canadian Review.* 1893- .
378.71372005   AP5 Q3

110.6 *Poetry.* 1912- . 11/yr.
PS301 P6

110.7 *Southwest Review.* 1915- . 4/yr. Until 1924 *Texas Review.*
051   AP2 S883

110.8 *Dalhousie Review.* 1921- . 4/yr.
AP5 D3

110.9 *Virginia Quarterly Review. A National Journal of Literature and Discussion.* 1925- .
051 AP2 V76

110.10 *Prairie Schooner.* 1927- . 4/yr.
051 AP2 P85285

110.11 *Soviet Literature.* 1931- . 12/yr. Until 1945 *International Literature.*

110.12 *Partisan Review.* 1934- . 4/yr.
335.05 HX1 P3

110.13 *University Review.* 1934- . 4/yr. Until 1963 *Univ. of Kansas City Review.*
AP2 U735

110.14 *American Prefaces. A Journal of Critical and Imaginative Writing.* 1935-43. 8 vols.
051 AP2 A3977

110.15 *Southern Review.* 1935-42. 7 vols. New Series 1965- . 4/yr.
051 AP2 S8555

110.16 *Kenyon Review.* 1939-70. 32 vols. 4/yr.
051 AP2 K426

110.17 *Accent. A Quarterly of New Literature.* 1940-60. 20 vols.
051 AP2 A243

110.18 *Horizon. A Review of Literature and Art.* 1940-50. 4/yr.
052 AP4 H88

110.19 *Phylon. The Atlanta University Review of Race and Culture.* 1940- . 4/yr.
325.260973 E185.5 P5

110.20 *Adam International Review. A Literary Journal in English and French.* 1941- . 4/yr.
052 AP1 A4

110.21 *Antioch Review.* 1941- . 4/yr.
AP2 A562

110.22 *Arizona Quarterly.* 1945- .
051 AP2 A7265

110.23 *Chicago Review.* 1946- . 4/yr.
AP2 C5152

110.24 *Irish Writing. The Magazine of Contemporary Irish Literature.* 1946-56.
820.82 AP4 I77

110.25 *Approach.* 1947-67. 64 nos.
051 AP2 A5955

110.26 *Georgia Review.* 1947- . 4/yr.
051 AP2 G375

110.27 *Landfall. A New Zealand Quarterly.* 1947- .
052 AP7 L35

110.28 *Western Humanities Review.* 1947- . 4/yr.
979.2 AP2 W426

110.29 *Carolina Quarterly.* 1948- . 3/yr.
378.756 LH1 N7 C3

110.30 *Hudson Review.* 1948- . 4/yr.
805 AP2 H886

110.31 *English Record.* 1950- . 4/yr.
420.7 PE1065 E65

110.32 *Shenandoah.* 1950- . 4/yr.
051 AP4 S56

110.33 *Black Mountain Review.* 1951-57. 4/yr. Rpt. N.Y., 1969.
810.5408 NX1 B52

110.34 *Colorado Quarterly.* 1952- .
AP2 C6634

110.35 *Delta. A Literary Review from Cambridge.* 1953- . 3/yr.

110.36 *Paris Review.* 1953- . 4/yr.
AP4 P245

110.37 *Tamarack Review.* 1956- . 4/yr.
AP5 T3

110.38 *Australian Letters. A Quarterly Review of Writing and Criticism.* 1957-68. 4/yr.
AP7 A85

110.39 *Evergreen Review.* 1957- . 12/yr.
051 AP2 E884

110.40 *Northwest Review.* 1957- . 3/yr.
AP2 N855

110.41 *Southern Poetry Review.* 1958- . 2/yr.

110.42 *Agenda.* 1959- . 4/yr.

110.43 *Critical Quarterly.* 1959- .
AP4 C887

110.44 *Midwest Quarterly. A Journal of Contemporary Thought.* 1959- .
AS30 M5

110.45 *Alphabet. The Iconography of the Imagination.* 1960- . 2/yr. Absorbed *Waterloo Review*, 1958-61.
     AP5 A4

110.46 *Carleton Miscellany.* 1960- . 2/yr.
     AS30 C34

110.47 *Minnesota Review.* 1960- . 4/yr.
     AP2 M5598

110.48 *Laurel Review.* 1961-71. 2/yr.

110.49 *Poet and Critic. A Gallery of Verse/A Worshop in Print/A Studio of Thought.* 1961- . 3/yr.

110.50 *Quartet.* 1962- . 4/yr.

110.51 *Southern Review.* Adelaide. 1963- . 2/yr.

110.52 *New South African Writing.* 1964-68. Annual.
     PR9852 N4

110.53 *University of Windsor Review.* 1965- . 2/yr.

110.54 *West Coast Review.* 1965- . 3/yr.
     AP2 W395

110.55 *Journal of Black Poetry.* 1966- . 4/yr.

110.56 *University of Denver Quarterly. A Journal of Modern Culture.* 1966- . 4/yr.
     AP2 U733

110.57 *Wascana Review.* 1966- . 2/yr.

110.58 *Caterpillar.* 1967- . 4/yr.
811.005   AP2 C27

110.59 *New American Review.* 1967- . 4/yr.
810.5   PS1 N4

110.60 *Voyages. A National Literary Magazine.* 1967- . 4/yr.
810.5   PS535.5 V6

110.61 *Works. A Quarterly of Writing.* 1967-

110.62 *Concerning Poetry.* 1968- . 2/yr.

110.63 *Kansas Quarterly.* 1968- . 4/yr.
051   AP2 K22

110.64 *New Orleans Review. A Journal of Literature and Culture.* 1968- . 4/yr.
051   AP2 N6212

110.65 *South Carolina Review.* 1968- . 2/yr. A subseries of *Furman Studies.*

110.66 *Antigonish Review.* 1970- . 4/yr.

110.67 *The Falcon.* 1970- . 2/yr.

110.68 *Mediterranean Review. An International Quarterly of New Literature.* 1970- .

110.69 *Prose.* 1970- . 2/yr.

110.70 *St. Andrews Review. A Twice Yearly Magazine of the Arts and Humanities.* 1970- .

110.71 *Seneca Review.* 1970- . 2/yr.

110.72 *California Quarterly.* 1971- .

§111. Literary Figure Periodicals

111.1 *Baconiana.* 1892- . Irreg. Formerly *Bacon Society Journal,* 1886-91.
PR2941 A3

111.2 *Blackmore Studies.* 1969- . Annual.

111.3 *Blake Newsletter.* 1967- . 4/yr.
700.924   PR4147 B47

111.4 *Blake Studies.* 1968- . 2/yr.
700.924   PR4147 B48

111.5 *Brontë Society Transactions.* 1894- . Annual.
823.81   PR4168 A4

111.6 *Browning Newsletter.* 1968- . 2/yr.
821.809   PR4229 B78

111.7 *Studies in Burke and His Time.* 1959- . 3/yr. Until 1967 *Burke Newsletter.*

111.8 *Kalki. Studies in James Branch Cabell.* 1966- . 4/yr.

111.9 *Cabellian. A Journal of the Second American Renaissance.* 1968- . 2/yr.
818.5208   PS3505 A153 C3

111.10 [William.] *Carleton Newsletter.* 1970- . 4/yr.

111.11 *Chaucer Review. A Journal of Medieval Studies and Literary Criticism.* 1966- . 4/yr.

111.12 *Conradiana.* 1968- . 3/yr.

111.13 *Stephen Crane Newsletter.* 1966- . 4/yr.

111.14 *Dickensian. A Magazine for Dickens Lovers.* 1905- . 3/yr.
PR4579 D5

111.15 *Dickens Studies.* 1965-69. 5 vols. 2/yr.
PR4579 D48

111.16 *Dickens Studies Annual.* 1970- .
823.8   PR4579 D49

111.17 *Dickens Studies Newsletter.* 1970- . 4/yr.

111.18 *Emily Dickinson Bulletin.* 1968- . 4/yr.
016.8114   Z8230.5 E44

111.19 *Auction of the Mind. A Journal of Emily Dickinson Studies.*
1970- . 2/yr.

111.20 *Dreiser Newsletter.* 1970- . 2/yr.

111.21 *Fitzgerald Newsletter.* 1958-68. 40 nos.
           PS3511 I9 Z62

111.22 *Fitzgerald/Hemingway Annual.* 1969- .
813.5209   PS3511 I9 Z617

111.23 *Frederic Herald.* 1967-70. Suspended. 3/yr.

111.24 *Gissing Newsletter.* 1965- . 4/yr.

111.25 *Hemingway Notes.* 1971- . 2/yr.

111.26 *New Rambler. Journal of the Johnson Society of London.*
1941- . 2/yr.

111.27 *James Joyce Review.* 1957-59.
828.912   PR6019 O9 Z64

111.28 *Wake Newslitter. Studies of James Joyce's "Finnegans Wake."*
1962- . 6/yr.
823   PR6019 O9 F594

111.29 *James Joyce Quarterly.* 1963- .
           PR6019 O9 Z637

111.30 *Bulletin of the Keats-Shelley Memorial, Rome.* London.
1910- . Annual.
           PR4836 A15

111.31 *Kipling Journal.* 1927- . 4/yr.
823.89   PR4856 A14

111.32 *C. L. S. Bulletin. Organ of the Charles Lamb Society.* 1935- .
4/yr.

111.33 *D. H. Lawrence Review.* 1969- . 3/yr.
823.912   PR6023 A93 Z6234

111.34 *Sinclair Lewis Newsletter.* 1969- . 2/yr.

111.35 *Jack London Newsletter.* 1967- . 3/yr.

111.36 *[Jack] London Collector.* 1970- . 2/yr.

111.37 *What's New About London, Jack.* 1971- .

111.38 *Markham Review.* 1968- . 3/yr.

111.39 *Melville Society Newsletter.* 1945-70. 4/yr.

111.40 *Menckeniana. A Quarterly Review.* 1962- . 4/yr.

111.41 *Mill News Letter.* 1965- . 2/yr.

111.42 *Milton Quarterly.* 1967- . Formerly *Milton Newsletter.*

111.43 *Milton Studies.* 1969- . Annual.
821.4   PR3579 M5

111.44 *Moreana. A Bilingual Quarterly.* Angers, France. 1963-

111.45 *William Morris Society Journal.* 1961- . Irreg.
AS122 W653

111.46 *Poe Newsletter.* 1968- . 2/yr.
818.309   PS2631 P63

111.47 *Shakespeare Jahrbuch.* 1865- . Weimar.
PR2889 D42

111.48 *Shakespeare Association of America Bulletin.* 1924-49. Succeeded by *Shakespeare Quarterly.*
PN2887 N5

111.49 *Shakespeare Survey. An Annual Survey of Shakespearian Study and Production.* 1948- .
822.33   PR2888 C3

111.50 *Shakespeare Quarterly.* 1950- .
PR2885 S63

111.51 *Shakespeare Newsletter.* 1951- . 6/yr.
822.33   PR2885 S48

111.52 *Deutsche Shakespeare-Gesellschaft West. Jahrbuch.* 1964- . West German continuation of *Shakespeare Jahrbuch.*

111.53 *Shakespeare Studies. An Annual Gathering of Research, Criticism, and Reviews.* 1965- .
822.33   PR2885 S64

111.54 *Shakespearean Research and Opportunities.* 1965- . Annual.

111.55 *Shavian. Journal of the Shaw Society.* London. 1946- . 3/yr.

111.56 *Shaw Review.* 1951- . 3/yr.
PR5366 A15

111.57 *Independent Shavian.* 1962- . 3/yr.

111.58 *Spenser Newsletter.* 1970- . 3/yr.

111.59 *Steinbeck Quarterly.* 1968- .

111.60 *Wallace Stevens Newsletter.* 1969- . 2/yr.
811.52   PS3537 T4753 Z88

111.61 *Tennyson Research Bulletin.* 1967- . Annual.
821.8   PR5579 T43

111.62 *Thoreau Society Bulletin.* 1941-   . Irreg.
PS3053 A23

111.63 Advena, Jean C., ed. *A Bibliography of the Thoreau Society Bulletin Bibliographies, 1941-1969. A Cumulation and Index.* Troy, N. Y., 1971.
016.818309   Z8873 A3

111.64 *Thoreau Journal, Quarterly.* 1969-   .
818.308   PS3053 T5

111.65 *Tolkien Journal.* 1965-   . 3/yr.

111.66 *Mark Twain Journal.* 1936-   . 2/yr.
817.44   PN2 M3

111.67 *Twainian. Mark Twain—Yesterday and Today.* 1939-   . 6/yr.
817.44   PS1329 T9

111.68 *Evelyn Waugh Newsletter.* 1967-   . 3/yr.

111.69 *Walt Whitman Foundation Bulletin.* Camden, N.J. 1948-55. Annual.
811.38   PS3229 W37

111.70 *Walt Whitman Review.* 1955-   . 4/yr.
PS3229 W39

111.71 *Calamus. An International Whitman Quarterly.* Tokyo. 1969-   . 3/yr.

111.72 *Wordsworth Circle.* 1970-   . 4/yr.

111.73 *Yeats Studies.* 1971-   .

Part Three. The Profession

19. The Purposes and Methods of Literary Scholarship

§112. Theory

112.1 Foerster, Norman. *The American Scholar. A Study in Litterae Inhumaniores.* Durham, N.C., 1929. Rpt. Pt. Washington, N.Y., 1965.
801.95   AZ508 F6

112.2 Earnest, Ernest P. *Academic Procession. An Informal History of the American College, 1636 to 1953.* Indianapolis, Ind., 1953.
378.73   LA229 E17

112.3 Daiches, David. *English Literature.* Englewood Cliffs, N.J., 1964. Princeton Studies: Humanistic Scholarship in America.
820.9   PN99 U52 D3

112.4 Knapp, Robert H. *The Origins of American Humanistic Scholars.* Englewood Cliffs, N.J., 1964.
378   LC1011 K6

112.5 Priestley, Francis E. *The Humanities in Canada.* Toronto, 1964. (Prev. ed. by Watson Kirkconnell and Arthur S. P. Woodhouse, 1947.) *Supplement to December 31, 1964.* Ed. Roy M. Wiles, 1966.
378.71   LA417.5 P7

112.6 Frye, Northrop, et al. *The Morality of Scholarship.* Ed. Max Black. Ithaca, N.Y., 1967.
001.2   AZ103 F75

112.7 Thorpe, James E., ed. *Relations of Literary Study. Essays on Interdisciplinary Contributions.* N.Y., 1967.

112.8 Royal Society of Canada. *Scholarship in Canada. Achievement and Outlook.* Toronto, 1968. Studia Varia Ser., 12.
001.20971   AZ515 R6

112.9 *The Future of the Humanities. The Papers Delivered at the Jubilee Congress of the Modern Humanities Research Association in August 1968.* Ed. J. C. Laidlaw. Cambridge, 1969.
001.3   AZ103 M65

§113. Practice

113.1 Altick, Richard D. *The Scholar Adventurers.* N.Y., 1950. Rpt. 1960, 1966.
820.72   PR99 A6

113.2 Harrison, George B. *Profession of English.* N.Y., 1962. Rpt. 1967.
378   LB2321 L282

113.3 Saunders, John W. *The Profession of English Letters.* London & Toronto, 1964.
820.023   PR401 S36

113.4 Allen, Don C. *The Ph.D. in English and American Literature.* N.Y., 1968.
407   PE66 A4

113.5 Shugrue, Michael F. *English in a Decade of Change.* N.Y., 1968.
420.7   PE1068 U5 S55

113.6 Enright, Dennis J. *Memoirs of a Mendicant Professor.* London, 1969.
828.91403   PR6009 N6 Z5

113.7 Mandel, Barrett J. *Literature and the English Department.* Champaign, Ill., 1970.
807.1173   PN70 M3

113.8 O'Toole, Simon [pseud.]. *Confessions of an American Scholar.* Minneapolis, 1970.

113.9 Ryan, Kevin, ed. *Don't Smile Until Christmas. Accounts of the First Year of Teaching.* Chicago, 1970.
371.1   LB2844.1 N4 R95

113.10 Watson, George G. *The Study of Literature.* London & N.Y., 1970.
801.95   PN81 W3

§114. Methods of Scholarship

114.1 Morize, André. *Problems and Methods of Literary History. With Special Reference to Modern French Literature. A Guide for Graduate Students.* Boston, 1922. Rpt. N.Y., 1966.
807   PN59 M6

114.2 Foerster, Norman, et al. *Literary Scholarship. Its Aims and Methods.* Chapel Hill, N.C., 1941.
801   PN45 L5

114.3 Leary, Lewis G., ed. *Contemporary Literary Scholarship. A Critical Review.* N.Y., 1958.
820.4   PR77 N3

114.4 Lyon, Harvey T. *Keats' Well-Read Urn. An Introduction to Literary Method.* N.Y., 1958.
821.78   PR4834 O5 L9

114.5 Altick, Richard D. *The Art of Literary Research.* N.Y., 1963.
807.2   PR33 A4

114.6 Thorpe, James E. *Literary Scholarship. A Handbook for Advanced Students of English and American Literature.* Boston, 1964.
             PR33 T5

114.7 Wellek, René, and Austin Warren. *Theory of Literature.* 3rd ed. N.Y., 1964. (Orig. ed. 1949.)
801   PN45 W36

114.8 Beaurline, Lester A., ed. *A Mirror for Modern Scholars. Essays in Methods of Research in Literature.* N.Y., 1966.
801.95   PN85 B34

114.9 Zitner, Sheldon P., ed. *The Practice of Modern Literary Scholarship.* Glenview, Ill., 1966.
801.95   PN85 Z5

114.10 Winks, Robin W., ed. *The Historian as Detective. Essays on Evidence.* N.Y., 1969.
907.2   D13 W65

114.11 Barzun, Jacques, and Henry F. Graff. *The Modern Researcher.* Rev. ed. N.Y., 1970. (Orig. ed. 1957.)
907   D13 B334

114.12 Thorpe, James E., ed. *The Aims and Methods of Scholarship in Modern Languages and Literatures.* 2nd ed. N.Y. 1970. (Orig. ed. 1963.)
407   PB21 T5

114.13 Watson, George G. *The Literary Thesis. A Guide to Research.* Harlow, Eng., 1970.
808.02   LB2369 W33

114.14 Bateson, Frederick W. *The Scholar Critic. An Introduction to Literary Research.* London, 1971.

§115. Scholarly Writing

115.1 *Scholarly Books in America. A Quarterly Bibliography Open to University Presses and Other Nonprofit Publishers of Scholarly Books.* 1959-   .
             Z231.5 U6 S3

115.2 *Scholarly Publishing. A Journal for Authors and Publishers.* 1969-   . 4/yr.
655.4   Z286 S37 S33

•

115.3 McCartney, Eugene S. *Recurrent Maladies in Scholarly Writing.* Ann Arbor, 1953. Rpt. N.Y., 1969.
808.042   PN147 M28

115.4 Modern Language Association. *Handbook for Editors of Learned Journals.* N.Y., 1959.
070.41   PN162 C6

115.5 Welter, Rush. *Problems of Scholarly Publication in the Humanities and Social Sciences.* N.Y., 1959.
655.5   Z479 W4

115.6 Cargill, Oscar, et al. *The Publication of Academic Writing.* N.Y., 1966.
PN155 C37

115.7 Nicholson, Margaret. *A Practical Style Guide for Authors and Editors.* N.Y., 1967.
808.02   PN147 N53

115.8 United States. Government Printing Office. *Style Manual.* Rev. ed. Washington, D.C., 1967.
655.258   Z253 U58

115.9 Wiles, Roy McK. *Scholarly Reporting in the Humanities.* 4th ed. Toronto, 1968. (Orig. ed. 1951.)
808.02   PN147 W52

115.10 University of Chicago Press. *A Manual of Style. For Authors, Editors, and Copywriters.* 12th ed. Chicago, 1969. (Orig. ed. 1906.)
655.25   Z253 C57

115.11 *The MLA Style Sheet.* 2nd ed. N.Y., 1970. (Orig. ed. 1951.)
808.02   Z253 M73

115.12 Bernstein, Theodore M. *Miss Thistlebottom's Hobgoblins. The Careful Writer's Guide to the Taboos, Bugbears and Outmoded Rules of English Usage.* N.Y., 1971.
428.2   PE1460 B4627

§116. Dissertations

116.1 Black, Dorothy M., ed. *Guide to Lists of Master's Theses.* Chicago, 1965.
016.011   Z5055 U49 B55

116.2 McNamee, Lawrence F. *Ninety-Nine Years of English Dissertations.* Commerce, Texas, 1969.

•

116.3 *List of American Doctoral Dissertations Printed, 1912-38.* Library of Congress. Washington, D. C., 1913-40. 27 vols. Rpt. N.Y., 1965.
Z5055 U49 U5

116.4 *Doctoral Dissertations Accepted by American Universities.* 1933/34—1954/55. 22 vols. Annual. Rpt. N.Y., 1964. Absorbed by *Dissertation Abstracts International.*
378.242   Z5055 U49 D6

116.5 Aslib [Assoc. of Special Libraries and Information Bureaux]. *Index to Theses Accepted for Higher Degrees in the Universities of Great Britain and Ireland.* 1953- . Annual.
016.01   Z5055 G69 A84

116.6 McNamee, Lawrence F. *Dissertations in English and American Literature. Theses Accepted by American, British and German Universities, 1865-1964.* N.Y., 1968. *Supplement One, 1964-1968* [adds Canadian, Australian, and New Zealand Universities]. N. Y., 1969.
016.82   Z5053 M32

116.7 *English and American Studies in German. Summaries of Theses and Monographs.* Tübingen, 1968- . Annual.

✓**116.8** *Dissertation Abstracts International.* 1938- . 12/yr. Formerly *Microfilm Abstracts,* 1938-51, and *Dissertation Abstracts,* 1952-68.
082   AS30 M5

  116.9 *Retrospective Index,* Vols. 1-29 (1938-69), 9 vols., 1970.
082   AS30 M5

Some universities have themselves published abstracts of their doctoral dissertations rather than submit them to *Dissertation Abstracts International* or before beginning to do so. The following check list contains such information as is available.

116.10 Boston. *Abstracts of Dissertations . . .* 1938-60[?].

116.11 California. *Summary of the Dissertations.* 1936-62.

116.12 Catholic. *Summaries of Dissertations . . .* 1937-66[?].
378.753   AS36 C33

116.13 Chicago. *Abstracts of Theses. Humanistic Series.* 1925-34 (covering 1922-32). 9 vols.
AS36 C34

116.14 Colorado. "Abstracts of Theses for Higher Degrees," in *Colorado Studies.* 1929-56.
AS36 C6

116.15 Cornell. *Abstracts of Theses . . .* 1938-49 (covering 1937-49). Annual.
378.747   LB7 C8

116.16 East Texas State. *Abstracts from Graduate Study.* 1964- . Annual.

116.17 Fordham. *Dissertations Accepted* . . . 1935-51. Continues as bibliography. Annual.
AS36 F6

116.18 George Peabody. *Abstracts of Dissertations* . . . 1942-62. Annual.
370.82   LB7 G4

116.19 George Washington. *Abstracts of Doctoral Dissertations* in *Bulletin,* 1902- . Continued in *Summaries of Theses.* 1931-70. Annual.
378.753   AS36 G37

116.20 Harvard. *Summaries of Theses Accepted* . . . 1928-47 (covering 1924-45). Annual.
AS36 H3

116.21 Iowa. *Doctoral Dissertation Abstracts and References.* 1940-54 (covering 1900-1952).
AS36 I975

116.22 Louisiana State. *Abstracts of Dissertations* . . . in *Bulletin.* 1936-55. 16 nos.
378.763   AS36 L87

116.23 Maryland. *Abstracts of Theses* . . . 1940-54 (covering 1938-54). 2/yr.
378.752   AS36 M353

116.24 Minnesota. *Summaries of Theses.* 1939-52.
378.776   AS36 M65

116.25 Nebraska. *Abstracts of Doctoral Dissertations.* 1940-53. 14 vols.
378.782   AS36 N19

116.26 North Carolina. *Research in Progress* in *Record.* 1920-63 (covering 1918-62).
LD3941.3 A2

116.27 North Dakota. *Abstracts of Doctoral Dissertations and Master's Theses.* 1951-62[?]. Annual.
378.784   AS36 N62

116.28 Northwestern. *Summaries of Ph. D. Dissertations.* 1933-52. 20 vols. Annual.
378.773   AS36 N65

116.29 Ohio State. *Abstracts of Dissertations* . . . 1929-57 (covering 1929-51).
378.771   AS36 O42

116.30 Oklahoma. *Abstracts of Theses* . . . 1930-54. 14 vols.
378.766   AS36 O45

116.31 Pennsylvania State. *Abstracts of Doctoral Dissertations* . . .
1938-55. 18 vols. Annual.
378.748   AS36 P45

116.32 Pittsburgh. *Abstracts of Theses* . . . 1925-53.
AS36 P8

116.33 St. John's. *Abstracts of Dissertations.* 1939-65. Annual.

116.34 St. Louis. *Publications and Research in Progress* . . . 1946-   .
Z5055 U5 S28

116.35 Southern California. *Abstracts of Dissertations* . . . 1936-58.
Annual.
378.794   AS36 L7

116.36 Stanford. *Abstracts of Dissertations* . . . 1927-53 (covering
1924-52). 27 vols.
AS36 L45

116.37 Temple. *Abstracts of Dissertations* . . . 1934-54[?].

116.38 Texas Tech. *Theses Accepted* . . . (1950-55), 1956; (1956-60),
1961.
013.764847   Z733 T43

116.39 Tulane. *Abstracts of Dissertations* . . . 1938-55. 12 vols.
Annual.
AS36 T9

116.40 Utah. *Abstracts of Doctoral Dissertations* . . . 1947-56.
013.378792   AS36 U815

116.41 Vanderbilt. *Abstracts of Theses* in *Bulletin.* 1932-53. Continues
with M.A. theses.
378.768   AS36 V3

116.42 Virginia. *Abstracts of Dissertations* . . . 1932-52 (covering
1924-52).
378.755   AS36 V56

116.43 Washington (Seattle). *Abstracts of Theses* . . . 1931-46 (covering 1914-46). 10 vols.
378.797   AS36 W28

116.44 Wisconsin. *Summaries of Doctoral Dissertations.* 1937-56 (covering 1935-55). 16 vols.
378.775   AS36 W78

•

116.45 Aberdeen. *Abstracts of Theses.* 1931-37..

254 / *Purposes and Methods of Literary Scholarship*

116.46 Cambridge. *Abstracts of Dissertations Approved* . . . 1925-57. Annual.
378.42   AS122 C3

116.47 Durham. *Abstracts of Theses* . . . 1931- .
AS122 D894

116.48 Glasgow. *Summaries of Theses Approved* . . . 1949- .

116.49 Hull. *Abstracts of Theses* . . . 1954/60- . Annual.
AS122 H783

116.50 Leeds. *Publications and Abstracts of Theses.* 1927-38. 1951- , as bibliography.

116.51 Oxford. *Abstracts of Dissertations* . . . 1928-47 (covering 1925-40). 13 vols.
062   AS122 O9

116.52 Reading. *Abstracts of Theses Approved* . . . 1957- .

116.53 Sheffield. *Summaries of Theses* . . . 1936- .

116.54 Southampton. *Abstracts of Theses Accepted* . . . 1953- . Annual.
AS122 S58 A3

20. Tools for the Student, Teacher, and Scholar

§117. Guides and Directories

117.1 *Study Abroad. International Scholarships and Courses.* 1948-
Annual.
378.3   LB2338 S86

117.2 *Directory of American Scholars. A Biographical Directory.*
4 vols. 5th ed. N.Y., 1969. (Orig. ed. 1942.)
923.773   LA2311 C32

117.3 Griffith, Benjamin W. *Barron's How to Prepare for the Graduate
Record Examination in Literature.* Woodbury, N.Y., 1969.
807.6   PN43 G65

117.4 Mildenberger, Kenneth W., ed. *MLA Guide to Federal Pro-
grams. An Analysis of Current Government Financial Assistance
Programs for Students, Teachers, Researchers, and Scholars in the
Fields of English and Foreign Languages.* N.Y., 1969.

117.5 Debrodt, Barbara R. *How to Put Your Husband Through College.* N.Y., 1970.
378.198   LB3613 M3 D4

117.6 *National Faculty Directory . . . . An Alphabetical List, with Ad-
dresses of . . . Faculty Members at Junior Colleges, Colleges, and
Universities in the United States.* 1970-   . Annual.
378.1202573   L901 N34

117.7 Spencer, Richard E., and Ruth Awe. *International Educational
Exchange. A Bibliography.* N.H., 1970.
016.3701916   Z5814 E23 S5

§118. Periodicals
These journals, representing professional organizations, combine creative, critical, or
humanistic interests with pedagogical matters.

118.1 *Leaflet.* New England Assoc. of Teachers of English. 1901-   .
4/yr.

118.2 *English Journal.* NCTE. 1912- . 9/yr.
420.5   PE1 E5

118.3 *Illinois English Bulletin.* 1913- . 8/yr.
PE11 I3

118.4 *AAUP Bulletin.* American Association of University Professors. 1915- . 4/yr.

118.5 *South Atlantic Bulletin.* A Quarterly Journal Devoted to Research and Teaching in the Modern Languages and Literature. 1935- .
405   PB1 S6

118.6 *English. Literature, Criticism, Teaching.* 1936- . 3/yr. Supersedes *Bulletin of the English Association,* 1906-35.
820.5   PR5 E5

118.7 *CEA Critic. An Official Journal of the College English Association.* 1939- . 9/yr.
PE1011 C22

118.8 *College English.* NCTE 1939- . 8/yr.
420.5   PE1 C6

118.9 *College Composition and Communication.* NCTE 1950- . 5/yr.
PE1001 C6

118.10 *Iowa English Yearbook.* 1956- .
PN59 I6

118.11 *CLA Journal.* College Language Assoc. 1957- . 4/yr.
P1 A1 C22

118.12 *California English Journal.* 1965- . 4/yr.

118.13 *Negro American Literature Forum. For School and University Teachers.* 1967- . 4/yr.

118.14 *English Quarterly.* Canada. 1968- . 4/yr.

§119. General Reference Tools

119.1 Walford, Albert J., ed. *Guide to Reference Material.* 3 vols. 2nd ed. London, 1966-70.
011.02   Z1035 W252

119.2 Winchell, Constance M. *Guide to Reference Books.* 8th ed. Chicago, 1967. (Orig. ed. 1902.) *Supplement 1965-66,* 1969, and *Supplement 1967-68,* 1970, ed. Eugene P. Sheehy.
011.02   Z1035 W79

119.3 Downs, Robert B. *How to Do Library Research.* Urbana, Ill., 1966.
028.7   Z1035 D63

119.4 Galin, Saul, and Peter Spielberg. *Reference Books. How to Select and Use Them.* N.Y., 1969.
011.92   Z1035.1 G3

119.5 *American Reference Books Annual.* Ed. Bohdan Wynar. 1970- .
011.02   Z1035.1 A55

119.6 Enoch Pratt Free Library. *Reference Books. A Brief Guide for Students and Other Users of the Library.* Ed. Mary N. Barton. 7th ed. Baltimore, 1970. (Orig. ed. 1938.)
016   Z1035.1 E5

●

119.7 [Palmer, Samuel.] *Palmer's Index to the Times Newspaper.* 1868-1943. 4/yr. Rpt. in 100 vols., Nendeln, Liechtenstein, 1965-66.
AI21 T5

119.8 *Official Index to the "Times."* London. 1906- . 6/yr.
AI21 T46

119.9 *New York Times Index.* 1913- . 24/yr with annual cumulations. Prior Series 1851-1913, N.Y., 1967- , in progress.
AI21 N44

119.10 Keller, Helen R. *The Dictionary of Dates.* 2 vols. N.Y., 1934. Rpt. 1971.
902.02   D9 K4

119.11 Hamilton, Edith. *Mythology.* 1942. Rpt. N.Y., almost annually.
292   BL310 H3

119.12 Von Ostermann, Georg F. *Manual of Foreign Languages. For the Use of Librarians, Bibliographers, Research Workers, Editors, Translators, and Printers.* 4th ed. N.Y., 1952. (Orig. ed. 1934.)
655.25   Z253 U581

119.13 Handlin, Oscar, et al., eds. *Harvard Guide to American History.* Cambridge, Mass., 1954. Rpt. N.Y., 1967.
016.917303   Z1236 H27

119.14 Cohen, John M., and Mark J. Cohen, eds. *The Penguin Dictionary of Quotations.* Harmondsworth, Eng. & Baltimore, 1960.
808.88   PN6081 C55

119.15 Powicke, Frederick M., and E. B. Fryde. *Handbook of British Chronology.* 2nd ed. London, 1961. (Orig. ed. 1939.)
942.002   DA34 P6

119.16 *New Century Classical Handbook.* Ed. Catherine B. Avery. N.Y., 1962.
913.38   DE5 N4

119.17 Clapp, Jane, ed. *International Dictionary of Literary Awards.* N.Y., 1963.
807.9   PN171 P75 C5

119.18 Freeman, William. *Dictionary of Fictional Characters.* London & Boston, 1963. *Author and Title Indexes* by J. M. F. Leaper, London, 1965.
820.3   PR19 F7

119.19 Brockett, Oscar G., et al. *A Bibliographical Guide to Research in Speech and Dramatic Art.* Chicago, 1963.
016   Z1002 B87

119.20 Walford, Albert J. *A Guide to Foreign Language Grammars and Dictionaries.* London, 1964.
Z7004 G7 W3

119.21 Grimal, Pierre, ed. *Larousse World Mythology.* Trans. Patricia Beardsworth. N.Y., 1965. (Orig. French ed. Paris, 1963.)
291   BL311 G683

119.22 Guinagh, Kevin, ed. *Dictionary of Foreign Phrases and Abbreviations.* N.Y., 1965.
418   P361 G8

119.23 *Brewer's Dictionary of Phrase and Fable.* 11th ed. N.Y., 1968.
803   PN43 B65

119.24 Learmonth, Andrew T., and Agnes M. Learmonth. *Encyclopedia of Australia.* London & N.H., 1968.
919.4003   DU90 L4

119.25 American Center of P. E. N. *List of Grants and Awards Available to American Writers.* 1969- . Annual.

119.26 *Acronyms and Initialisms Dictionary.* 3rd ed. by Ellen T. Crowley and Robert C. Thomas. Detroit, 1970. (Orig. ed. 1960.) *Supplement*, 1971.
421.8   PE1693 G3

119.27 *Literary and Library Prizes.* Ed. Olga S. Weber. 7th ed. N. Y., 1970. (Orig. ed. 1935.)
807.9   PN171 P75 L5

119.28 *Oxford Classical Dictionary.* 2nd ed. by Nicholas G. Hammond and Howard H. Scullard. Oxford, 1970. (Orig. ed. by Max Cary et al., 1949.)
913.38   DE5 O9

§120. Biographical Reference Works

120.1 *Dictionary of National Biography.* Ed. Leslie Stephen and Sidney Lee. 66 vols. London, 1885-1901. Freq. rpts. in 22 vols. Decennial supplements.
920.042   DA28 D4

120.2 *Corrections and Additions to the Dictionary of National Biography. Cumulated from the Bulletin of the Institute of Historical Research Covering the Years 1923-1963.* Boston, 1966.
920.04203   DA28 L65

120.3 Foster, Joseph, ed. *Alumni oxonienses. The Members of the University of Oxford, 1500-1886.* 8 vols. London, 1887-92. Rpt. in 4 vols. Nendeln, Liechtenstein, 1968.
LF524 A22

120.4 Boase, Frederic. *Modern English Biography. Containing Many Thousand Concise Memoirs of Persons Who Have Died Between the Years 1850-1900.* 3 vols. Truro, Eng., 1892-1901. *Supplement.* 3 vols., 1908-12. Rpt. 6 vols. London & N.Y., 1965.
920.042   CT773 B6

120.5 *Alumni cantabrigienses. A Biographical List of All Known Students, Graduates, and Holders of Office at the University of Cambridge from the Earliest Times to 1900.* Ed. John Venn and John A. Venn. 10 vols. Cambridge, 1922-54.
LF124 A2

120.6 *Dictionary of American Biography.* Ed. Allen Johnson and Dumas Malone. 21 vols. N. Y., 1928-37. *Supplement One.* Ed. Harris E. Starr. 1944. Rpt. in 22 vols., 1946. *Supplement Two.* Ed. Robert L. Schuyler and Edward T. James, 1958.
290.073   E176 D56

120.7 Emden, Alfred B. *A Biographical Register of the University of Oxford to A. D. 1500.* 3 vols. Oxford, 1957-59.
378.42   LF525 E5

120.8 Emden, Alfred B. "Additions and Corrections to *A Biographical Register . . . of Oxford . . . :* Supplemental List No. 1." *Bodleian Library Record,* 6 (1961), 668-88.

120.9 Emden, Alfred B. *A Biographical Register of the University of Cambridge to 1500.* Cambridge, 1963.
378.42   LF113 E4

120.10 Wallace, William S. *The Macmillan Dictionary of Canadian Biography.* 3rd ed. London & N.Y., 1963. (Orig. ed. Toronto, 1926.)
920.071   F1005 D5

120.11 Slocum, Robert B. *Biographical Dictionaries and Related Works.* Detroit, 1967.
016.92   Z5301 S55

•

120.12 *Current Biography.* 1940-   . 11/yr cumulated as *Current Biography Yearbook.*
          CT100 C8

120.13 *Biography Index. A Quarterly Index to Biographical Material in Books and Magazines.* 1946-   . Annual cumulation.
016.92   Z5301 B5

120.14 *New York Times Obituaries Index, 1858-1968.* N.Y., 1970.
929.3   CT213 N47

21. Works in Allied Fields

§121. Translation and World Literature

121.1 *Index translationum. Répertoire international des traductions/ International Bibliography of Translations.* New Series. 1948- . Annual. Quarterly 1932-40.
016   Z6514 T7 I42

121.2 Line, Maurice B. *A Bibliography of Russian Literature in English Translation to 1900 (Excluding Periodicals).* London, 1963.
016.891709   Z2504 T8 L5

121.3 Hulet, Claude L., ed. *Latin American Poetry in English Translation. A Bibliography.* Washington, D.C., 1965.
        Z1609 T7 H81

•

121.4 *Babel. International Journal of Translation.* 1955- . 4/yr.
        PN241 A1 B15

121.5 *Contemporary Literature in Translation.* 1968- .
808.8004   PN6013 C55

121.6 *Delos. A Journal On and Of Translation.* 1968- . 2/yr irreg. Each issue lists translations in progress.
428.02   PN241 A1 D4

121.7 Brower, Reuben A., ed. *On Translation.* Cambridge, Mass., 1959. Harvard Studies in Comp. Lit., 23.
808   PN241 B7

121.8 Arrowsmith, William, and Roger Shattuck, eds. *The Craft and Context of Translation. A Symposium.* Austin, Tex., 1961. Rpt. 1971.
410.28   PN241 A74

121.9 Cohen, John M. *English Translators and Translations.* London, 1962. Writers and Their Work, 142.
820.9   PR131 C6

121.10 Savory, Theodore H. *The Art of Translation.* Boston, 1968.
418.02   PN241 S25

121.11 Proetz, Victor. *The Astonishment of Words. An Experiment in the Comparison of Languages.* Austin, Tex., 1971.
418.02   PN241 P75

•

121.12 *Year's Work in Modern Language Studies by a Number of Scholars.* Mod. Hum. Res. Assoc. 1931 (for 1930)- . Annual.
405.8   PB1 Y45

121.13 Baldensperger, Fernand, and Werner P. Friederich. *Bibliography of Comparative Literature.* Chapel Hill, 1950. Rpt. N. Y., 1960. Univ. of N.C. Studies in Comp. Lit., 1.
016.809   Z6514 C7 B3

121.14 *Yearbook of Comparative and General Literature.* 1952- . Includes bibliography.
805.8   PN851 Y4

121.15 Zell, Hans M., et al., eds. *Literature of Africa. An Annotated Bibliographical Guide to Creative Writing by Black African Authors.* N.Y., 1969.

121.16 Zell, Hans M. *A Reader's Guide to African Literature.* London, 1971.

•

121.17 *Modern Langage Journal.* 1916- . 8/yr.
PB1 M47

121.18 *Comparative Literature.* 1949- . 4/yr.
805   PN851 C595

121.19 *Mahfil. A Quarterly of South Asian Literature.* 1953- .

121.20 *WLWE Newsletter. World Literature Written in English.* 1962- . 2/yr.

121.21 *Comparative Literature Studies.* 1964- . 4/yr.
809   PN851 C63

121.22 *Forum for Modern Language Studies.* 1965- . 4/yr.
PB1 F63

121.23 *African Literature Today. A Journal of Explanatory Criticism.* 1968- . 2/yr.
896   PL8010 A4

121.24 *Conch. A Sociological Journal of African Cultures and Literatures.* 1969- . 2/yr.

121.25 *Research in African Literatures.* 1970- . 2/yr.

121.26 *Savacou. A Journal of the Caribbean Artists Movement.*
1970- . 4/yr.
917.290676   F1601 S26

•

121.27 *Cassell's Encyclopaedia of World Literature.* Ed. Sigfrid H.
Steinberg. 2 vols. N.Y., 1954.
803   PN41 C3

121.28 Friederich, Werner P., and David H. Malone. *Outline of Comparative Literature from Dante Alighieri to Eugene O'Neill.* Chapel
Hill, 1954. Univ. of N.C. Studies in Comp. Lit., 11.
809   PN871 F7

121.29 Tyler, Priscilla, ed. *Writers the Other Side of the Horizon. A
Guide to Developing Literatures of the World.* Champaign, Ill., 1964.
820.904   PR473 T9

121.30 Fleischmann, Wolfgang B., ed. *Encyclopedia of World Literature in the Twentieth Century.* 3 vols. N.Y., 1967-71. Includes U. S.
and British.
803   PN774 L433

121.31 Kunitz, Stanley J., and Vineta Colby, eds. *European Authors,
1000-1900. A Biographical Dictionary of European Literature.* N.Y.,
1967.
920.04   PN451 K8

121.32 Hargreaves-Mawdsley, William N. *Everyman's Dictionary of
European Writers.* London & N.Y., 1968.
803   PN451 H3

121.33 Laurence, Margaret. *Long Drums and Cannons. Nigerian Dramatists and Novelists.* N.Y., 1968.
820.9   PR9898 N5 L3

121.34 Parks, George B., and Ruth Z. Temple, eds. *The Literatures of
the World in English Translation.* N. Y.
Vol. I. *The Greek and Latin Literatures.* 1968.
016.88   Z7018 T7 E85
Vol. II. *The Slavic Literatures.* Ed. Richard C. Lewanski. 1967.
016.8917   Z7041 L59
Vol. III. *The Romance Languages.* 1970
016.84009   Z7033 T7 E56

121.35 Aldridge, Alfred O., ed. *Comparative Literature. Matter and
Method.* Urbana, Ill., 1969.
809   PN863 A6

121.36 Lang, David M., ed. *Guide to Eastern Literatures.* N.Y., 1971.
809.895   PJ307 G8

121.37 Roscoe, Adrian A. *Mother Is Gold. A Study in West African Literature.* Cambridge, 1971.
820   PR9898 W4 R6

§122. Children's Literature

122.1 Haviland, Virginia, ed. *Children's Literature. A Guide to Reference Sources.* Washington, D.C., 1966.
016.80989282   Z1037 A1 H35

122.2 Pellowski, Anne. *The World of Children's Literature.* N.Y., 1968.
028.52   Z1037 P37

122.3 Meigs, Cornelia L., et al. *A Critical History of Children's Literature. A Survey of Children's Books in English.* Rev. ed. N.Y., 1969. (Orig. ed. 1953.)
028.509   PN1009 A1 M4

§123. Folklore

123.1 Bonser, Wilfrid. *A Bibliography of Folklore. As Contained in the First Eighty Years of the Publication of the Folklore Society.* London, 1961. Pubs. of the FL Soc., 121.
Z5981 B6

123.2 Thompson, Stith. *Motif-Index of Folk-Literature. A Classification of Narrative Elements in Folktales, Ballads, Myths, Fables, Mediaeval Romances, Exempla, Fabliaux, Jest-Books, and Local Legends.* Rev. ed. 6 vols. Bloomington, Ind., 1955-58. (Orig. ed. 1932-36.)
398.012   GR67 T52

123.3 Leach, Maria, and Jerome Fried, eds. *Funk and Wagnalls Standard Dictionary of Folklore, Mythology and Legend.* 2 vols. N. Y., 1949-50.
398.03   GR35 F8

123.4 Tallman, Marjorie. *Dictionary of American Folklore.* N.Y., 1960.

398.0973   GR105 T3

123.5 Aarne, Antti. *The Types of the Folk-Tale. A Classification and Bibliography.* Rev. trans. by Stith Thompson. Helsinki, 1961. (Orig. German ed. 1910; orig. trans. 1928.) Rpt. N.Y., 1971.
016.3982   GR40 A1513

123.6 Briggs, Katherine M., ed. *A Dictionary of British Folk-Tales in the English Language, Incorporating the F. J. Norton Collection.* 4 vols. Bloomington, Ind., 1970-71.
398.20942   GR141 B69

•

123.7 *Southern Folklore Quarterly.* 1937- . Annual bibliography.
398.0975   GR1 S65

123.8 *Journal of American Folklore.* 1888- . 4/yr.
GR1 J8

123.9 *Journal of the Folklore Institute.* 1964- . 3/yr. Formerly *Midwest Folklore,* 1951-63.
398   GR1 I5

•

123.10 Thompson, Stith. *The Folktale.* N.Y., 1946. Rpt. 1960.
398.21   PN1001 T5

123.11 Jobes, Gertrude. *Dictionary of Mythology, Folklore and Symbols.* 3 vols. N.H., 1961-62.
398.03   GR35 J6

123.12 Anderson, George K. *The Legend of the Wandering Jew.* Providence, R.§ffl 1965.
398.35   GR75 W3 A5

123.13 Rosenberg, Bruce A. *The Art of the American Folk Preacher.* N.Y., 1970.
251.00973   BV4208 U6 R67

123.14 Edmonson, Munro S. *Lore. An Introduction to the Science of Folklore and Literature.* N.Y., 1971.
801.9   PN871 E3

§124. Linguistics

124.1 Scheurweghs, Gustave. *Analytical Bibliography of Writings on Modern English Morphology and Syntax, 1877-1960.* 4 vols. Louvain, 1963-68.
Z2015 S32

124.2 Alston, Robin C., ed. *A Bibliography of the English Language from the Invention of Printing to the Year 1800. A Systematic Record of Writings on English, and in Other Languages on English, Based on the Collections of the Principal Libraries of the World.* Leeds, Eng., 1965- .
Z2015 A1 A4

124.3 Permanent International Committee of Linguistics. *Linguistics Bibliography for the Year, with Supplement for Previous Years*. 1948 (for 1937-47)– . Annual.
016.4   Z7001 P4

124.4 *General Linguistics*. 1955- . 4/yr plus MLA Linguistics bibliography 1970 (for 1969)– .

124.5 *Quarterly Check List of Linguistics. An International Index of Current Books, Monographs, Brochures and Separates*. 1958- .
Z7003 Q35

124.6 Allen, Harold B., ed. *Linguistics and English Linguistics*. Goldentree Bibliographies. N.Y., 1966.
016.41   Z7001 A4

124.7 Wawrzyszko, Aleksandra K. *Bibliography of General Linguistics, English and American*. Hamden, Conn., 1971.
016.41   Z7001 W35

●

124.8 *American Speech. A Quarterly of Linguistic Usage*. 1925- . Suspended 1968. Annual bibliography.
PE2801 A6

124.9 *Word Study*. 1925-70. 45 vols. Irreg.
420.5   PE1 W6

124.10 *Journal of Linguistics*. 1965- . 2/yr.
410.5   P1 J65

124.11 *Journal of English Linguistics*. 1967- . Annual.
420.05   PE1001 J65

●

124.12 Nash, Rose. *Multilingual Lexicon of Linguistics and Philology. English, Russian, German, French*. Coral Gables, Fla., 1968.
413   P29 N34

§125. Miscellaneous Periodicals

125.1 *English Historical Review*. 1886- . 4/yr.
DA20 E58

125.2 *Isis. International Review Devoted to the History of Science and Its Cultural Influences*. 1913- . 4/yr.
Q1 I7

125.3 *New England Quarterly. A Historical Review of New England Life and Letters*. 1928-
F1 N62

125.4 *Speech Monographs.* 1934- . 4/yr.
808.5   PN4077 S6

125.5 *Journal of Aesthetics and Art Criticism.* 1941- . 4/yr. Annual
bibliography since 1946.
          N1 J6

125.6 *Etc. A Review of General Semantics.* 1943- . 4/yr.
149.9   B840 E85

125.7 *JGE. The Journal of General Education.* 1946- . 4/yr.
          L11 J775

125.8 *General Semantics Bulletin.* 1949- . Annual.
149.9   B820 G4

125.9 *Journal of Communication. Devoted to Communication in
Human Relations.* 1951- . 4/yr.
          P90 J6

125.10 *Form.* 1966- . 4/yr.
          N1 F66

125.11 *Journal of Aesthetic Education.* 1966- . 4/yr.
701.1707   N1 J58

Indexes

Index of Periodicals

Index of Authors, Editors, Collaborators, Revisers, Translators, and Assistants

Because this is a computer-generated index, an author whose name appears in different forms on different title pages is listed as if he were more than one author. Thus, for example, Anne Jane Dyson is indexed as Anne J. Dyson for item 76.5 and as Jane A. Dyson for item 28.17, and Stanley J. Kunitz appears both in this form and as S. J. Kunitz.

282 / *Index of Authors, Editors, Etc.*

Cowie, Alexander, 38.17
Cowley, Malcolm, 74.17, 74.27, 74.51, 74.65
Cox, Charles B., 72.23
Craig, Alec, 103.10, 103.14
Craig, Edward G., 32.2
Craig, Hardin, 13.24, 32.9, 51.8, 53.13, 53.28
Craigie, William A., 23.3
Craik, Thomas W., 55.29
Crane, R. S., 81.2
Crane, Ronald S., 56.3, 81.2, 82.26, 82.51, 104.2
Crawford, James L., 97.15
Creed, Robert P., 47.21, 50.24
Creizenach, Wilhelm, 55.9
Crews, Frederick C., 79.9, 83.88
Crick, Bernard R., 88.5
Cronin, Anthony, 74.60
Crook, Arthur, 74.38
Crooke, William, 18.3
Crowley, Ellen T., 119.26
Cruise O'Brien, Conor, 74.55
Crum, Margaret, 24.7
Cruse, Amy, 102.3, 102.5, 102.6
Crutchley, Brooke, 91.14
Cruttwell, Patrick, 27.35, 54.20
Cunliffe, John W., 64.5, 73.10
Cunliffe, Marcus, 13.51, 13.52
Cunliffe, Marcus F., 21.13
Cunningham, James V., 82.35
Cunningham, John E., 59.19
Curley, Dorothy N., 73.19
Currey, Ralph N., 75.30
Curti, Merle E., 22.33
Cushing, Helen G., 107.5
Cushing, William, 6.19
Cuthbert, Eleanora I., 24.4
Cutler, Bradley D., 73.1
Cutler, John L., 50.1

Daghlian, Philip B., 35.15
Daiches, David, 5.11, 13.7, 13.42, 75.13, 77.43, 79.6, 82.53, 112.3
Damon, Philip, 83.59
Danby, John F., 54.18
Dargan, Marion, 35.4
Daunt, Marjorie, 48.3
Davenport, Basil, 44.15
Davidson, Angus, 62.8, 70.10
Davie, Donald, 26.29, 27.38, 75.48, 77.66
Davies, David L., 23.8
Davis, Hallie Flanagan, 76.16
Davis, Herbert J., 62.3

Davis, Mary W., 69.3
Davis, Norman, 47.19
Davis, Richard B., 19.29
Dawson, Giles E., 89.9
Dawson, S. W., 32.38
Day, Arthur G., 26.23
Day, Donald B., 44.3
Day, Robert A., 60.17
Deane, Cecil V., 32.6
Dearing, Vinton, 107.3
Dearing, Vinton A., 87.13
Debrodt, Barbara R., 117.5
DeFord, Sara, 27.49
De Grazia, Edward, 103.21
De La Mare, Walter, 64.3
Delany, Paul, 34.13
De Laura, David J., 64.29
Dembo, Lawrence S., 75.43
Demetz, Peter, 80.22, 81.11
Denholm-Young, Noël, 89.8
Denomy, Alexander J., 47.10
Dent, Thomas C., 76.45
Derrett, M. E., 77.73
De Selincourt, Ernest, 26.4
Deutsch, Babette, 27.40, 75.35
Dickinson, Arthur T., 41.16
Dipple, Elizabeth, 83.80
Dix, Ernest R., 93.33
Dobbie, Elliott V., 50.4, 50.5, 50.7
Dobell, Bertram, 93.66
Dobrée, Bonamy, 13.6, 13.17, 59.8, 59.10, 102.8
Dodsworth, Martin, 75.48
Dolezel, Lubomir, 8.2
Dondore, Dorothy A., 22.2
Donoghue, Denis, 75.40, 76.23
Donovan, Robert A., 60.18
Doran, Madeleine, 55.27
Dormon, James H., 69.9
Douce, Francis, 90.16
Downer, Alan S., 31.10, 32.27, 76.20, 76.24
Downs, Robert B., 86.9, 95.1, 103.1, 119.3
Drinkwater, John, 64.4
Drury, Francis K., 29.8
Dudek, Louis, 75.44
Dudley, Donald R., 5.14
Dudley, Fred A., 7.1
Duff, Edward G., 90.42, 91.7, 92.1, 93.4, 93.12, 93.21
Dugan, C. Winston, 93.33
Dukore, Bernard F., 28.9
Duncan, Joseph E., 27.21
Dunn, Esther C., 53.2
Dunn, Waldo H., 64.25

Durling, Dwight L., 27.9
Durr, Robert A., 74.79
Duthie, G. I., 7.7
Dutton, Geoffrey, 14.7
Dworkin, Rita, 76.4
Dyde, Jessie W., 35.1
Dykes, Eva B., 62.4
Dyson, Anne J., 76.5
Dyson, Anthony E., 83.52
Dyson, Henry, 13.5
Dyson, Jane A., 28.17

Eager, Alan R., 1.6
Eagle, Dorothy, 12.4, 12.5
Eagleton, Terence, 74.80
Eames, Wilberforce, 93.1
Earnest, Ernest P., 22.65, 112.2
Eastwood, Wilfred, 73.17
Edel, Leon, 35.9, 77.57, 83.54
Edgar, Pelham, 39.8
Edmonson, Munro S., 123.14
Edwards, Herbert W., 22.16
Edwards, Murray D., 31.30
Egger, E., 95.3
Ehrsam, Theodore G., 63.1
Ehrstine, John W., 15.15
Eichelberger, Clayton L., 71.7
Eisinger, Chester E., 77.53
Eldershaw, M. Barnard, 77.15
Eldredge, H. J., 28.1
Eleanore, Sister Mary, 36.2
Eliade, Mircea, 83.73
Eliot, T. S., 26.22, 26.27, 26.31, 26.41, 53.9, 82.5, 82.20, 82.21
Elledge, W. Paul, 62.28
Elliott, Robert C., 83.33, 83.81
Ellis, Henry, 90.16
Ellis-Fermor, Una, 72.24
Ellis-Fermor, Una M., 55.36
Ellmann, Mary, 7.22
Ellmann, Richard, 72.22, 74.56
Elton, Oliver, 26.2, 56.8, 61.9, 63.15
Elton, William, 79.1
Elwin, Malcolm, 72.12
Emden, Alfred B., 120.7, 120.8, 120.9
Empson, William, 26.5, 26.25
English, Thomas H., 95.19
Enright, Dennis J., 74.61, 113.6
Enscoe, Gerald E., 62.25
Enser, A. G. S., 101.6
Erdman, David V., 8.11
Ernst, Morris L., 103.7
Esdaile, Arundell, 60.1, 86.10, 95.12, 95.13

284 / *Index of Authors, Editors, Etc.*

Gold, Herbert, 74.43
Gold, Robert S., 78.6
Goldberg, Gerald J., 79.7
Golden, Joseph, 76.37
Goldfarb, Russell M., 64.33
Goldwater, Walter, 104.13
Good, John T., 73.17
Goode, Clement T., 12.1
Goode, Stephen H., 109.2, 109.3, 109.4
Goodheart, Eugene, 74.71
Goodman, Paul, 83.21
Goodwin, Kenneth, 16.18
Gordon, Ian A., 33.15
Gossett, Louise Y., 77.68
Gottesman, Ronald, 87.26
Gove, Philip B., 44.1
Gowers, Ernest, 18.8
Gradon, Pamela, 47.33
Graff, Henry F., 114.11
Graham, George K., 70.19
Graham, Walter J., 106.1, 106.2
Grannis, Chandler B., 91.25
Grant, Damian, 83.83
Grant, Douglas, 22.40
Granville-Barker, Harley, 32.7, 64.1
Graves, Robert, 26.19, 27.6, 33.6, 83.18
Gray, George J., 93.28
Gray, Richard A., 3.1, 84.1
Grebstein, Sheldon N., 81.12
Green, David B., 61.5
Green, Elizabeth A., 73.11
Green, Henry M., 14.6, 73.13
Green, Martin B., 22.24, 22.30
Green, Roger L., 44.12
Greenberger, Allen J., 72.39
Greene, Donald J., 56.12
Greene, Thomas M., 26.39
Greenfield, Stanley B., 45.5, 46.8, 47.20
Greenwood, Joseph A., 18.9
Greg, Walter W., 28.4, 55.5, 55.17, 87.4, 93.18, 93.19
Gregor, Ian, 40.8
Gregory, Horace, 75.14
Gregory, Winifred, 104.5, 104.15
Grieder, Theodore, 97.20
Grierson, Herbert, 53.16
Grierson, Herbert J., 25.2
Grierson, Herbert J. C., 53.7
Griest, Guinevere L., 70.24
Griffith, Benjamin W., 117.3
Grimal, Pierre, 119.21
Grimstead, David, 69.11

Griswold, William M., 37.1
Groom, Bernard, 27.18
Gross, Harvey S., 27.29, 27.36
Gross, John, 80.25
Gross, Seymour L., 22.48
Gross, Theodore L., 22.85
Growoll, Adolf, 93.1, 94.1
Grundy, Joan, 54.41
Guinagh, Kevin, 119.22
Gurko, Leo, 74.7, 74.15
Guttenberg, Antoine C. V., 65.42
Guttmann, Allen, 22.86
Gwynn, Stephen L., 13.2

Haber, Tom B., 50.11
Hackett, Alice P., 102.12
Hackman, Martha L., 86.14
Hadgraft, Cecil, 14.5
Hagen, Ordean A., 43.6
Hagstrum, Jean H., 58.10
Haight, Anne L., 103.25
Haight, Willet R., 94.31
Halkett, Samuel, 6.20
Hall, Donald, 24.5
Hall, James W., 77.85
Hall, Vernon, 79.2, 80.18
Hall, Wade H., 65.36
Halle, Morris, 27.50
Haller, William, 53.15
Hamer, Enid H., 27.30
Hamer, Philip M., 88.6
Hamilton, Edith, 119.11
Hamilton, George R., 27.33
Hamilton, Kenneth G., 53.31
Hammond, Nicholas G., 119.28
Handley-Taylor, Geoffrey, 6.18
Handlin, Oscar, 119.13
Handy, William J., 83.53
Hansen, Harry, 74.1
Harbage, Alfred, 28.8, 55.25
Harbert, Earl N., 65.45
Harding, Denys C., 26.40
Hardison, Osborne B., 51.14, 53.29
Hardy, Barbara, 39.24, 75.48
Hardy, John E., 22.48, 77.59
Hargreaves-Mawdsley, William N., 121.32
Harman, Eleanor, 91.19
Harmon, Maurice, 11.10
Harper, Howard M., 77.81
Harris, Ronald W., 62.22
Harris, Victor, 53.20
Harris, Wilson, 16.12
Harrison, George B., 113.2

Harrod, Leonard M., 95.9
Hart, Horace, 86.1
Hart, James D., 20.2, 102.9
Harte, Barbara, 6.16
Hartman, Carl, 74.35
Hartnoll, Phyllis, 29.6
Hartwick, Harry, 77.11
Harvey, Paul, 12.4
Harvey, William J., 39.26
Haslam, Gerald W., 22.80
Hassan, Ihab H., 77.44
Hatch, James V., 28.22
Hatcher, Anna, 7.19
Hatcher, Harlan H., 77.12
Hauck, Richard B., 41.17
Haviland, Virginia, 122.1
Hawes, Gene R., 91.26
Hawken, William R., 99.6
Haycraft, Howard, 6.2, 6.4, 6.6, 6.8, 43.5
Hayden, John O., 62.23
Hayman, Allen, 74.59
Hazard, Lucy L., 22.4
Hazlitt, William C., 93.27, 93.32
Heaney, Howell J., 86.23
Heath-Stubbs, John, 27.42
Heath-Stubbs, John F., 27.41
Hector, Leonard C., 89.10
Hefling, Helen, 35.1
Heilbronner, Walter L., 92.9
Heiney, Donald W., 74.24
Hemenway, Robert, 41.14
Henderson, Stephen E., 22.74
Hendrick, George, 37.12, 105.10
Henkin, Leo J., 70.7
Hepworth, Philip, 88.9
Herrick, Marvin T., 32.18
Herron, Ima H., 32.36
Hertzberger, Menno, 98.7
Herzberg, Max J., 20.1
Hetherington, John A., 6.12
Heusinkveld, Arthur H., 45.2
Hewitt, Barnard W., 31.20, 31.31
Hewitt, Cecil R., 103.22
Hibbard, Addison, 5.4
Hibbard, Laura A., 49.11
Hicks, Granville, 72.13, 74.4, 77.38
Hieatt, Constance B., 48.5
Highet, Gilbert, 7.4, 83.41
Hilfer, Anthony C., 74.76
Hill, Francis J., 95.13
Hill, Frank P., 69.2

Subject Index

Numbers refer to individual entries; when several works appear together, only the section number is given.

Abbreviations: acronyms, 119.26; foreign, 119.22; in manuscripts and archives, 88; of periodical titles, 3.6, 105
Aberdeen University library: manuscript collections, 90.10; theses abstracts, 116.45
Abstracts: American literature, 19.19; book reviews, 84.2; dissertations, 116; English literature, 3.8; periodicals, 105.2
Aesthetics, 83, 125
Age of Transition, 72
Allegory: general studies, 83; Medieval, 47, 51; Renaissance, 53
Alumni directories, 120
American language: bibliographies, 1, 2, 3, 78; general studies and dictionaries, 23, 78; style, 8, 27, 33, 78. *See also* English language; Linguistics
American literature: annals, 20.5; authors, 6, 76.9, 111, 121.30; autobiography, 34; bibliographies, 1, 2, 3, 19 *(see also subject and period headings);* biography, 35; chronology, 20.5; criticism, 79–85; diaries, 34; dissertations, 116; drama and theater, 28–32, 69, 72, 76; essay, 36; fiction, 37–39, 41–44, 71, 72, 77; general studies, 7, 22, 65, 72, 74; guides, 5, 20, 73; manuscripts, 88–90; periodicals, 3, 9, 10, 19, 21.1, 30, 39, 42.4, 43, 44, 65, 72.1, 73, 76–79, 83–85, 108–11; poetry 24, 25,

26, 27, 67, 72, 75; subject indexes, 4; surveys, 21, 65, 72, 73 *(see also* 13). *See also* Black literature; Southern literature
American national bibliography, 94
American studies: bibliographies, 19; general studies, 22; periodicals, 9, 10
Analytical bibliography, *see* Bibliography, technical
Anglo-Saxon, *see* Medieval
Annals: American literature, 20.5; Australian literature, 12.6; British literature, 12.2, 119.15; English drama, 28.8
Annals, *see* Periodicals
Anonyms and pseudonyms, 6.19–6.22
Antiquarian books, 98
Archives, 88
Arthurian literature, 45, 49
Auction records, 98
Audience: censorship, 103; general studies, 102; Medieval, 47.15, 50; Renaissance 53.35, 55; Restoration and Eighteenth century, 59.12, 60, 102; Nineteenth century, 70.17, 102
Augustan, *see* Restoration and Eighteenth century
Australian language, 17.7, 18, 78.4
Australian literature: annals, 12.6; authors, 6, 11.9, 26.8, 75.2; bibliographies, 1, 2, 3, 11, 14, 24, 75.2, 77; criticism, 81, 85; fiction, 38.14, 77; general studies, 16, 64.35; manuscripts, 90.9; periodicals, 9,

Usage: dictionaries and studies, 17, 18, 23, 48, 78; scholarly writing, 115
Utopias, 44, 83.81

Verse, *see* Poetry
Versification, 27
Victorian Period, *see* Nineteenth century

Watermarks, 87.3
Welsh (Anglo-Welsh) literature: bibliography, 3.6, 73.6; periodicals, 9, 10, 104.1; surveys, 13
West Indian literature: bibliographies, 3, 11.6, 14; general studies, 16, 121; guide, 12.7; novel, 77.97

Women in literature: as authors, 6, 41.9, 70.23; as subjects, 7, 40.10, 47, 53.24
World literature: authors, 6, 121; bibliographies, 1, 2, 3, 73, 76, 121: criticism 37, 77, 79–85; drama and theater, 29, 30, 76; encyclopedias, 121; fiction, 37, 42, 77; general studies, 7.10, 62.19, 74, 77, 121; guides, 5; periodicals, 9, 10, 30, 73, 84, 85, 108–11, 121; poetry, 75; surveys, 5, 74, 75, 121. *See also* Commonwealth literature
Writers, *see* Authors

Yearbooks, *see* Periodicals